THE ECONOMICS OF INTERNATIONAL BUSINESS

THE ECONOMICS OF INTERNATIONAL BUSINESS

William A. Kerr
Professor of Economics, Department of Economics,
University of Calgary, Calgary, Canada

and
Nicholas Perdikis
Lecturer in International Economics, Department of Economics,
University of Wales – Aberystwyth, Aberystwyth, UK

CHAPMAN & HALL
London · Glasgow · Weinheim · New York · Tokyo · Melbourne · Madras

Published by Chapman & Hall, 2–6 Boundary Row, London SE1 8HN

Chapman & Hall, 2–6 Boundary Row, London SE1 8HN, UK

Blackie Academic & Professional, Wester Cleddens Road, Bishopbriggs, Glasgow G64 2NZ, UK

Chapman & Hall GmbH, Pappelallee 3, 69469 Weinheim, Germany

Chapman & Hall USA, One Penn Plaza, 41st Floor, New York NY 10119, USA

Chapman & Hall Japan, ITP-Japan, Kyowa Building, 3F, 2-2-1 Hirakawacho, Chiyoda-ku, Tokyo 102, Japan

Chapman & Hall Australia, Thomas Nelson Australia, 102 Dodds Street, South Melbourne, Victoria 3205, Australia

Chapman & Hall India, R. Seshadri, 32 Second Main Road, CIT East, Madras 600 035, India

First edition 1995 and reprinted 1996

© 1995 William Kerr and Nicholas Perdikis

Typeset in 10½/12 pt Times by Colset
Printed in Great Britain by The Alden Press, Oxford.

ISBN 0 412 60860 X

Apart from any fair dealing for the purposes of research or private study, or criticism or review, as permitted under the UK Copyright Designs and Patents Act, 1988, this publication may not be reproduced, stored, or transmitted, in any form or by any means, without the prior permission in writing of the publishers, or in the case of reprographic reproduction only in accordance with the terms of the licences issued by the Copyright Licensing Agency in the UK, or in accordance with the terms of licences issued by the appropriate Reproduction Rights Organization outside the UK. Enquiries concerning reproduction outside the terms stated here should be sent to the publishers at the London address printed on this page.
  The publishers makes no representation, express or implied, with regard to the accuracy of the information contained in this book and cannot accept any legal responsibility or liability for any errors or omissions that may be made.

A catalogue record for this book is available from the British Library

Library of Congress Catalog Card Number: 95-67599

∞ Printed on permanent acid-free text paper, manufactured in accordance with ANSI/NISO Z 39.48-1992 and ANSI/NISO Z 39.48-1984 (Permanence of Paper).

For Helen, Laurie and Jill

Contents

Preface	xi
Part One: Introduction	1
1 Why study the economics of international business?	3
One executive's story	3
International trade in the post World War II period	6
Plan of the book	13
Part Two: What insights does trade theory provide?	15
Introduction to Part Two	17
2 International trade and economic theory	19
What determines competitiveness?	19
Classical trade theory	20
Neo-classical trade theory	23
Alternatives to neo-classical trade theory	25
Intra-industry trade	27
What do trade theories tell us about trade patterns?	31
The determinants of trade intensity and competitiveness	33
What can be concluded?	35
References	36
3 The great debate – free trade versus protectionism	39
The middle ground of managed trade	39
The case for an open trade regime	39
The political economy of protectionism and trade liberalization	43
Static arguments for protection	46
The strategic or dynamic reasons for protection	53
Lessons for business	56
References	57
Summary of Part Two	59
Part Three: The international trading system	61
Introduction to Part Three	63
4 The search for an orderly system for trade	65
The nation state and economic sovereignty	65
The state and the structure of international trade	66
The nature of the international trading system	67

	The international trading system through history	69
	Bilateral and multilateral trade relationships	71
	References	74
5	**Regional trade associations**	**75**
	Economic blocs and regional economic integration	75
	Definitions and levels of economic integration	75
	The theory of regional economic integration	77
	Regional economic blocs	82
	Economic blocs and the nation state	91
	References	91
6	**Institutions of the multilateral trading system**	**93**
	The basis of the multilateral system	93
	The World Trade Organization	94
	The United Nations Conference on Trade and Development	95
	The General Agreement on Tariffs and Trade	96
	References	99
7	**Orderly markets**	**100**
	Why orderly markets are desired	100
	International commodity agreements	100
	Voluntary export restraints	102
	Countertrade	104
	References	106
8	**How countries restrict trade**	**107**
	Unilateral action by countries	107
	Trade restricting measures	107
9	**Control of the use of trade barriers**	**117**
	The need for multilateral controls	117
	Measures to control the use of trade restrictions	117
	References	125
10	**'Fair' trade**	**126**
	Contingent protection	126
	Dumping	126
	Countervail	128
	References	129

Summary of Part Three   130

Part Four: The economic actors who conduct international trade   131

Introduction to Part Four   133

11	**National firms and transnational firms**	**135**
	Do transnationals make sense?	135
	The cost of organizing international transactions	135
	Capturing the returns to research and development	138
	Using goodwill to international advantage	140

	Protecting vulnerable assets	141
	Exercising market power	142
	Strategic use of transfer prices	143
	Long-term contracts	143
	Joint ventures	144
	Greenfield investments versus acquisitions	145
	Limits on foreign direct investments	146
	References	147
12	**Private firms and state trading agencies**	148
	Government involvement in international commerce	148
	State trading agencies in command economies	148
	State trading agencies in mixed economies	151
	Payment in kind	152
	References	156
13	**Production firms and trading houses**	157
	What is a trading house?	157
	Why use a trading house?	157
	Questions of culture	162
	The cost of identifying new markets	164

Summary of Part Four — 166

Part Five: Institutions that facilitate international trade — 167

Introduction to Part Five — 169

14	**Financing international transactions**	173
	Arranging for payment	173
	Acquiring foreign exchange	184
	Changes in exchange rates	188
	References	192
15	**Moving products between countries**	193
	The movement of goods and international transportation	193
	A taxonomy of seaborne trade and cargoes	193
	Air freight and transportation	198
	References	199
16	**The settlement of international commercial disputes**	200
	Why disputes arise	200
	Differences in national legal systems	201
	International arbitration versus national courts	203
	The institutions of international commercial arbitration	210
	Enforcement of arbitration awards by national courts	217
	References	219

Summary of Part Five — 220

Part Six: Future trends in international trade and commerce — 223

Introduction to Part Six — 225

17	**Facing the future**	229
	Disequilibrium and change	229
	Resource mobility	229
	Increased diversity	231
	Developing countries and former command economies	233
18	**Issues for the international trading system**	235
	Liberalization versus protectionism	235
	Trade in services	238
	Protection of intellectual property	242
	Government procurement	245
	Trade blocs	247
	Business input into trade issues	248
	References	250

Summary of Part Six	251
Exercise 1	253
Glossary of terms	255
Index	271

Preface

The globalization of business in the last 40 years has made it essential that business people and those pursuing business studies courses understand the economic forces that shape the international business environment.

Our experience, gained on both sides of the Atlantic from teaching economics to business studies students and those not majoring in economics, led to our dissatisfaction with existing texts. While excellent in themselves, the approach adopted by the standard international economics books is largely inappropriate for the 'business' student. The texts on 'international business' while being less 'theoretical' than their economics counter-parts tend to include areas such as accounting, human resource management, marketing and strategic management. As a result international economic issues are not dealt with in sufficient detail. Our aim then in writing this book is to provide business studies students with a text that deals with these issues both rigorously and in depth but in a way that is sympathetic to their needs.

Books do not just appear. A great many people, apart from the authors, influence their genesis. In writing this book we too are indebted to a number of people. In particular we would like to thank Jill Hobbs who read numerous drafts and whose advice and influence has been invaluable in shaping this book. We would also like to thank Professor L. J. Williams of the Department of Economics UWA who read and commented on some of the earlier chapters. Bill Kerr would like to thank the University of Calgary for granting him a sabbatical during which this book was written. He would also like to express his thanks to Professor Ken Thompson and the academic and secretarial staff of the Economics Division of the Department of Agriculture, University of Aberdeen for their hospitality and their support while on his sabbatical leave. Nick Perdikis would like to thank David Law of the Department of Economics UWA for his encouragement and useful advice.

Our thanks also go out to Linda Jones of the Department of Economics UWA and Wendy Devonish of Flying Fingers Typing Services who had the onerous tasks of deciphering our writing and typing the book.

We would also like to mention in appreciation the support given to us by Steven Reed and the rest of the staff at Chapman & Hall.

Last but not least we would like to thank our wives and Laurie for putting up with us while we were writing this book.

Calgary 1994
Aberystwyth 1994

PART 1
Introduction

Why study the economics of international business? 1

ONE EXECUTIVE'S STORY

It had all been so easy. It had all gone so wrong! Tony had finished clearing out his desk and was waiting, as he had been told, for security to come and escort him out of the building. Until they had told him just over an hour ago, Tony had been manager of the international division of a medium sized British manufacturer of patient monitoring equipment used in hospitals. He had joined the firm 10 years ago after completing an MBA in the US. In his first 8 years he had been in domestic sales and worked his way up to be one of four assistant managers. Then one day, 2 years ago, he got the call.

The purchasing manager for a chain of private hospitals in a large Latin American country wanted to know if Tony's firm would be interested in providing monitors to re-equip their hospitals. The potential order was large but Tony's company had never had any export dealings. After a meeting with senior management it was decided that the company should pursue the order and Tony was put in charge of the project. He flew to Latin America, met with the hospital chain's management, was wined and dined, and a deal was sketched out. The order was too large for the company's existing manufacturing capacity and new investment would be required.

Back in the UK Tony drew up a formal business plan. The price the company would have to charge after accounting for all the additional transportation and insurance charges would make a competitive bid difficult. Tony was, however, able to find an Asian company which could supply a costly and crucial computer component at a far lower price than their local British supplier. Tony was also able to secure a British government grant which was available to assist new exporters. The lower cost Asian component and the grant would allow the exported monitors to be profitably sold at a price less than monitors sold in the British market. The imported component would also improve profit margins on monitors sold in the domestic market.

Tony presented his plan to the Board of Directors and the expansion in manufacturing capacity was approved. After a successful bid, a

4 Why study the economics of international business?

lucrative formal contract was negotiated in Latin America. Tony was made manager of a new International Division which was to be responsible for fulfilling the contract and searching out other foreign markets. The expansion of manufacturing facilities was completed on schedule and regular shipments of monitors to Latin America began. Tony began travelling the world seeking out additional sales while his division waited for the profits to roll in.

It was then that things began to go wrong. The first inkling that all was not going according to plan came when the profits did not begin to roll in. The payments from Latin America were always late and were never the amount agreed in the contract. A stream of complaints that the monitors were defective upon arrival was used to justify the reduced payments. Tony and the company's engineers had to make a number of expensive trips to Latin America to check the state of the equipment. The engineers could find no faults but the hospital chain's management still insisted that the monitors were not performing to the specifications in the contract. On the advice of the company's British solicitors, Tony reluctantly hired legal council in the hospital chain's country to sue for payment. Negotiations with the hospital chain continued while the lawyers prepared their case. Legal bills began to roll in.

The lawyers in Latin America were informed by their government that the imported monitors were now the subject of two trade actions. A manufacturer of competing monitors located in the country was bringing an anti-dumping suit with the government's Dumping Tribunal. The suit was based on the imported monitors being sold at a lower price in Latin America than in the UK. Further, the country's Unfair Trade Practices Commission was conducting an 'export subsidy' investigation into the grant Tony's company had received. If either investigation found against Tony's company, large import duties would be applied to any imported monitors. While the lawyers thought the investigations were instigated largely for their nuisance and political value, good cases would have to be prepared for both hearings. Legal costs increased.

Back in the UK, there were other problems. The switch to the Asian supplier of computer components had led to job losses at the company's former British supplier. The union representing the workers who had been made redundant was accusing Tony's company of exploiting low paid Asian workers and contributing to the demise of British manufacturing. Tony remembered one particularly difficult session when the press asked him about this point – he did not have any good counter arguments and, in fact, he wasn't sure that he didn't agree. The Chairman of the Board had made it known that he thought the adverse publicity was damaging the company's reputation.

The management of the former British supplier had obtained one of the Asian company's components. Their computer people suspected that the Asian manufacturer had pirated their technology. The British government was being asked to take action against imports from the Asian supplier on the basis of patent violations.

Back in Latin America, the country was going through a period of sustained inflation and the value of the local currency was falling dramatically against the pound. As the contract price had been specified in the local currency, those payments that were received from the hospital chain could be exchanged for less and less pounds. Meanwhile, the legal wheels were grinding slowly and the case for non-payment was finally going to court. The Latin American law firm sent a fax suggesting that the case be dropped because the judge appointed to hear the case was the cousin of the doctor who was head of the company which owned the chain of hospitals. That had been this morning.

An emergency meeting of the Board of Directors had been called and a decision taken to cut the company's losses and abandon the Latin American contract. The International Division was to be wound up and Tony let go. Tony wondered what he could have done differently. He did not have long to ponder as the company's security escort had arrived.

While Tony, and his company, might have been particularly naïve, the catalogue of woes listed above are all real problems which must be addressed by business people wishing to engage in international commercial activity. If they are not anticipated, or dealt with without careful investigation, they can sour even the most lucrative of foreign business opportunities. Most of these problems – and many others – can be effectively dealt with if the workings of the international economy are well understood. Specialized institutions, both public and private, often exist which can lower the costs and reduce the risks associated with international business. This book is an attempt to provide a guide to the complex system which constitutes the international commercial environment within which companies operate. The intent is to prepare business people – or future business people – and others interested in international commerce to anticipate problems like those faced by Tony, our fictional executive. The book also lays out the choice of options which can be used to eliminate, or at least mitigate, the costs and risks associated with any anticipated problems. International business will never be as easy as Tony thought but a good understanding of the economics of international business can prevent it from going wrong.

It is said that no man is an island, and in international business and commerce this is no less true for nations, companies or individuals whether they are located on one of the world's largest continents or even one of its islands. When listening to news bulletins on the radio or watching television one is struck by the way individuals, companies and national leaders appreciate this fact. Reactions, however, often vary from the – 'we should keep all foreign goods out and meet our needs from home production' to the 'an open world economy is best for business because trade increases our standard of living'. There are many variants in between these extremes.

Often those commentating on trade see the need for other countries to open up their economies to foreign competition but never see the case for opening their own markets. Nowhere have the arguments been better rehearsed than in the multilateral trade negotiations that take place in Geneva or in bilateral discussions such as those between the US and Japan. The recent negotiations with Japan, in particular, have highlighted the bearing that domestic factors, such as the organization of distribution systems, have on international trade and business. Countries' social policies are also affected by and affect international competitiveness. No one is totally isolated from changes in the international commercial environment. Hence businesses, whether directly involved in, or only indirectly affected by, international commerce cannot afford to ignore international economic issues nor the way in which these issues will impinge on their activities.

INTERNATIONAL TRADE IN THE POST WORLD WAR II PERIOD

The end of World War II ushered in a new era in international trade. New institutions were put in place at post war conferences which, while they have been considerably altered over time, still provide the framework within which international trade takes place. The most important of the institutions were the **General Agreement on Tariffs and Trade (GATT)***, which defined the environment for trade in goods, and the **International Monetary Fund (IMF)**, which regulated the exchange rate environment. While the influence of these organizations has grown or declined over time, they have presided over the greatest increase in international commerce ever seen.

The growth of world trade

World trade in goods and services has grown rapidly in the period since the end of World War II. In value, trade has increased from US$53 300 million in 1948 to US$4 640 000 million in 1992. This growth has been characterized by several phases. In the period between 1948 and 1960 trade grew on average at the annual rate of 6%, between 1960 and 1973 it grew by 8% annually, between 1973 and 1980 there was a period of slower growth of 4% with even lower growth, averaging 2%, between 1980 and 1985. The period 1985–1990 saw a resumption of more rapid growth, of approximately 6%. Growth declined somewhat in 1991 and 1992 with annual rates of 3% and 4%, respectively.

A further feature of post war trade is that, in volume terms, the growth in world trade has outstripped the growth in world output. As a result, the world's trading nations have become more integrated.

What caused this rapid increase in trade? Two post war phenomena are largely responsible:

*Terms in **bold** are further defined in the Glossary of terms.

1. The rise in real incomes and, hence, demand for goods and services in the world's leading economies.
2. A general reduction in the restrictions imposed on trade.

The continued increase in activity in the world's principal economies was the result of several factors. Firstly, the period of reconstruction after the war in Europe, especially with the arrival of considerable US aid through the Marshall Plan, led to an increase in demand. Reconstruction stimulated trade since in the initial stages capital goods had to be imported. It also laid the foundations of future growth. Secondly, the Korean War acted as a stimulus to reconstruction in the Japanese economy, in particular, but also helped to keep demand for commodities high in the rest of the world. Thirdly, and especially after the Korean War, the general stability in commodity prices, in particular oil – the principal source of energy – enabled world wide rising incomes to be translated into demand for additional products rather than inflationary increases in prices.

Fourthly, there was a major switch in national economic policies away from attempting to stabilize prices and towards employment stability during the post war period and up to the mid-1970s. In using **Keynesian** techniques to control the level of employment, governments pursued policies that encouraged spending and economic growth.

Fifthly, the post war period also saw the establishment of international arrangements, especially multilateral institutions, that would give the world international financial stability and encourage growth in trade. The various rounds of trade negotiations held under the auspices of GATT, especially the so-called Kennedy Round in the 1960s, enhanced the post war growth in world trade.

Slowing rates of economic growth in general and subsequently the slowdown in the expansion of international trade can be attributed, to a large extent, to the reversal in Keynesian economic policies, the rise in commodity prices, the collapse of the post war international financial arrangement and a decline in countries' willingness to abide by international trade commitments. By the early 1970s inflationary pressures were making themselves felt in the major industrialized economies. It was not long before the free spending policies of governments were reversed and the goal of full employment was sacrificed in favour of price stability. This was achieved largely by the adoption of deflationary **monetarist** policies based on high interest rates. While a degree of price stability was achieved, real incomes and spending power in the industrial economies were severely affected.

Inflation in the US, largely brought about by expensive social policies and an unwillingness to finance the Vietnam War by taxation, had two major international effects. The first was on commodity prices. The second was on the international financial system. Commodity producers around the world were mainly paid in US dollars for their products which meant that their real incomes declined as the purchasing power of the dollar fell. By the early 1970s, fed up with receiving less in real terms for their product and upset with the industrial countries support for the Israelis in the Arab–Israeli war, the mainly Middle Eastern **Organization of Petroleum Exporting Countries (OPEC)** unilaterally raised the price for crude oil. Other commodity producers following OPEC's example quickly formed cartels and raised their prices.

The period of stable commodity prices was over. Companies could no longer make long-term plans based on stable input prices. Business confidence declined which led to a reduction in investment and consequently a decline in economic growth. This decline was compounded by the policy response of the industrial countries who initially responded to the demand dampening effect of the rise in commodity prices by attempting to stimulate their economies. These expansionary policies were soon reversed in order to squeeze out the inflation they had caused. This policy roller coaster was especially prevalent after the second oil shock in 1981.

Inflation in the US had an indirect but still important effect on trade via its impact on the international financial system. The US dollar was – and still is – the principal currency with which international payments were made. Hence, most countries held the majority of their foreign currency reserves in dollars. They also fixed the rate at which their currencies could be exchanged for dollars. The post war international financial system was predicated on the principle of fixed exchange rates and the conversion of currencies into the US dollar. Any loss of confidence or willingness to hold the dollar would, therefore, have a detrimental effect on the world monetary system. As the US dollar's purchasing power declined, countries became less and less happy with holding large quantities of dollars. Fixed exchange rates were abandoned for floating exchange rates in 1972. This increased the risks of doing business and receiving payments internationally. Uncertainty in international financial relations was bound to have an adverse effect on trade flows.

Slow economic growth led many countries to tackle problems of industrial restructuring and unemployment by restricting imports. From the mid-1970s to the mid-1980s countries began trying to protect their industries using measures that circumvented the commitments they had made through the GATT. In this period a number of agreements were concluded bilaterally between pairs and groups of countries. For example, weaker countries were bullied by stronger economic powers into 'voluntarily' restricting their exports. Although not outlawed at the time, these agreements certainly contravened the spirit of GATT and had an adverse effect on world trade and, hence, economic growth.

The improved rates of growth in international trade from the mid-1980s can be accounted for by the strong performance of major economies. Recessions in the US, Europe and Japan contributed to the slowdown in the growth of trade in 1991 and 1992.

Table 1.1 The Composition of World Trade (% share in total)

	1955	1965	1970	1975	1980	1985	1992
Agricultural Products	34.7	25.4	20.5	17.1	14.9	13.5	12.2
Food	21.8	18.2	14.7	13.2	11.1	10.3	9.6
Raw Materials	12.9	7.2	5.8	3.9	3.8	3.2	2.6
Mining Products	14.7	12.9	12.7	21.8	26.1	20.1	12.2
Ores, Minerals, etc.	3.7	3.3	3.4	2.4	2.1	1.7	3.1
Fuels	11.0	9.6	9.3	19.4	24.0	18.4	9.1
Manufactures	49.0	58.5	64.9	59.4	57.3	62.6	72.8
Chemicals	5.0	6.5	7.1	7.0	7.4	8.0	9.0
Machinery and Transport Equipment	18.0	24.6	28.8	28.0	25.6	30.4	37.3
Other Manufactures	26.0	27.4	29.0	24.4	24.3	24.2	26.5

Sources: *GATT International Trade Statistics* (several issues) and *UNCTAD Handbook on International Trade* (several issues).

The structure of world trade

Table 1.1 shows the composition or structure of world trade and how it has changed over the period 1955 to 1992. It is clear that trade in manufactures has dominated – except in 1975 when the upsurge in oil prices during the 1970s upset the trend. In 1992, manufactures accounted for nearly 73% of all merchandise exports. Within the manufactures category the most important single group of products is machinery and transport equipment. Trade in these products has grown steadily over the period and now accounts for just over 37%. While trade in manufactures has increased steadily, the share of agricultural commodities, both as raw materials and processed food products, has declined, as has that of mining products such as ores, minerals and non-ferrous metals.

What forces have brought about these changes? The continued upsurge in the trade in manufactures at the expense of other categories can be attributed to the fact that consumers spend relatively more on these goods as their incomes rise – in economist' terms they have higher **income elasticities**. As incomes have risen, the demand for manufactures has risen at a faster rate than other groups such as agricultural products which have lower income elasticities. The exception was, of course, fuels in the 1970s. The special circumstances that applied to energy due to the sharp OPEC price increases have already been mentioned. As the power of OPEC has declined, however, the original downward trend in energy's share in the value of trade has reasserted itself.

So far only the trade in goods, or what is also called visible or merchandised trade has been discussed; however, services are also traded. Trade in services constitutes approximately one quarter of the value of the trade in visible goods. From 1980 to 1990 the growth of trade in services has roughly matched that of manufactures.

Table 1.2 shows the composition of the trade in services in 1980 and

Table 1.2 The Composition of World Service Trade

	1980	1990	Annual Growth 1980–1990 (%)
Shipping	57.3	88.7	4.5
Passenger Services	17.9	48.1	10.4
Other Transport	54.8	79.7	3.8
Travel	91.8	233.9	9.8
Royalties and Fees	11.6	32.2	10.8
Other Services	111.6	274.6	9.4
TOTAL	345.0	757.2	8.2

Source: *World Economic Survey* 1993. United Nations, New York. Value Billions of $US.

1990, and their annual average rate of growth over that period. The principal causes of the overall growth in services can be attributed to the substantial growth seen in some of the component parts. For example, travel and passenger services have been influenced by the rapid growth in tourism itself and is a function of the growth of real incomes in the richer countries of the world. The rapid rise in royalties and fees accruing to the owners of patents, copyrights and trademarks reflects the increasing proportion of the value of goods which can be attributed to inputs of intellectual property. Other private services including, amongst other things, the use of telecommunications equipment (telephone, satellite and computer networks) underlines the importance of the revolution in information technology. In fact, these elements of the trade in services grew much faster than merchandise trade. The only items that grew slower and had a dampening effect on the overall growth of services were shipping and other transportation items. The reason for this slower growth can be attributed to the reduction in transportation costs per ton loaded and the less than proportionate growth in the trade of bulk commodities.

The distribution and concentration of world trade

Trade is not distributed evenly across countries and it is highly concentrated amongst the so-called developed or industrial countries of the world. Trade has also grown faster for these countries than the growth of world trade. As a result, these advanced nations now account for 72% of world trade. The principal explanation for the dominance of the industrial countries in the distribution of trade is that they are the most efficient producers of the goods that are in greatest demand. Within this group of rich nations, the relative decline in the US and UK's share of world trade and the rise of that of Japan has been a clear trend.

Those developing countries that have been able to industrialize – the so-called newly industrialized countries (NICs) – have also benefited from the growth in world trade. Their export performance in the 1980s and early 1990s has been particularly strong. Originally utilizing their abundant resource of cheap labour, they produced and exported mainly labour intensive goods such as textiles and clothing. As their skill base has developed they have moved on to include electronics components, electronic goods and communications equipment as major exports. Their ability to break into markets where trade barriers were high makes their achievements even more remarkable. The precise grouping of NICs usually varies according to the sources one examines but they usually include Singapore, Taiwan, Hong Kong, South Korea, Malaysia – the Asian Tigers – as well as Thailand. Portugal and Spain are also included in the list as well as Brazil and Colombia in Latin America.

It is the concentration of NICs in Asia that has led to the recent rapid growth of trade in that area. For example, an average rate of export growth of 14% was achieved in 1992 by Taiwan, Korea, Singapore and Hong Kong. Malaysia, Thailand and Indonesia achieved almost as high rates of growth.

Perhaps the most important recent development in Asia has been the reappearance of China as a trading nation. The communist regime of Mao Tse-tung followed a policy of self-sufficiency for most of the post war period. Since the late 1970s, the opening up of the Chinese economy to world trade has been an integral part of its development strategy. It has achieved an annual average growth in trade of 15% with exports currently accounting for 19% of GNP. Over 77% of its exports are manufactures with the majority, approximately 64%, going to the developed economies of Japan, the US and Europe.

In Latin America and the Caribbean, trade has also expanded, again largely as a result of economic liberalization, the renewed availability of finance and stronger economic performance. By the late 1980s a previous decline in export earnings was reversed and annual growth rates averaged just over 12.5% over the period. The value of exports would have been higher but for the weakness of agricultural and natural resource markets. The regions' substantial growth in trade reflects the rapid expansion of Brazil, Chile and some of the countries of Central America, and the more moderate but strong increases experienced by Argentina, Ecuador, Uruguay and Mexico. The principal trading partners of this area are still the developed market or industrialized economies which account for just over 60% of its exports and 70% of its imports. Intra-area trade, however, constitutes only 15% of the regions' total trade.

Africa's export trade is dominated by primary products with over 70% coming from agricultural and mining products. This concentration has had its drawbacks since the demand for primary products grows at a slower rate than the growth in world incomes. Debt problems, falling commodity prices and stagnant economic growth have contributed to keeping African import growth in check.

The participation of the former communist countries – or command economies – in the international trading system prior to their economic transformation can be said to be minimal and still only accounts for approximately 2.5% of world trade. The basis on which this trade was carried out was mainly in the form of bilateral trade deals that limited transactions to specific goods or groups of products. Even the trade that was conducted between communist countries was restricted and, hence, did not contribute greatly to the economic development of these countries. With the widespread change in regimes and accompanying ideologies, a major shift has taken place in trade relations. Whereas in the early 1980s approximately 50% of their exports were traded within the area, this had fallen to just over 30% by 1992. This decline in trade among the former command economies has been accompanied by an increase in exports to the developed market economies – up from 28% in 1980 to just under 44% in 1992. A similar pattern can be discerned in imports.

To summarize, it is clear that over the post war period international trade has been increasing rapidly and much faster than world output. The post war period has also seen the continued increase in the share of manufactures and decline of primary products traded in the world economy. Latterly, services have increased their share of total trade. The world economy has become much more integrated. The major growth has been experienced by the developed, market, or industrial countries. Other economies that have shown spectacular success in the trading area are the so-called NICs, particularly those in South and East Asia. China is becoming a growing market and a major exporter. Other developing countries, particularly those in Africa, burdened by major economic difficulties have not participated fully in the growth in international trade. The former central and eastern European countries are also experiencing problems as they attempt to re-orient their trade.

Foreign direct investment

The post war period has not only seen the rapid growth of trade in both goods and services but also the growth of foreign investment. This has been of two types:

1. Indirect made up of equity investment (the purchasing of shares in foreign companies), private debt investment (the acquisition of foreign bonds and other debt instruments), and inter-governmental transfers principally made up of loans, gifts and economic aid.
2. **Foreign direct investment (FDI)** whereby firms extend their operations into foreign countries.

The major objective of FDI is to gain or maintain control of markets and/or resources. Manufacturing and the extractive industries such as oil, coal and ores have been the most important areas for FDI but it is also prominent in the services sector – banking and finance, legal services, marketing and distribution. The bulk of foreign direct investment originates in the US, Japan and the countries of the European Union (EU), which together account for over 90% of the total value of these investments.

The reason for the rise in FDI is a subtle combination of both push and pull factors. As the world economy grew and national incomes rose, the increase in the size of foreign markets enabled companies to set up facilities abroad which could attain the same cost structures as could be achieved in their home country. In many cases, the simplification of production procedures – which reduced the need for skilled labour – enabled firms to transfer production abroad to countries where labour costs were lower.

Trade barriers have also played their part in the expansion of FDI. By acting as a brake on the international movement of goods and services, trade barriers have encouraged firms to set up production facilities abroad in order to break into or maintain their foothold in foreign markets. This is the case even if production facilities required to service the local market in the initial phases of development have not been of a size necessary to be internationally competitive.

The formation of regional trade associations has acted as a stimulus to FDI not only because of the possibility that the association may wish to restrict external trade in the future but also that with the adoption of free trade amongst member states the potential market increases. As a result, one often sees substantial FDI from other rich nations such as the US and Japan into regional associations such as the EU.

It must not be forgotten that some nations have actively encouraged FDI either in an attempt to fulfil industrialization plans, to improve the efficiency of domestic firms through competition and/or in the hope that foreign firms with their perceived superiority in organization and production will spur domestic firms to copy their example. Foreign countries have often encouraged FDI by offering a series of incentives linked to tax breaks, allowances and rebates, grants, guarantees to allow the repatriation of profits, the provision of land for development, and the improvement of infrastructure.

PLAN OF THE BOOK

World trade is, therefore, important both for the countries that participate in the international economy and for the businesses that engage in international commercial activity. The rest of this book is devoted to explaining the determinants of trade and trade patterns and the institutions that shape and influence the international trading environment.

In Part Two we discuss the determinants of trade patterns from the perspective of economic theory. We examine the concepts economists use to explain why nations trade and show how the resources available to be used in production, whether natural resource endowments or the results of past investments in physical facilities and people, influence the types of goods a country trades. We also discuss the factors that can lead some countries to be more successful traders than others. The factors that shape the international trading system are also examined.

Emphasis is placed on the reasons for openness in trade and the political and economic factors that might lead to restrictions on the movements of goods and services internationally.

Part Three examines the nature of the international trading system. Chapter 4 concentrates on the role of the nation state, especially in the development of trading relationships via bilateral agreements. Chapter 5 explores the formation of regional trade associations.

Multilateralism is dealt with in Chapter 6. Particular emphasis is placed on the role of the relatively new **World Trade Organization (WTO)** as well as the GATT in overseeing the trading system. Chapter 7 deals with the various arrangements that contribute to orderly trade such as commodity agreements, voluntary export restraints and counter trade. Chapter 8 provides a detailed discussion of the policy measures used by countries to restrict trade while Chapter 9 explains how the multilateral system attempts to control the use of trade restrictions. The means of addressing problems considered 'unfair' trade are the subject of Chapter 10.

The role and function of the major participants in international commerce are studied in Part Four. Emphasis is placed on the rationale for the growth and development of transnational companies, although other players such as trading houses are not neglected. State trading organizations are also covered despite the collapse of the centrally planned economies that favoured this form of trading. The reason for this is that many countries still pursue some of their trade objectives through the use of state institutions.

Part Five examines closely the system that facilitates international commercial transactions. These largely private sector institutions reduce the risks involved in trade by providing finance, guaranteeing payment, providing insurance and organizing the transportation of goods. Since trade involves buying and selling across frontiers between countries having different business ethics, cultures and legal systems, disputes between the parties involved are bound to arise. We, therefore, examine closely the means available to businesses to settle international disputes.

The final section examines some of the likely future developments in the world trading system. While the future appears to hold further growth in trade and closer economic integration, we would not be performing our duty as dismal scientists if we did not emphasize some of the potential difficulties that may arise and impact adversely on international business.

PART 2

What insights does trade theory provide?

Introduction to Part Two

Why should one study the trade theories of economists? In the economics profession, the pure theory of international trade has a reputation for being extremely abstract. It is considered by many outside the economics profession as being more of a rigorous intellectual exercise than being useful in solving real world problems. While these perceptions are, to some extent correct, being familiar with the major trade theories is important for anyone interested in international commerce. The foremost reason is that the influence of trade theory on government attitudes toward international trade is considerable. The conclusions of some of the major theories are used (and misused) to support a wide variety of international political initiatives, trade policies and lobbying positions. Some popular theories have not withstood the tests of close intellectual scrutiny or rigorous empirical investigation. Others are not theories at all but, rather, the well disguised propaganda of particular vested interests.

Technological advancement, particularly the revolution in communications, is fostering greater economic integration. Debates over trade policy will continue. Business people will increasingly be drawn into those debates. Hence, a basic understanding of the theories upon which many of the arguments are based is vital. The input which business people can have on trade policy will be enhanced if they are informed participants in trade discussions. This section attempts to provide an introduction to the insights which trade theory provides.

International trade and economic theory 2

WHAT DETERMINES COMPETITIVENESS?

The purpose of this chapter is to briefly outline the theories that economists have used to explain the pattern of world trade. The models presented will appear simple. They will be framed in terms of two countries or two products or two inputs to production. Those engaging in international commerce are faced with a complex world with many countries, an industry producing a wide range of goods and production processes using enough inputs to justify employing a department full of cost accountants. It is often therefore difficult to see the relevance of the simple models of economists.

Models, however, are by their very nature simplifications. Economists justify their simple models in two ways. Firstly, while more complex systems can be modelled, they require sophisticated mathematical treatment which only specialists can understand. For the sake of communication, the models are kept simple. This would not be a valid justification if adding complexity altered fundamentally the conclusions generated by the models. The second reason that economists use to justify the use of simple models is that adding complexity, at least in terms of more countries, products or inputs, seldom changes the conclusions of the simple models. Economists say that the results of the simple models can be 'generalized'. The models presented in this chapter will continue the tradition of simplicity. What is important is the insights generated by their conclusions.

Since Adam Smith's day it has been assumed that nations trade because it will bring them some advantage. [Adam Smith was professor of Moral Philosophy at the University of Glasgow from 1752 to 1763 and is commonly thought of as the father of modern economics. His famous book *The Wealth of Nations* was originally published in 1776 (Smith, 1961).] This issue will be discussed in greater detail in Chapter 3. The differences in the products that countries trade is determined by their competitiveness in producing goods which in turn is determined by the productivity of the inputs used in the productive process. What trade theories try to do is explain how this competitiveness comes about. The views of the **'classical' economists** on this topic are outlined before proceeding to the more modern theories and explanations for trade in differentiated products.

Table 2.1 Absolute advantage (output per unit of labour)

Goods	Apples	Pencils
Britania	1	5
Americana	6	4

CLASSICAL TRADE THEORY

The classical approach to trade was mainly concerned with showing that trade was beneficial to the parties that undertook it. These theories still provide much of the popular intellectual underpinnings for the belief in trade liberalization.

Absolute advantage

Adam Smith's proposition was simple. He argued that if two nations voluntarily traded with each other then both must gain if each country specialized in the production of the good in which it had an **absolute advantage**. The country would then exchange what it produced for the commodity in which it had an absolute disadvantage. Advantage is defined by efficiency in the use of resources in production.

Absolute advantage can best be illustrated numerically by referring to Table 2.1.

Here we have two countries (Britania and Americana) and two goods (apples and pencils). By expending 1 unit of labour (per hour/week/month, etc.) Britania can produce 1 apple. Alternatively, Britania could use 1 unit of labour to produce 5 pencils. For the same commitment of labour Americana can produce 6 apples or 4 pencils. From this we can see clearly that Britania has an absolute advantage in producing pencils while Americana has an absolute advantage in the production of apples.

Assume that people in Britania are willing to exchange pencils for apples on a one for one basis. Americana could shift 1 unit of labour from producing pencils to producing apples (it is beginning to specialize in apple production). If Americana can trade 6 of its apples for 6 pencils produced by Britania, it will gain 2 pencils (i.e. by moving 1 unit of labour from its own production of pencils, 4 pencils less are produced but 6 pencils are gained from trading). Alternatively, if it only wanted to produce four extra apples for trade it would save itself one third of the labour time expended. The 6 units of apples that Britania receives from trading would have required it to expend 6 units of labour time if it had produced these domestically. If Britania had used this labour time in the production of pencils it could have produced 30 pencils. By specializing and trading Britania can make a net gain of 24 pencils (30 minus the 6 pencils it must trade). Of course, people in Britania are as well off as they were before because the 6 apples they are no longer

Table 2.2 Comparative advantage (output per unit of labour)

Goods	Beef	Lamb
Britania	1	2
Americana	6	4

producing have been acquired by trading. If Britania did not wish for all 24 extra pencils, it could choose to save some of the labour. The saved labour could be used to produce other goods or could be taken as leisure. The major point is that both countries gain from specializing and then trading.

Our example has shown that by specializing in the production of the good in which it has an absolute advantage and then engaging in international exchanges – trade – a country can make gains. What should a country do, however, when it is more efficient than other countries in the production of all goods? To answer this question the 19th century economist David Ricardo developed the concept of comparative advantage (Ricardo, 1951).

Comparative advantage

The theory of **comparative advantage** concentrates not on the absolute differences in countries' efficiency in producing goods but on the differences in relative efficiencies. The law of comparative advantage states that a country with an absolute advantage in the production of both goods in a two good world should specialize in the production and export of the good in which its absolute advantage is greatest. Consumption of the other good would be satisfied by importing it from the other country which, in turn, would specialize in the good in which its absolute disadvantage would be least. This can be numerically illustrated in Table 2.2.

Here again we have two countries (Britania and Americana) each producing two goods (beef and lamb). In this example Britania has an absolute disadvantage in the production of both goods while Americana is more efficient at producing both of them. Americana is six times more efficient at producing beef and twice as efficient at producing lamb. Its major advantage, however, clearly lies in the production of beef and so it can be said that Americana's comparative advantage lies in the production of beef. Compared to Americana, Britania is least inefficient in the production of lamb producing only half as much per unit of labour (2:4) compared to one sixth as much beef (1:6). Thus, Britania can be said to have a comparative advantage in the production of lamb. If both nations specialize in and export the good in which they have a comparative advantage they will both benefit from trade.

To illustrate the gain from trade let us assume as in our previous example that Americana can exchange 6 kg of beef for 6 kg of lamb. If Americana chooses to shift 1 unit of labour out of the production of lamb and into the production of beef, it could produce an extra 6 kg of beef. This extra beef could be traded for 6 kg of lamb, as only 4 kg less lamb was produced, Americana would gain 2 units of lamb compared to its autarkic (no trade) position. Britania would also gain in that the 6 kg of beef it would receive in exchange for its lamb which would have taken it 6 units of labour time to produce. Britania could now use that labour effort to produce 12 kg of lamb and trade 6 kg of this extra lamb production for 6 kg of beef. Hence, it would have the same quantity of beef and an extra 6 kg of lamb by specializing and trading. Britania gains more (6 kg of lamb) than Americana (2 kg of lamb), but they have both gained by specializing and entering into trade with one another. This is the fundamental lesson of the theory of comparative advantage.

It should not be assumed that mutually beneficial trade only arises when 6 kg of beef are exchanged for 6 kg of lamb. Exchange rates other than this 1:1 ratio can also lead to gains. As long as Americana can achieve more than 4 kg of lamb by giving up 6 kg of beef it will gain. Similarly if Britania can give up less than 12 kg of lamb for 6 kg of beef then it too will gain. Thus the range within which advantageous trade can take place lies between 4 kg of lamb < 6 kg of beef < 12 kg of lamb. When the two countries trade 6 kg of beef for 6 kg of lamb Americana gains 2 kg of lamb and Britania 6 kg of lamb, 8 kg in total. This would be the case whenever both countries shifted a unit of labour and continued the move toward specialization. Of course, once one country shifted all its labour out of the production of the good which it had a comparative disadvantage, no more gains from trade could be achieved. As the ratio of exchange moves closer to 4 kg of lamb for 6 kg of beef, the smaller is the share of the gain occurring to Britania. Conversely, the closer the ratio of exchange approaches 6 kg of beef for 12 kg of lamb, the greater is the gain for Americana. For example, if Americana could exchange 6 kg of beef for 8 kg of lamb then Americana would gain 4 kg of lamb. Britania would also gain 4 kg of lamb. If, on the other hand, Americana exchanges 6 kg of beef for 10 kg of lamb it would gain 6 kg of lamb but Britania would only gain 2 kg of lamb. Thus, differences in the ratio of exchange would determine the actual as opposed to the possible gains from trade and, more relevant to our discussion, the type and quantity of goods traded, i.e. the pattern and the volume of trade. The determination of the ratio of exchange was, however, not addressed by the theory of comparative advantage. It was only able to describe the conditions of supply and the benefits once demand was known.

While the classical economist focus was on the benefits to be gained from trade their analysis did not answer the question, 'what determines comparative advantage?'. The classical view suggested that climate and differences in the quality of natural resources led to differences in the productivity of labour between countries. As a result, nations would have different comparative advantages and, hence, they would export different products to one another. This may well have been a reasonable explanation in a period when the products traded were agricultural and/or when labour was the predominant input. Many of the goods which are actually traded require inputs other than labour and natural resources. In a world where labour skills can be learned and production know-how is widely available, the classical view loses a great deal of its explanatory power. Economists of the neo-classical school attempted to address the issue by relating comparative advantage to the productive factors with which a country was endowed. The major contribution of the classical theory was, however, to prove that if a difference in productive efficiency existed, gains could be expected from engaging in trade. The simple but powerful logic of the theories of absolute and comparative advantage has withstood the test of long-term intellectual scrutiny, and still provides one of the major cornerstones underpinning the case for trade liberalization.

NEO-CLASSICAL TRADE THEORY

The **neo-classical** theory of international trade was developed by the Swedish economists Heckscher and Ohlin (Ohlin, 1933). It is also known as the factor proportion theory.

The basic 2 × 2 model

Neo-classical theory still accepts as its starting point the two country-two commodity world that the classicists assumed but differed on a number of points. Firstly, more than one factor of production was assumed. Capital was included along with labour. Secondly, the two goods produced were assumed to have different **factor intensities**, one using relatively more capital than labour while the reverse was the case for the other good. Thirdly, while factor intensities differed between products, the production technologies used to produce each of the goods were assumed to be the same in both countries. In other words, a good which requires relatively more capital than labour in its production in one country is be said to be capital intensive. It is also produced capital intensively in the other country.

Given the above production conditions, how does the theory operate or what does it predict? Let us take two countries that are distinguished from one another by an inequality in the distribution of resources between them, i.e. one country is capital abundant while the other is labour abundant. The capital abundant country has a higher capital to labour ratio than the labour abundant country. If demand conditions are the same in the two countries, then the prices of the factors are determined by their supply as reflected by the quantities available in the country – its endowment. In the capital abundant country, capital becomes relatively cheaper while in the labour abundant country, labour is relatively cheaper. By linking these relative prices to the production conditions outlined above, neo-classical theory produces the conclusion that goods which use capital intensively in their production will be produced at lower cost in the relatively capital abundant country. The opposite will be the case in the labour abundant country which will have a comparative advantage in producing labour intensive goods. Thus, countries that are relatively well endowed with capital will produce and export goods that use capital intensively in their production while labour abundant countries will export labour intensive goods.

The neo-classical theory went deeper than the classical approach in that it not only predicted trade patterns but could also account for the differences in comparative advantage between countries. Classical theory would suggest that labour productivity would determine what goods a country would produce and export. Heckscher and Ohlin went beyond this and gave a reason for the difference in labour productivity. For example, in capital abundant countries labour productivity would be high because it had more capital to work with than in labour abundant countries.

The Leontief paradox

The neo-classical explanation held sway in economics until mathematical and statistical tools were developed which could test it empirically. Examining the trade patterns of the US, which was considered to be a capital-rich country, **Leontief** (1953) discovered that its exports were in fact labour intensive while its imports were capital intensive. This paradoxical result was also found for other countries and was furthermore confirmed for the US by later studies (Leontief, 1956). This led economists to re-examine the assumptions on which neo-classical theory was based and either to modify it so that it explained the facts or to seek alternative explanations.

A number of justifications were put forward to reconcile the empirical results with the theory. One of the first, which was proposed by Leontief, was that US labour was roughly three times more productive that its foreign counterparts as a result of superior management, first-rate training and better motivation. By taking US labour superiority into account one could recalculate the figures to show that the US was, in fact, a labour abundant country.

The second influence to be examined was the impact of US restrictions on imports. It was argued that labour intensive industries in the US were highly protected so that imports were biased in favour of capital intensive goods (Travis, 1964).

Neo-classical theory's concentration on only two of the many factors of production was also suggested as a possible explanation. For example, it was pointed out that the US was really an importer of natural resource intensive goods which also happened to require a great deal of capital but little labour. On a straight capital/labour measurement they would show up to be capital intensive whereas they were actually natural resource intensive (Vanek, 1953).

A further explanation of the paradox was the possible influence of demand factors. It was suggested that US demand was heavily biased in favour of capital intensive goods which raised their price, hence neutralizing the comparative advantage of home produced goods while re-enforcing that of imports (Valvanis-Vail, 1954). These and many other explanations were put forward to explain the paradox and rehabilitate the neo-classical theory of trade.

ALTERNATIVES TO NEO-CLASSICAL TRADE THEORY

Other economists, as we have pointed out, took a different view and tried to explain trade patterns by expounding alternative theories. These were usually developed by holding constant the factors that Heckscher and Ohlin assumed variable and assuming variable the factors they held constant! For example, **economies of scale** (an economic concept which suggests that, over at least some range of production, efficiency will improve as the quantity of output a factory is designed to produce increases) were allowed to exist whereas under Heckscher and Ohlin there were only **constant returns to scale** (where production facilities are equally efficient no matter what their size), labour was no longer assumed to be homogeneous but had different skills, factor intensity was allowed to vary over the life of the product and so on. We will now examine some of these so-called alternative theories and the light they shed for determining a country's comparative advantage and, in turn, its trading pattern.

Human skills

More as an extension of the Heckscher–Ohlin theory rather than a true alternative, economists have suggested that skilled labour inputs are an important source of comparative advantage and, hence, trade patterns (Keesing, 1966). It has been argued that countries which are well endowed with professional personnel and highly skilled labour will specialize in the export of skill intensive goods. The opposite is also true. Countries that have abundant supplies of unskilled labour concentrate on the production and export of goods employing untrained labour. By defining skills in terms of either educational attainment or the average wage rates in the industry (since wages are assumed to reflect training and professionalism) empirical support has been found for this theory. This evidence is particularly strong from tests where labour has been 'decomposed' into its various skill components and then has been used along with capital to explain trade patterns (Baldwin, 1971).

Economies of scale

One of the assumptions on which the factor endowments theory was based was that of constant returns to scale. Firms, however, are known to achieve economies of scale and a large home market has been said to contribute positively in bringing these about. As a result, large countries would be expected to benefit over small countries in the production of goods whose methods of production allowed them to reap economies of scale. Although ostensibly at a disadvantage, small countries could achieve economies of scale and gain comparative advantage if they concentrated on the production of goods to satisfy international markets and did not rely on national characteristics as a selling feature (Drèze, 1960).

One interesting aspect of the economies of scale argument is that trading patterns could be determined by which country's firms had established an early lead over its rivals in one or a range of industries. By gaining a lead, a country would achieve lower costs and would therefore make it potentially difficult for rival countries to compete successfully. Under these circumstances it becomes possible for a country to export a good or a range of goods that are contrary to those expected from an examination of its factor endowments.

Technological theories

While explanations of trading patterns were sought by incorporating static economies of scale into the analysis, these theories relied upon historical accident as an explanation for why a country's industry gained the lead. As this explanation was not entirely satisfactory, another approach incorporating dynamic economies of scale and technical progress was advanced. This group of theories assumes that there is a link between high national income levels and innovativeness or dynamism. The argument suggests that industrially advanced countries are the initiators of new products. As a result, they are able to reap both static and dynamic economies of scale in production given their large and expanding markets. As long as identical innovations do not take place simultaneously in different countries or imitation is not instantaneous, then one country will gain a lead or comparative advantage over another in the development and production of a specific commodity (Posner, 1961; Hufbauer, 1965). In this way, trade will be generated between countries. Each country will exchange with the other, goods which it has not yet been able to imitate and produce at home. Once the importing country's firms have succeeded in reproducing the good at comparable cost, trade in the commodity will cease. Studies have shown that this technological approach to trade can explain some of the trade between developed countries and between developed and developing countries (Hufbauer, 1970).

The product life cycle

Although a link between income and dynamism or innovativeness can be established, it is not so clear why the production of new goods should be located in advanced countries. An answer to this question was, however, provided by Vernon (1966) who suggested that as a good matures its characteristics change which also leads to a change in the location of its production.

In the initial phase of a product's development there are major uncertainties regarding styling and the appropriate production process. These uncertainties can be reduced if changes in consumer desires can be translated quickly into alterations in the product or the production process. The first can be acted on if production is carried out close to the point of sale while the second can be achieved if flexible skilled labour is substituted for machines. As the product matures and becomes standardized, marketing and production uncertainties become less and competitive pressure increases. This will, in turn, encourage firms to find cheaper locations for their production and comparative advantage moves from the innovating country to those with the lowest production costs.

Income similarity

As well as encouraging the development of new goods, income can also be looked upon as shaping tastes and, hence, demand patterns. Income similarity was put forward by Linder (1961) to explain the increasing volume of trade between advanced countries with similar factor endowments. His argument went like this: entrepreneurs initially concentrate on supplying the home market but once this has become saturated they seek new outlets, principally in countries or amongst social groups within those countries that have similar incomes and, hence, tastes to those in their own country. Trade will, therefore, be greatest in intensity between countries that have similar national incomes. Again, there is considerable evidence to suggest that these demand factors have played an important role in the determination of trade patterns between countries. This hypothesis has been particularly useful when coupled with the notion of economies of scale for explaining the phenomenon of intra-industry trade or trade in similar products.

INTRA-INDUSTRY TRADE

During the late 1950s and early 1960s it became obvious that trade was growing fastest between the advanced industrial countries and that this trade was in similar – from the same industry in the other country – but differentiated products (Verdoorn, 1960; Balassa, 1975). Both neo-classical and alternative theories predicted that trade would take place between countries with dissimilar factor endowments and, hence, in dissimilar goods so this new phenomenon needed an explanation. To place the role of this intra-industry trade in context, one merely has to examine the following figures. For example, it has been estimated that 60% of world trade is in manufactured goods and half of this is accounted for by intra-industry trade (Greenaway and Miller, 1986).

Trade in non-manufactures is also subject to this phenomenon. Other researchers have concluded that for some individual countries, up to 70% of their trade in manufactures is subject to intra-industry trade (Aquino, 1978). It has, furthermore, been increasing over time (Hesse, 1974).

The measurement of intra-industry trade

There are a variety of ways to measure intra-industry trade but the simplest is to measure the extent of overlapping trade in a particular commodity or good and express this as a proportion of overall trade, i.e. exports plus imports.

Intra-industry trade can then be expressed as

$$B_i = \frac{(X_i + M_i) - |X_i - M_i|}{(X_i + M_i)} \times 100$$

where B_i stands for intra-industry trade in commodity i, and X_i and M_i the level of exports and imports of the commodity, respectively.

Thus if exports equal $200 and imports $120 then $240 is overlapping trade (i.e. $120 of imports and $120 of exports) while $80 does not overlap. Intra-industry would thus be 75% of the total.

Using our formula this can be deduced from:

$$B_i = \frac{(200 + 120) - |200 - 120|}{(200 + 120)} \times 100$$

$$= \frac{320 - 80}{320} \times 100$$

$$= \frac{240}{320} \times 100$$

$$= 75\%$$

The aggregation and classification of goods

When discussing intra-industry trade, it is essential to know what is meant by similar goods because the extent of this type of trade can be affected by the definitions used. Let us take chocolates as an example and define Belgian chocolates as a totally different product to British chocolates. With this definition, no intra-industry trade can take place. This would, however, be stretching the point since in another sense chocolate is chocolate all the world over. It may differ in colour, texture and taste but its basic make up is the same. At the other extreme, all manufactured goods could be defined as a single product. In this case exporting advanced medical equipment in return for bicycles would be considered intra-industry trade. Thus, the degree to which goods are aggregated and disaggregated has important implications for intra-industry trade. It has led some economists to regard it as nothing more

Table 2.3 An Illustration of Standard Industrial Trade Classification

SECTION 5	CHEMICALS AND RELATED PRODUCTS
DIVISION 51	Organic Chemicals
GROUP 511	Hydrocarbons n.e.s. Derivatives
SUB-GROUP 511.1	Acyclic Hydrocarbons

Source: Commodity Trade Statistics 1993, United Nations, New York.

than a statistical artefact (Pomfret, 1986). Other researchers, however, discovered that as trade was disaggregated into finer classifications and intra-industry trade declined, it nevertheless remained at levels that still required an explanation (Grubel and Lloyd, 1975).

At this juncture it may be pertinent to explain or show how commodity trade is classified. Most countries present their trade statistics in the form adopted by the United Nations, the so-called Standard International Trade Classification. It is a numerical classification with each commodity being allocated a section number. Each section is then sub divided into divisions groups and sub groups with each of these being given a number prefixed by that allocated to the section. Table 2.3 illustrates this clearly. Thus the first digit refers to the section number and the second to the division while the third and fourth digits refer to the group and sub group, respectively.

Explaining intra-industry trade

The first explanation of intra-industry trade was advanced by Grubel and Lloyd, (1975) who emphasized product differentiation and economies of scale as potential causes. It soon became evident, however, that intra-industry trade also existed among non-differentiated or homogenous products. A further explanation for trade in differentiated products was also required.

Homogeneous goods

Intra-industry trade in **homogeneous goods** can be explained fairly easily by three factors. The first is the existence of entrepôt or the re-export trade. A considerable proportion of Hong Kong and Singapore's trade is of this type. A country may import goods in bulk which may be shipped out to other neighbouring countries possibly having been broken down into smaller consignments. In this way, one would see the simultaneous importing and exporting of the same goods. The second explanation is seasonality, where products are exported during one part of the year and imported during another. This is quite common for agricultural products. The third explanation is the cost of transport which may encourage users of a particular good to import it from a bordering country rather than a domestic producer who is located say at the other end of its own country. For similar reasons, the domestic producer may export his good to another country that is located nearby.

It is quite common to see this type of cross-border trade take place between land-locked countries such as those found in Europe.

Differentiated goods

For differentiated goods, a more sophisticated explanation is required. Differences in tastes amongst consumers and economies of scale in production have been suggested. Consumer tastes are, at least in part, determined by income (Linder, 1961). As people become richer, they will demand better quality goods and greater variety. Under **autarky**, domestic producers can only cater for dominant domestic tastes and choice will be limited. Consumers could buy their preferred choices from abroad but may be discouraged from doing so by high transport costs and other barriers which add to the purchase price of the imports. As incomes rise, however, consumers may well be able to afford these premiums (Barker, 1977).

The opening up of trade between countries and the expansion of markets will allow firms to specialize in the production of varieties. Under autarky, domestic firms will concentrate their production on one or a few varieties. To expand on the number of varieties produced would lead to increased costs and lower profits for the firms concerned. Once trade is opened up, however, market segments appear which are large enough for suppliers to reap economies of scale and, as a result, they are able to produce more varied goods. Which country achieves a lead and, hence, a comparative advantage is very much a matter of chance, company strategy or government policies which promote particular industries (Krugman, 1979). The latter is known as industrial policy. Major policy debates take place over whether governments can improve on market signals by identifying future leading industries and put policies in place to ensure they secure the comparative advantage.

Another explanation of intra-industry trade builds on the Heckscher-Ohlin framework (Pomfret, 1986). This approach suggests that different varieties require different factor inputs and, as a result, each country will specialize in the products that use its abundant factor intensively. It will then exchange this variety in return for the other. This theory suggests that a product, say chairs, can be produced from different materials (e.g. wood and plastic). Those countries that are abundant in wood will produce and export wooden chairs, and satisfy their demand for plastic chairs by importing them. This theory suggests, however, that products are being misclassified in that chairs should really be sub-categories of the wood and plastics industries and not grouped together. While this explanation of intra-industry trade is plausible a number of writers do not feel that it explains the phenomenon of intra-industry trade fully (Lloyd, 1989).

How do the theoretical explanations of intra-industry trade measure up in practice? As with all empirical work, methodological problems arise when one tries to test theoretical concepts in practice. The variables that need to be used to model homogeneity, product differentiation, market structure and scale economies are sometimes not available, and the proxies developed are often at best rough approximations. Without minimizing the problem involved in estimating the relationships, the principal empirical works show that variables such as overlapping tastes, product differentiation, market structure, technology, and economies of scale have a positive influence on the level of intra-industry trade between countries (Greenaway and Miller, 1986). Other factors that were found to have a negative influence were trade barriers and foreign direct investment. Neither of these needs much explanation as one restricts the volume of trade and, hence, the opportunity for intra-industry trade to take place, while the other acts as a replacement for trade.

WHAT DO TRADE THEORIES TELL US ABOUT TRADE PATTERNS?

Probably the first thing to note is that it is unlikely that any one particular theory can account for the existing pattern of world trade. The economics profession tends to conduct analyses on the basis of the Heckscher–Ohlin model despite its limitations and its poor showing in empirical tests. There are several reasons for this. Firstly, it is a simple theory whereby, with a few assumptions concerning the use of abundant resources and knowing the factor endowments of a country, one can make predictions about its trade pattern. Secondly, the tests that tend to refute the Heckscher–Ohlin model are not without their own flaws. For example, they rarely take into account trade policies and distortions and so cannot be said to refute the neo-classical theories directly. Thirdly, if Heckscher–Ohlin is modified to include human capital, as some researchers have done, then this modified version gives reasonable results (Baldwin, 1971). Finally, empirical evidence for the alternative theories is not strong enough for any one of these to be regarded as a completely adequate alternative. It has been suggested that the product life cycle theory is probably better at explaining changing trade patterns over time than explaining trade at any one point in time.

As the issue of a general trade theory has not been totally settled, some trade economists have, however, suggested trade theories are useful at explaining trade patterns in certain groups of goods (Hufbauer, 1970; Hirsch, 1974). Those that require either heavy natural resource, climatic influenced or unsophisticated labour inputs could be classed as **Ricardian-type goods**. Thus, trade in goods coming from the extractive industries (i.e. coal, petroleum, minerals) or food products such as wheat and corn can be explained adequately by Ricardian trade theory. Typically, one would expect a flow of these products from developing countries, although in the case of food grains and some minerals, many of the developed countries, e.g. the US, Canada and Australia, also export these goods.

Those goods that require standardized technologies and no single specific factor inputs will be located in countries which offer the best combination of factor prices. In other words, industries such as textile manufacturing, ferrous metal production and such like would be regarded as Heckscher–Ohlin-type goods and that theory would describe the location of those industries and their pattern of trade. In particular, this theory would explain the trade between developed and developing countries.

Following the scheme just outlined one would, therefore, expect that trade in technologically advanced goods would be explained by the technology theories. Given that these theories emphasize the advanced nature of the economies involved in producing such goods, both in terms of income level and innovative skill, these goods will be produced in advanced countries and exported to either other advanced and/or developing countries. Thus, exports of micro-electronic goods and sophisticated transport equipment such as aircraft will usually emanate from the developed economies. That is not to say that this will always be the case for, as already suggested, once the production technologies become standardized these goods can come under the Heckscher–Ohlin category.

Several country studies testing this approach have found that the US exports are concentrated in the technology and Ricardian groups. Japan's exports are found predominately in the Heckscher–Ohlin group while the Ricardian group is absent. The EU is fairly strong in both the Heckscher–Ohlin and technology groups but weak in the Ricardian (Hirsch, 1974). The UK's exports were shifting away from technological goods to Heckscher–Ohlin varieties (Katrak, 1982). In contrast the evidence from Japan suggested a movement into technological goods (Heller, 1976).

One question that might be asked is what role do the theories of intra-industry trade play in this analysis? The answer is that countries whose industries had gained substantial economies of scale, and hence had specialized in particular product lines, would export these products to countries with similar income levels and tastes. Thus Heckscher–Ohlin-type goods such as cars can be traded between countries with similar factor endowments as can technological goods such as medical equipment and sophisticated computer equipment.

Assuming that goods can be categorized by the inputs required in their production – which should not be too difficult – then our trade theories enable us to explain trade patterns and, to be more precise, explain which countries will produce and export which goods. A question that still remains to be answered is why some countries are more prone to trade than others. This is covered in the next section.

THE DETERMINANTS OF TRADE INTENSITY AND COMPETITIVENESS

Economists have tried to identify the factors that determine:

1. Trade dependency, i.e. the ratio of imports to GDP.
2. Net exports.

Leamer (1974, 1984) related these measures to three groups of variables:

1. The state of development, i.e. GDP and population.
2. Resistance variables such as trade restrictions and transport distances.
3. Variables that reflect resource endowments such as capital intensity, research and development expenditure, skills and education, and the consumption of electricity.

This last variable was used to proxy the industrial complexity and sophistication of a country.

The results showed that there was a close link between trade dependency and the development variables while resource endowments contributed little. In other words, countries with high GDPs and large populations are the major traders. The results for net exports, however, were contrary in that resource variables were more important. In Leamer's (1974) study, research and development was the most important factor while in his 1984 study the factor intensity variables predominated.

A recent approach has attempted to explain why some nations are more successful than others in exporting (Porter, 1990). In particular, an explanation is provided for why some countries' industries continued to be successful even when factors such as exchange rates, resource endowments and so on worked against them. The answer, it was suggested, lay in the maintenance and growth of national productivity and, in particular, how companies formulate their strategies.

Four major determinants of international competitiveness or '**competitive advantage**' were identified. These were:

1. Factor endowments both basic (natural resources, climate, labour and capital) and advanced (telecommunications, infrastructure, labour skills, resource facilities and technical knowledge). It is argued that these advanced factors are critical for competitiveness. While basic factors can initially give a country a competitive edge in the production of certain goods, it is the availability of the advanced variety that maintain and enhance it.
2. Demand conditions such as the size and composition of the home market relative to foreign demand but more specifically the demands placed on local firms by domestic customers with regard to the quality and the upgrading of their products. A demanding home market will often prepare firms for selling in the international arena.
3. The existence of internationally competitive related and support

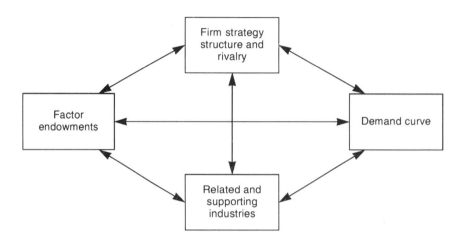

Figure 2.1 Porter's diamond and national competitive advantage. Source: Porter, M. E. (1990) *The Competitive Advantage of Nations*, The Free Press, New York.

industries. These will enhance the success of firms using their products and services by lowering their users costs and/or providing better support than those available to their rivals.
4. Firm strategy, structure and competitiveness. It is suggested that ownership, management and operational strategy are important in enhancing competitiveness.

No one form of these is necessarily correct but those that allow flexibility and rapid response to changing circumstances are the most successful. Domestic rivalry amongst firms also enhances competitiveness as firms strive to increase their efficiency and provide better quality goods.

These four, mutually reinforcing, determinants constitute Porter's diamond (see Figure 2.1). Industries and companies within them would succeed where the 'diamond' pulled in their favour. A nation's competitiveness in a particular area would be achieved and enhanced if favourable demand conditions coexisted with plentiful factor endowments, successful and competitive support industries and a group of producers whose rivalry encouraged them to make full use of these conditions, and to continually upgrade and improve their products.

It was also suggested that two other factors played an important part, i.e. government policy and chance. The role of the government was particularly crucial in the formulation and execution of policy. It could affect dramatically all four determinants in Porter's diamond. Government's attitudes towards education, research and development, the provision of telecommunications, and infrastructure could affect factor conditions. Its industrial and competition policies and its fiscal and monetary policies could influence firms strategy, structure and security as well as support industries and demand conditions. Government policy was then crucial to successful working of the mutually reinforcing diamond.

The integration of these factors determined not only which industries were established in which countries, but how successful they were in the international market place. Evidence from 100 case studies drawn from 10 leading industrial countries, among them the US, UK, Italy, Germany, Japan, Sweden and Switzerland, supported this hypothesis. In many ways this hypothesis confirmed the earlier work mentioned above, but departed from it by emphasizing the strategic behaviour of companies.

WHAT CAN BE CONCLUDED?

Since Ricardo's time, economists have sought to explain the pattern of trade by making use of the concept of comparative advantage. Countries will export those goods in which they have such an advantage and will import goods in which they do not. They will gain by doing so. The question that later economists sought to answer was what factors determine comparative advantage? The Heckscher–Ohlin approach emphasized a country's factor endowments as being the key. Hence, a relatively capital abundant country exported goods that used capital intensively in their production process while it imported labour intensive goods. The Leontief paradox highlighted the limitations of this approach and encouraged not only a recasting of the original theory to take into account factors such as land and human skills/capital but also the development of alternative theoretical models. In this way, the influence of technology, innovativeness and research and development were brought to the fore as were economies of scale and income similarity.

While these theories enriched the explanations of trade patterns they did not, at least directly, explain the growth of intra-industry trade – particularly trade in differentiated goods. This phenomenon needed the interaction of income similarities and economies of scale in production to provide theoretical insights. Intra-industry trade in non-differentiated goods could be largely accounted for by the existence of entrepôt trade, seasonality in the production of goods and transport costs.

Trade theories also allowed economists to isolate the factors that influenced a country's trade intensity and competitiveness. Trade dependency was closely related to the stage of an economy's development as shown by GDP and population. Success in exporting, though, was linked closely to innovativeness as measured by research and development and factor intensity.

Some countries did well at exporting in areas in which they did not apparently have a comparative advantage. This led some researchers to search for explanations other than factor endowments and research and development expenditures. These included inter industry linkages and support, the competitive environment, socio-economic factors, infrastructure and government policy.

Theoretical explanations of trade patterns lead directly into policy debates regarding what governments can do to improve a country's competitiveness. Some policy prescriptions are fairly straightforward. If labour skill levels or expenditures on research and development improve competitiveness, then governments should make and also encourage these investments. However, the returns on these expenditures will depend upon whether the types of goods which can take advantage of these improvements are important to a country's trade. Other more dynamic theories may suggest to government that they get involved in trying to identify potential growth or 'winner' industries. Their record has been mixed at best.

The importance of this work for business is clear. At the most basic level, the theories should improve company planning by being able to classify the type of industry the firm is in. If domestic markets are not growing, insights can be gained into the likely prospects for exporting.

Dynamic theories may provide insights for the future. Which markets are likely to grow? Should investments in research and development take place and into which product lines? Of equal, if not more importance, the dynamic theories may point to likely sources of future foreign competition. Finally, business will be called on to advise government on industrial policy. Trade theory can improve the impact firms are able to exert on the direction of policy. It can provide powerful arguments which may be particularly useful in preventing governments from following inappropriate industrial policies. In other words, while trade theory may not be able to precisely identify future 'winners', it can help identify potential 'losers'. Japan's orderly restructuring of its once pre-eminent export oriented shipbuilding industry and no longer internationally competitive steel industry are obvious examples.

The main classical conclusion – that countries gain from trade – has also been the subject of considerable theoretical effort. This work contributes to the long standing debate on trade liberalization and protectionism, and is the basis for the discussion in Chapter 3.

REFERENCES

Aquino, A. (1978) Intra-industry trade and intra-industry specialization as concurrent sources of international trade in manufactures. *Weltwirtshaftliches Archiv*, **114**(2), 275–96.

Balassa, B. (1975) *European Economic Integration*, North Holland, Amsterdam.

Baldwin, R. E. (1971) The determinants of the commodity structure of US trade. *American Economic Review*, **61**, 126–46.

Barker, T. S. (1977) International trade and economic growth: an alternative to the neo-classical approach. *Cambridge Journal of Economics*, **1**(2), 153–72.

Drèze, J. (1960) Quelques reflections sereins sur l'adaptation de l'industrie Belge au Marché commun. *Comptes Rendus des Travaux de la Société Royale d'Economie Politique de Belgique*, **275**.

Greenaway, D. and Miller, C. R. (1986) *The Economics of Intra Industry Trade*, Blackwell, Oxford.

Grubel, H. G. and Lloyd, P. S. (1975) *Intra industry Trade: The Theory and Measurement of Trade in Differentiated Products*, Macmillan, London.

Heller, P. S. (1976) Factor endowment change and comparative advantage: the case of Japan 1956–1969. *Review of Economics and Statistics*, **58**, 283–92.

Hesse, H. (1974) Hypothesis for the explanation of trade between industrial countries, 1953–1970, in *On the Economics of Intra-industry Trade*, (ed. H. Gierch), JCB Mohr, Tubingen, pp. 39–59.

Hirsch, S. (1974) Hypotheses regarding trade between developing and industrial countries, in *The International Division of Labour: Problems and Prospects*, (ed. H. Gierch), JCB Mohr, Tubingen, pp. 65–82.

Hufbauer, G. (1965) *Synthetic Materials and the Theory of International Trade*, Duckworth, London.

Hufbauer, G. (1970) The impact of national characteristics and technology on the Commodity Composition of trade in manufactured goods, in *The Technology Factor in International Trade*, (ed. R. Vernon), National Bureau of Economic Research, New York, pp. 145–231.

Katrak, H. (1982) Labour skills, R & D and capital requirements in the international trade and investment of the UK 1968–78. *National Institute Economic Review*, **101**, 38–47.

Keesing, D. (1966) Labour skills and comparative advantage. *American Economic Review*, **56**, 249–67.

Krugman, P. R. (1979) Increasing returns, monopolistic competition and international trade. *Journal of International Economics*, **9**, 469–79.

Leamer, E. E. (1974) The commodity composition of international trade in manufacture: an empirical analysis. *Oxford Economic Papers*, **26**(3), 350–74.

Leamer, E. E. (1984) *Sources of International Comparative Advantage*, MIT Press, Cambridge, MA.

Leontief, W. A. (1953) Domestic production and foreign trade: the American capital position re-examined. *Proceedings of the American Philosophical Society*, **97**, 332–49.

Leontief, W. A. (1956) Factor proportions and the structure of American trade: further theoretical and empirical analysis. *Review of Economics and Statistics*, **38**, 386–407.

Linder, S. B. (1961) *An Essay on Trade and Transformation*, John Wiley, New York.

Lloyd, P. J. (1989) Reflections on intra-industry trade and factor proportions, in *Intra-industry Trade*, (eds P. K. M. Tharakan and J. Kol), Macmillan, London, pp. 15–30.

Ohlin, B. (1933) *Inter-regional Trade and International Trade*, Harvard University Press, Cambridge, MA.

Pomfret, R. (1986) On the division of labour and international trade: or Adam Smith's explanation of intra-industry trade. *Journal of Economic Studies*, **13**(4), 56–63.

Porter, M. E. (1990) *The Comparative Advantage of Nations*, The Free Press, New York.

Posner, M. V. (1961) International trade and technical change. *Oxford Economic Papers*, **13**, 323–41.

Ricardo, D. (1951) on the *Principles of Political Economy and Taxation*, in *The Works and Correspondence of David Ricardo*, (ed. P. Sraffa), Cambridge University Press, Cambridge.

Smith, A. (1961) *An Inquiry into the Nature and Causes of the Wealth of Nations*, (ed. E. Cannan), reprinted by Methuen, London.

Travis, W. P. (1964) *The Theory of Trade and Protection*, Harvard University Press, Cambridge, MA.

Valvanis-Vail, S. (1954) Leontief's scarce factor paradox. *Journal of Political Economy*, 62, 523–8.

Vanek, J. (1953) The natural resource content of foreign trade, 1870–1955 and the relative abundance of natural resources in the United States. *Review of Economics and Statistics*, **41**, 146–53.

Verdoorn, P. J. (1960) The intra block trade of the Benelux, in *Economic Consequences of the Size of Nations*, (ed. E.A.G. Robinson) Macmillan, London.

Vernon, R. (1966) International investment and international trade in the product cycle. *Quarterly Journal of Economics*, **80**, 190–207.

The great debate – free trade versus protectionism

3

THE MIDDLE GROUND OF MANAGED TRADE

The environment within which international trade and commerce takes place is neither one of free trade nor one of total restriction. Most of the world's trade is carried out somewhere in between, in what can be called a managed environment. This middle ground is not fixed and can change over time and oscillate between a more and less open system. As we will see, theory suggests that a less restrictive system leads to an increase in trade which of course is beneficial to firms engaged in international commerce and, furthermore, maximizes the welfare of all countries. It might then seem surprising that some of the main proponents of protective measures are firms. Businessmen, nevertheless, are heard to claim that they face 'unfair' foreign competition and want their home governments to do something about it (Cuthbertson, 1986). Governments, while accepting the arguments for free trade, will ignore such requests at their peril if the power and influence business people and their supporters is strong. Participating in international business is risky and requires firms to carry out heavy investment so an understanding of the forces that engender liberalization and protection and their consequences is both important and useful.

This chapter outlines the theoretical arguments for trade liberalization and protectionism, and the pressures that bring these trade regimes into being. The institutional structure of the international trading system will be discussed in Part Three. We will begin by discussing first the early views on protection – known as **mercantilism**. Then the free trade arguments will be developed before addressing the more modern approaches to trade restriction and the political forces that foster them.

THE CASE FOR AN OPEN TRADE REGIME

Mercantilist writers in the 18th and 19th centuries proposed that nations limit their imports as much as possible in order to run a trade surplus – more exports than imports (Heckscher, 1935). In the mercantilist era, international accounts were settled in gold and silver. A trade surplus would lead to the accumulation of precious metals which could be used to finance government expenditure. By spending these surpluses in the home economy and restricting the purchases of foreign goods, the flow of precious metals abroad was minimized. Domestic business activity would be stimulated as consumers were forced to purchase domestically produced goods. Restricting foreign purchases might reduce consumers' choice but it maximized the revenue accruing to the state. In the mercantilists' scheme of things, maximizing the state's revenue was akin to maximizing a country's welfare. This view of society's welfare was totally opposite to that of the classical economists such as Adam Smith (1961) and Ricardo (1951) who equated the nation's welfare with the sum of each individual's welfare. In other words, what benefited the individual benefited the country. How did the classical economists reach this conclusion?

The conclusion can be derived by using some basic economic theory. Figure 3.1 shows the **production possibility frontier** (PP) of a country producing two goods – wheat and cars. The production possibility frontier shows the maximum combinations of outputs it is possible for a country to produce if it uses all of its available resources. As one moves along the frontier from left to right more cars are obtained at the cost of producing less wheat. This is accomplished by shifting resources out of wheat production and into car production. At any point on the frontier, the quantity of wheat given up for an additional car is known as a car's **opportunity cost**. The concavity of the curve illustrates that as one moves along the curve from left to right, the opportunity cost of giving up wheat in order to obtain cars increases. In other words, to produce an additional car, the country must forgo increasing quantities of wheat. The reason for this is that some factors of production may be more suited to the production of one commodity rather than another and so more of a factor must be used to obtain one more unit of the chosen good. For example, wheat farmers are likely to be less efficient than skilled auto workers at producing cars. Hence, if farmers have to be shifted to car production, the extra output of cars they produce will be less than if additional auto workers were available. Although the production possibility frontier shows us how much of each good a country can produce it does not tell us how much of each is produced. This can be derived in turn by imposing the country's or community's indifference map onto the diagram.

Community indifference curves are constructed, in theory, by aggregating the **indifference curves** of all the individual consumers residing in the country (Leontief, 1933). An individual's indifference curve shows his/her willingness to trade off possible combinations of consumption goods. Each curve shows the individual's trade offs at a fixed level of satisfaction, in other words, the combinations of goods among which he/she is indifferent. For example, a person may be equally satisfied if they have two beers and six pieces of pizza or three beers and four pieces of pizza. Of course, each individual will value beer and pizza in his or her own way. Combinations which give greater satisfaction put the individual on a higher curve.

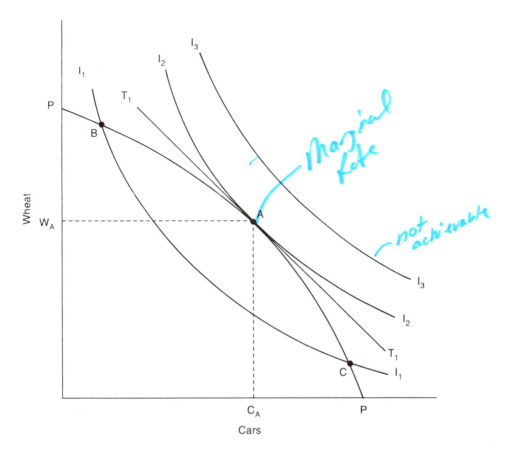

Figure 3.1 Consumption and production under autarky.

Rational individuals are assumed to want to consume combinations of products which give them the highest level of satisfactions. As with the individual, it is assumed that a nation attempts to achieve the greatest satisfaction, which means that it tries to carry out consumption somewhere on the highest attainable community indifference curve. What constrains the nation in achieving this is the productive capacity of the domestic economy as shown by the production possibility frontier. In Figure 3.1, consumption (and production) choice of the nation is illustrated by point A where the community indifference curve $I_2 I_2$ is tangential to the production possibility frontier PP. Reading off the axis, the country consumes $0\text{-}C_A$ cars and $0\text{-}W_A$ wheat. To put it more technically, at point A the nation's marginal (meaning one more) rate of substitution between wheat and cars (i.e. the rate at which it will give up wheat to consume one more car or vice versa) as shown by the community indifference curve is equal to the nation's marginal rate of transformation or opportunity cost of producing these two goods.

Why point A is the optimum point can be shown by a little counterfactual logic. For example, community indifference curve $I_1 I_1$ intersects

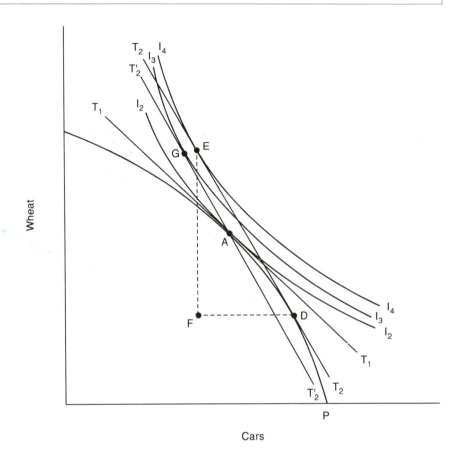

Figure 3.2 Consumption and production under free trade.

PP at points B and C and these points could be chosen – because they could be produced – but the community or nation would not be maximizing its satisfaction since by changing the combination of wheat and cars, a point on a higher community indifference curve could be chosen. For example, if the country was producing and consuming at point B, by reducing the amount of wheat and increasing the quantity of cars produced, point A on community indifference curve I_2I_2 can be achieved. Points on an even higher indifference curve such as I_3I_3 cannot be achieved as production possibility frontier PP shows the boundary of the nation's productive potential.

Under autarky, the situation without trade, the nation will produce and consume at point A which is reproduced on Figure 3.2. The tangent line T_1T_1 gives the price line or internal terms of trade between wheat and cars for community indifference curve I_2I_2 (i.e. the price of cars in terms of wheat or visa versa is indicated by the slope of the line – the steeper the line the more wheat must be given up for an additional car). Once we open up the country to international trade it can now produce and consume at prices that are different to those prevailing under autarky. This is illustrated by the price line or international terms of trade line T_2T_2. This indicates that cars are now more expensive – in terms of wheat – in the international market than they were in the home market. Domestic producers will now take advantage of these higher prices by moving out of wheat production and into car production. This will continue until point D is reached where the international terms of trade line is tangential to the production possibility frontier. We can also see in Figure 3.2 that T_2T_2 is not tangential to community indifference curve I_2I_2 but it is tangential to I_4I_4 at point E. As I_4I_4 is to the right of I_2I_2, if the nation could consume the bundle of goods illustrated by point E it would be better off. It can in fact achieve this through international trade. The country could exchange D–F cars for F–E wheat.

Despite there having been a change in the composition of its consumption pattern – more wheat, less cars – as it has moved from autarky to free trade, the nation has been able to achieve a higher level of satisfaction and is in material terms better off. Even if it could not change its pattern of production (therefore leaving production at point A), opening up its economy to world prices will still lead to an improvement for the country. This is again illustrated in Figure 3.2. In contrast to the free trade situation, the international terms of trade line $T_2'T_2'$ (which is parallel to T_2T_2 indicating the same international prices) passes through the original autarkic production point A. Although indifference curve I_4I_4 cannot be reached, $T_2'T_2'$ is now tangential to I_3I_3 at point G which is to the right of I_2I_2 and therefore an improvement on the original autarkic consumption point A. Again cars – although less of them – could be traded for wheat. By having opened it up its economy to the forces of international competition, the country's citizens are able to alter their consumption and achieve greater satisfaction. Moving resources from one industry to another may impose costs on society – for retraining or workers – and individuals – who must relocate. Hence, this is an important point. Even if a country wishes to keep its resources employed in the same production activities, it is advantageous to engage in international trade.

This illustration shows us that the overall gain from adopting an open trading system falls into two parts:

1. That which comes from exchange, i.e. moving from position A to G.
2. That from adjusting production to international competitive pressures, i.e moving from position G to E.

THE POLITICAL ECONOMY OF PROTECTION AND TRADE LIBERALIZATION

Given the analysis in the above section it seems inconceivable that arguments against free trade would be advanced but they are, and governments are seen to legislate for protection and argue strongly against the reduction of trade barriers at international negotiations. Again we may ask ourselves, why are trade restrictions so prevalent? To answer this question, a discussion of the political economy of protection is required [for further reading on this topic see Finger (1979), Baldwin (1979), Becker (1983) and Pincus (1975)].

Let us return to Figure 3.2 where we saw that as the economy was opened up and the international, rather than the domestic, terms of trade imposed themselves, production shifted from A to D. One consequence of this change is to shift the distribution of income away from wheat producers and towards car producers. One of the assumptions made in deriving community indifference curves is that the distribution of income does not change. (If it did, individual's indifference curves would also change thus rendering impossible the aggregation process and invalidating the conclusions drawn from our diagrammatic analysis.) To make our theoretical conclusions still valid would require that those who benefit from free trade should compensate the losers out of their gains so that the distribution of income between car and wheat producers remained constant. In order to generate benefits for the country as a whole when moving to a free trade system, the gainers are required to compensate the losers. Unless the gainers are altruistic (or have an acquaintance with economic theory so they can see the need to compensate the losers), a third agency in the shape of the government will have to intervene and secure the benefits on behalf of the nation as a whole.

Whether the government will act in this foresighted way is, of course, questionable. Governments are made up of the members of political parties whose prime function is to represent the interests of their supporters (Frey, 1984). If the government relies on the votes of the gainers to keep it in power then it might not wish to alienate this support by taxing some of their gains in order to give the proceeds to the losers. Even if both the government and its supporters wished to compensate the losers there may be practical difficulties in identifying the losers and compensating them for their losses.

It is with these possibilities in mind that potential losers may form groups to lobby governments for the imposition of trade barriers. The strength of this **protectionist** lobby can be substantial. Firstly, the pressure to organize is greater amongst the losers because they are a well defined group while the gainers – the rest of society – are a more diverse body. For the gainers, the benefits of trade barrier reductions and free trade accrue over time and are spread thinly over many individuals. Hence, those who gain may not be as willing, or as likely, to organize to prevent trade restrictions from being put in place or to lobby for them to be removed as those who lose out.

Secondly, the losers may well be better represented in parliaments and legislatures than the prospective gainers. This is particularly the case where the losers are favourably distributed regionally. For example, if the losers have a majority of 51% in two out of three constituencies, then they need only 34% of the total vote to command a majority in parliament. If they have the same majority in say 13 out of 25 constituencies, then they can command a majority in parliament with only 27% of the total vote.

Thirdly, the political power of potential losers can be strengthened further or a majority can be assembled together if the political group supporting protection in the legislature is willing to trade its votes with another group in order to achieve mutually beneficial legislation. This process is also called **log rolling** and works as follows: say there are two groups of voters engaged in industries threatened by competitive imports. Group I is strongly in favour of import barriers to protect its industry – proposition A – but weakly in favour of reducing the levels of protection afforded to group II's industry – proposition B. Group II takes the opposite line. If groups I and II are minorities in parliament then their proposals will be voted down and free trade will be the result. If, however, they can combine and agree to support one another then they may be able to form a majority and get their respective proposals through parliament and into law.

There can, therefore be, a political market for protection. The composition of the demand and supply side of this market will now be examined in greater detail. Demand for protection will come from groups that can identify a reduction in trade barriers which will lead to a loss of sales, lower output and unemployment. In practice, this means domestic firms in competition with foreign firms supplying the home market, trade unions and worker organizations representing the workers employed in the domestic firms and component suppliers to the domestic firms. Of course, demand for the imposition of barriers when trade is free will come from those who perceive a threat from a new source of competition.

The pressure of demand will be reduced by opposition from groups that will lose out from protection, e.g. companies that rely on an open trading system to sell their goods such as multinational companies and domestic companies with a higher proportion of their output geared to export. Other interest groups that will support this anti-protectionist stance include the component suppliers to these export oriented companies and workers who rely on them for their employment, as well as consumer groups who may fear that barriers will lead to higher prices.

On the supply side, those willing to grant protection are politicians and bureaucrats/civil servants. Politicians wanting to remain in power may be willing to make concessions to the pro-protectionist lobby if it is stronger and has more political clout than the anti-protectionist lobby. This sort of pressure has been brought to bear on politicians in many countries. It is said that the over-representation of rural areas, in terms of seats in the parliaments of France and Japan, has coloured their governments views towards the liberalization of agricultural trade.

Although supposedly neutral, civil servants can also have an important role to play in the granting of protection. Their **utility** function – or what makes them happy – can be expressed as being made up of the 'prestige, power and influence' that they enjoy relative to the economic group they serve, e.g. positions of the civil servants in ministries of agriculture vis-à-vis the farmers and the agribusiness sector in general. The main constraint that a civil service faces is the power of parliament and the executive arm of the government; however, since both these institutions may rely on the civil service for advice, its discretionary power in policy making can be great.

In the political market place, therefore, a strong homogeneous group in favour of protectionism, faced by a weaker more heterogeneous opposition and a weak government seeking to stay in power and advised by a sympathetic civil service, may well achieve its protectionist aims, despite the economic arguments against such a policy. Potential losers have also had a large number of theoretical arguments which can be used to disguise their vested interests in the cloak of societies best interest.

STATIC ARGUMENTS FOR PROTECTION

The static case for protection, which implies intervention in the trading system on a permanent basis, evolves from:

1. The existence of distortions in the domestic economy in both the consumer markets and factor (raw material, labour, capital) markets.
2. Domestic desires for increased employment or stable exchange rates.
3. The need for national security.
4. Governments' revenue requirements.

These will be examined in turn (a more detailed discussion of these theories can be found in Corden, 1957).

Distortions in commodity and factor markets

The existence of **externalities** will bring about distortions in commodity markets (this section draws heavily on Bhagwati and Ramaswami, 1963). A classic example of this type of distortion is the possibility that farmers, in carrying out their activities, employ techniques that lead to soil erosion. In the long run, this will lead to reduced farm output. This loss of output means that society as a whole will lose – there is a social cost. These consequences may not, however, be perceived in the short run. Hence, the private costs of these farming activities do not reflect their true social costs. The divergence between private and social cost could also arise if, for some reason, producers were not using techniques that led to economies of scale being reaped in the long run.

To illustrate, let us return to our example of a wheat and car producing economy now represented by Figure 3.3. Again PP is the country's production possibility frontier but because of the existence of externalities in the wheat producing sector, the domestic terms of trade line T_1T_1 is not tangential to it. The slope of T_1T_1 represents the private

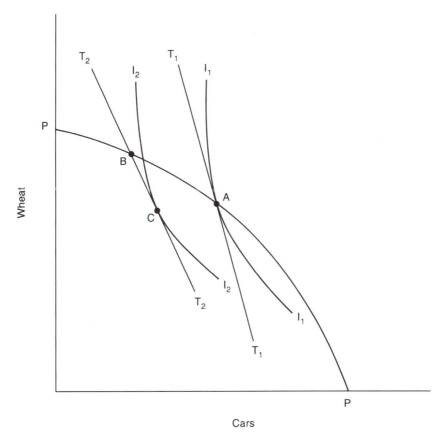

Figure 3.3 Production, consumption and commodity market distortions.

cost trade off rather than the true social cost trade off. Rather than being tangential to PP, T_1T_1 cuts through PP at point A with the country's community indifference I_1I_1 curve tangential to T_1T_1 at this point. Hence, consumption and production takes place at A. If the economy is opened up to trade and T_2T_2 represents the new international terms of trade, production will take place at B and consumption at C on the lower indifference curve I_2I_2. As a result of the distortion in its commodity markets, the country is now worse off by trading because its comparative advantage in wheat at distorted prices has moved it into increased wheat production. Re-imposition of trade restrictions will change the price line back to T_1T_1 and allow the country to achieve higher levels of satisfaction.

Is this, however, the best policy to be followed? The answer is no. A preferred policy would be one of taxing wheat production, which is prone to external diseconomies, and subsidizing car production where the country's true comparative advantage lies (remember that the distorted price line T_2T_2 moved the country's production away from cars and towards more wheat production). By examining Figure 3.4 we

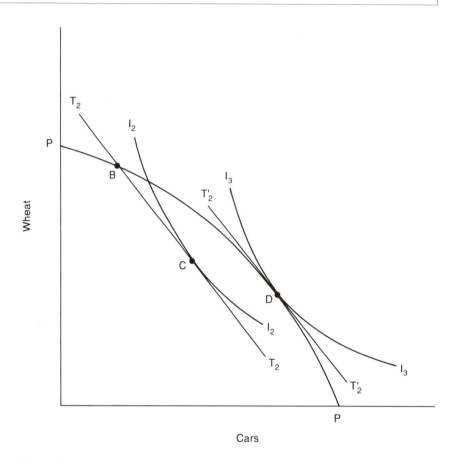

Figure 3.4 Production and consumption after the removal of commodity market distortions.

will see why this is the case. As in Figure 3.3, point B is the free trade production point. If we impose taxes on wheat production and subsidies on car production then production will be shifted in favour of the latter which is illustrated by point D. At this point the international terms of trade line $T_2'T_2'$ becomes tangential to the production possibility frontier PP ($T_2'T_2'$ being parallel to T_2T_2). This terms of trade line is also tangential to the community indifference curve I_3I_3 and as a result the marginal rate of substitution is equal to the opportunity cost of production and, moreover, the nation achieves a higher level of satisfaction than hitherto as I_3I_3 is to the right of I_2I_2.

Distortions in factor markets arise when a particular factor is paid more than the value it contributes to production – its **marginal product**. It has been asserted that the abundance of labour concentrated in the agricultural sectors of some developing countries means the marginal product of labour is close to zero. For a number of reasons, however, such as tradition, or on humanitarian grounds, labour is paid a wage which is above this level. Trade unions may also be successful in raising

Static arguments for protection | 49

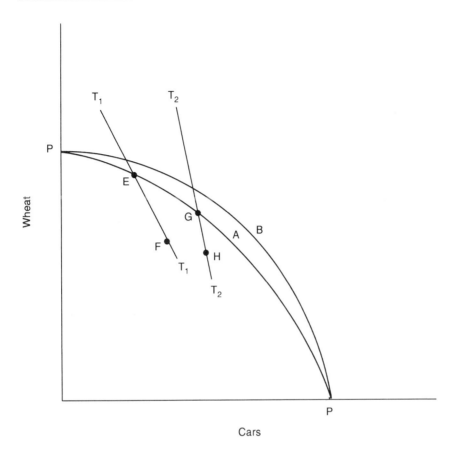

Figure 3.5 Production, consumption and distortions in the factor markets.

workers wages above their marginal product by exerting their collective bargaining power in a particular labour market. For whatever reasons, these distortions have implications for the consumption/production patterns in an economy, in that they bias production against the product.

Figure 3.5 illustrates the effect of factor market distortion on an economy. In this case, labour in the car industry is paid a wage greater than its marginal product. This might arise if workers in the car industry had a particularly effective trade union. As in our previous examples, the economy produces wheat and cars, and its production possibility frontier is shown by the curve PAP. If distortions did not exist, then the productive potential would be greater, as illustrated by the curve PBP. In a free trade situation, let us assume that production takes place at point E (through which the international price line passes) and consumption takes place at F. If a tariff is placed on car imports to redress the distortion existing in that industry, the slope of the price line changes and production moves in favour of car production from E to G. The new price line $T_2 T_2$ will now become tangential to a higher indifference curve, say at point H, and the nation's consumers will now be better off than they were at point F.

Is this the best outcome for the nation? The optimum would be to rid the economy of its distortions and capture the potential shown by the production possibility curve PBP and then allow free trade. How can this potential be realized? The simplest way is by subsidizing, or taxing, the use of the factor in question. For example, if trade union power has raised wages above the marginal product of labour in the car industry, then subsidizing this factor will equalize the marginal product of labour in both industries. Taxing the use of labour in the wheat sector would have the same effect. Without distortions existing in the labour market, the production possibility curve facing the economy would move out from PAP to PBP.

Distortions in both the commodity and factor markets can, hence, be overcome by the imposition of trade barriers in the form of tariffs. Tariffs are taxes collected as goods enter a country and, hence, raise their price. As we have seen though, this may not be the best policy. A systems of subsidies and/or taxation will lead to a greater level of welfare. It is for these reasons that economists often call the imposition of tariffs a **second best** policy.

Full employment and the balance of payments

It is often argued that unemployment can be alleviated by the imposition of tariffs and restrictions on foreign goods entering the home market. The logic behind this argument often runs like this: restricting imports and, hence, making them more expensive will force domestic purchasers of these goods to switch their expenditure from foreign produced goods to home produced goods. This increase in demand for home produced goods will lead to an expansion of the sectors involved in their production and an increase in the demand for labour. The beauty of this policy, or so the argument runs, is that the domestic economy can be expanded without a deterioration in the **balance of trade**. (The balance of trade is the net result of subtracting the sum of the value of a country's imports and financial outflows from the sum of the value of its exports and financial inflows). The importance of the balance of trade can be explained through an example. Suppose imports – for simplicity, assume that financial inflows equal financial outflows – exceed exports for a sustained period at the current exchange rate. This would mean that more of a nation's currency would be flowing into international exchange markets than foreigners would need to buy exports. A surplus of the country's currency would exist. This would put downward pressure on the exchange rate. The value of the currency relative to its trading partners would eventually have to fall. Certainly the influential economist John Maynard Keynes advocated the adoption of such a policy for Britain in the 1930s (Keynes, 1972).

For this analysis to be applied, rigidities in the labour market must exist. Traditional trade theory assumes that factor markets are perfect.

This means that factors of production could move costlessly and instantaneously from one industry to another, hence, no sustained unemployment could exist. Of course, in the real world unemployment can persist and become a major social problem. The question again arises: is it better to impose a tariff or to tackle the root of the problem and encourage the market to work more efficiently? It may be the case that as, for example, wheat workers are made redundant they will not be able to find employment in the expanding car industry because they lack the necessary skills. In this situation it might make more sense to subsidize the retraining of these workers and, hence, provide the labour required to further the expansion of the car industry where the country has a long-term comparative advantage. For example, if the balance of payments was the main constraint, then it may be better to devalue the currency. That would increase not only domestic demand, as people switched from the now more expensive imports to domestic products. As well, foreign demand for the country's goods would increase as exports will now be less expensive in the eyes of foreigners. As a result unemployment would be reduced. Keyne's advocacy of tariffs was based on the premise that Britain could not devalue its currency. Once it did, he withdrew his suggestion for an employment stimulating tariff.

A slightly more subtle argument concerning the balance of payments has been put forward by a group of economists known as the New **Cambridge School** (this view is clearly expressed in the *Cambridge Economics Policy Review*, especially the 1978 issue). They point out that devaluation no longer works because the reduction in workers' real incomes as a consequence of the increase in foreign prices leads them to argue for, and be granted, higher wages. This stimulates inflation and domestic labour costs rise until the original impact of the devaluation is neutralized. The Cambridge school suggests that a tariff will not have the same inflationary impact if the revenue raised by the tariff is paid to workers to offset the price rises created. The redistribution of this tariff revenue thus keeps real wages constant and helps maintain the stimulus on the economy. Furthermore, a tariff on final goods will not affect input prices and so, in turn, will not adversely affect the labour component of home industries costs as would a devaluation.

While balance of payments arguments are accepted by multilateral organizations as a legitimate reason for imposing tariffs, and both the US and the UK have resorted to them, albeit temporarily, once again counter-arguments suggest that this may not be the best policy to follow (Hindley, 1983). For instance, the protection of real wages is at the expense of profits which could have an adverse effect on investment in the long run. The dampening of foreign competition could also lead to the long run deterioration of the home industry's productivity. It is also questionable that wage pressure would be less under a tariff policy than under devaluation for two reasons. Firstly, since the reduction in the choice of goods is equivalent to a reduction in the average wage, workers may attempt to offset this decline through demands for higher wages. Secondly, it is quite likely that the reduction of foreign competition caused by tariffs would encourage home producers to raise their own domestic prices. It thus seems unlikely that a policy of tariff protection is preferable to that of devaluation. Again, it seems that tariffs should only be imposed when alternative policies are not available and even then only in the short run. In the longer term, it is probably better for the country to attempt to overcome the problems its industries face by tackling them head on rather than to protect the industries indefinitely.

Reasons of national security

Nations may feel that if they follow the free trade path then they may become totally dependent – or at least greatly dependent – on another country for imports of sensitive goods. If something should happen to disrupt the flow of these goods then the country might find itself in major difficulties. It is for this reason that countries have often protected their agricultural and primary products sectors. The argument is made that if a war occurred and a country's food imports were disrupted then, a major disruption would arise and hardship created. Hence, it is important to protect the sector in question so that it provides enough products to cover basic needs, or at least a core which can be expanded in times of trouble. The agricultural policies of the US, Japan and the EU have, to some extent, been based on this premise. Whether trade barriers are the best form of protection is once more a contentious point (a sceptical view of this protectionist argument is found in Winters, 1990). It could well be the case that stockpiling essential goods might be a cheaper policy. Subsidizing important sectors directly rather than using tariffs can also lead to higher benefits to society. Which of these policies should be adopted depends on the cost and benefits of each and the probabilities that the worst scenarios would result.

The optimum tariff

If a country is a major purchaser of a particular commodity then it might move the terms of trade in its favour by imposing tariffs on the import in question (Metzler, 1949). How would this work? When a country places a tariff on an import it pushes up its price in the domestic market and, as a result, demand falls. As sales to this country are very important to the exporting country, it will be forced to reduce its prices to recapture the lost market. As prices fall, the **terms of trade** (the rate it can exchange domestic products for imports) of the tariff imposing country will improve and this will allow it to achieve a position on a higher indifference curve than before. While this argument is valid and recognized by many economists, it was also noted that both countries can play the tariff game and the country on whose goods the tariff has been placed can retaliate with one of its own on imports from the imposing country (Johnson, 1965). The result of this retaliation would be a reduction in the volume of trade taking place between the two countries. Neither country, nor the firms involved in trade, would benefit.

The revenue raising tariff

Many countries, especially those with low incomes and ineffective governments have difficulties in raising adequate revenues via the usual routes of taxing incomes and/or the sale of goods. By taxing imports they are able to supplement their sources of tax revenue and for many middle income developing countries this has now become a prime source of funding (Greenaway and Sapsford, 1987). The wisdom of carrying out this practice has been questioned (IBRD, 1987). Tariffs distort the economy by protecting home industries and thereby hinder the competitive process. Further, they mask the true cost of government expenditure.

THE STRATEGIC OR DYNAMIC REASONS FOR PROTECTION

The strategic and dynamic reasons for protection differ from the static arguments in that they do not envisage the permanent maintenance of barriers to trade. Barriers are to be adopted only to attain a specific objective. Once this has been achieved, then the barriers to trade can be removed and the home economy exposed to the full rigours of international competition. Barriers are, therefore, justified on the basis of countering the strategic use of market advantage by foreign companies or acquiring a comparative advantage for an industry.

Countering strategic behaviour

Large or technically sophisticated firms may be able to formulate and carry out strategic plans of action which can increase their competitiveness in the long run. Foreign firms may attempt to capitalize on the weaknesses of domestic firms to increase their market share. They may be able to deny domestic firms the technology required to become competitive through the manipulation of other firms that own the technology. If the foreign firm is a large user of the technology, they may be able to pressure the supplier not to sell the technology to firms in the importing country. As a result, domestic firms will not be able to increase their market share. Imposing trade restrictions on the foreign firm's products can eliminate the incentive for the exporter to limit access to the technology. Sophisticated marketing programs, which are beyond the capability of domestic firms, may be used to increase or protect the market share of foreign firms. Trade restrictions can limit market shares.

The most important use of strategic advantage by large transnational firms is the international version of predatory pricing – **dumping**. The issue of dumping has gained more prominence recently both among businessmen and academic economists (Yarrow, 1987). Dumping is claimed to exist when prices charged for imports do not reflect the true costs of production.

In economic theory, dumping is defined as the selling of goods in a foreign market at prices below the cost of production in the home market. In the static sense, a country able to purchase goods at prices below domestic levels can only benefit at the expense of the country producing the good. Why should a country complain if a foreign firm wishes to beneficially price imports for consumers? The static approach, however, ignores longer-term implications which can be damaging. For example, the undercutting of home producers could be part of a strategy whereby once they were put out of business the foreign firm could then exploit a new found monopoly position and raise prices, possibly above original levels. In order to prevent this happening and the country incurring the start up costs to re-establish the industry, anti-dumping duties in the form of tariffs may be levied on the foreign firm's exports.

The case for infant industries

New businesses facing competition from well established industries in exporting countries may find it difficult to establish themselves because of high initial start up costs (Myint, 1963). In order that economies of scale can be reaped and competitiveness vis-à-vis foreign producers established, the home market needs to be protected for domestic producers. High initial costs need not only arise from high fixed costs, they can also arise from the inexperience of the managers and workers in producing and selling the good in question. As output expands and familiarity with production and sales increases, costs will fall and competitiveness attained. Protecting the home market for the domestic firm would allow it to achieve lower costs.

There are many problems with this argument (Baldwin, 1969). The first is trying to identify **infant industries**. Secondly, even if the current industries can be identified, it is possible that behind the protective barrier, the domestic industry may not actually 'grow up'. It may choose to continue to plead it is a special case that cannot be expected to compete with imports. This may well become the case if the industry achieves the role of an important employer and investor in the domestic economy and, hence, becomes politically influential.

Finally, it is necessary to consider whether protection via tariffs is the best policy, or would an alternative such as a subsidy be just as effective and less of a distortion for the economy? Tariffs will raise the prices of goods to the consumer, whereas subsidizing the high initial costs will keep prices at world levels and, thereby, not harm the consumer. This, however, shifts the burden from the consumer to the taxpayer. For the infant industry argument to be valid requires that the costs of fostering the industry's development, whether imposed on consumers or taxpayers, is outweighed by the future benefits. While some industries in some countries have been successfully established in this way, it is not totally clear that one can predict the benefits streams at the outset. There are, in fact, many industries in a variety of countries where adopting this type of policy has led to the establishment of industries that never became competitive internationally and proved to be a burden on their home economies rather than a benefit. This leads us to the 'infant economy' arguments which we discuss below.

Before we do this, let us examine a variant of the infant industry argument which is the **'senile industry'** argument. This suggests that an industry which has lost its comparative advantage may regain it if it receives protection so that it can re-equip its factories and retrain its work force and managers. These costs could be recouped if it acquires a greater share of the home market. Whether one can distinguish between a loss of competitiveness due to bad management or some other reason, or a genuine change in the country's comparative advantage is questionable. Both the infant and senile industry arguments depend on entrepreneurs being unable to see the future benefits of making the investments needed to improve international competitiveness themselves, thus requiring a third agency in the form of the government to step in.

The infant economy and import substitution

The German economist List, seeing that the British economy had developed into the world's major industrial power, argued that the only way that other countries could catch up was to erect barriers to trade and industrialize behind these (List, 1841). Many colonies, on gaining their independence in the 1950s and 1960s took up this theme in their development plans. A number of Latin American countries also adopted this development strategy. The basic argument ran like this (Lewis, 1969; Prebish, 1969); traditional agricultural and raw materials exports could not be relied upon to underpin economic development. As supply increased, prices would fall and revenues would decrease. Further, as incomes in developed countries grew, the demand for developing countries' products would not increase in line with incomes – they have relatively low **income elasticities**. Developing countries would be condemned to a position always behind that of developed countries. To overcome this problem, developing countries would have to pursue industrialization policies in order to produce goods with better market potential. Industrialization had to be carried out behind high barriers so that economies of scale could be achieved. In the development stage, domestic products would be substituted for products previously imported – this strategy became formally known as **import substitution**.

As with the infant industry argument, many inefficient industries might arise which would be unable to compete internationally. They would then act as a brake on economic development rather than a spur (Flanders, 1964; Morgan, 1969). Studies have shown that the more successful countries were those that adopted open policies and promoted exports.

Trade barriers have also been used to encourage a foreign firm to come and set up an operation to supply the economy from within its own borders. The main benefit that can flow from this policy is that it may encourage industrialization, as firms such as component suppliers are set up to supply the new firm. The major disadvantage is that barriers may encourage sub-optimal sized plants to be established. Much of Canada's manufacturing industry may suffer from this problem. Having higher costs than foreign firms, these operations can be potentially detrimental to the long run development of the economy and, thus, contrary to the original goal.

LESSONS FOR BUSINESS

It is said that the free traders win all the arguments but the protectionists get the votes. Firms threatened by foreign competition can always find arguments for protection. It is natural to make those arguments. There is a lot to lose. We have not even presented some of these arguments (e.g. the inability to compete with 'cheap foreign labour'). Although for an individual firm, it is argued, raising trade barriers for this reason simply protects a particular vested interest. The cost to the society is the gains to trade foregone. Sometimes such simple arguments win public support. It is important, however, for the long run consequences of protectionism to be well understood by business people. They will mean slower growth and less national income. In the short run, protectionism may even appear to provide general benefits but only if there is no retaliation by other countries. Protectionism can lead to a downward spiral of reduced trade and the loss of its benefits.

The more sophisticated arguments for protection have been explored in this chapter. It is important that businesses understand these arguments and their flaws. Each must be judged within the context within which they are proposed. Alternatives to trade restrictions are almost always available to address problems of competitiveness. Governments will often consult with the business community before proceeding with trade measures or other policies aimed at improving the ability of domestic firms to compete with foreign firms. Trade restrictions often appear to be 'cheap policies' when compared with subsidies or retraining schemes. This is because the costs of trade restrictions, often spread over a large number of consumers, are not as obvious as budgetary expenditures. The lesson of economic theory is, however, that protection will almost always be more expensive. This is particularly true over time if a country becomes saddled with an uncompetitive industrial base. Currently, protectionism's acceptability as a government objective is on the wane. It is clearly identified with particular vested interests rather than the national good. This is an important result of the work of trade theorists. It means that firms relying on the protection provided by trade restrictions may be vulnerable and should consider alternative long-term company strategies and/or alternative avenues of government support.

REFERENCES

Baldwin, R. E. (1969) The case against infant industry protection. *Journal of Political Economy*, 77, 295–305.

Baldwin R. E. (1979) *The Political Economy of US Import Trade Policy*, MIT Press, Cambridge, MA.

Becker, G. S. (1983) A theory of competition among pressure groups for political influence. *Quarterly Journal of Economics*, **98**(3), 371–400.

Bhagwati, J. and Ramaswami V. K. (1963) Domestic distortions, tariffs and the theory of optimum subsidy. *Journal of Political Economy*, **71**, 44–50.

Corden, W. M. (1957) Tariffs, subsidies and the terms of trade. *Economica*, **24**, 235–42.

Cuthbertson, J. M. (1986) The folly of free trade. *Harvard Business Review*, NS **86**(5), 122–8.

Finger J. M. (1979) Trade liberalization and public choice perspective, in *Challenges to a Liberal Economic Order*, (eds R. C. Amacher, G. Haberler and T. D. Willet), American Enterprise Institute, Washington, DC, pp. 421–53.

Flanders, M. J. (1964) Prebisch on protectionism: an evaluation. *The Economic Journal*, **71**, 305–26.

Frey, B. (1984) *International Political Economics*, Blackwells, Oxford.

Greenaway, D and Sapsford, D. (1987) Further econometric analysis of the relationship between fiscal dependence on trade taxes and economic development. *Public Finance*, **42**(2), 309–19.

Heckscher, E. (1935) *Mercantilism*, George Allen & Unwin, London.

Hindley, B. (1983) Trade policy economic performance and Britain's economic problem, in *Policy and Performance in International Trade*, (eds J. Black and A. Winters), Macmillan, London, pp. 25–42.

IBRD (1987) *World Bank Development Report*, International Bank for Reconstruction and Development, Washington, DC.

Johnson, H. G. (1965) Optimal trade intervention in the presence of domestic distortions, in *Trade Growth and the Balance of Payments*, (eds R. E. Caves, P. Kenen and H. G. Johnson), North Holland, Amsterdam, pp. 3–34.

Keynes, J. M. (1972) The Collected writings of John Maynard Keynes, Vol. 9, 'Essays in Persuasion'. Mitigation by tariff, in *Essays in Persuasion, Vol. 9, Collected Writings*, Macmillan, pp. 231–44.

Leontief, W. (1933) The use of indifference curves in international trade. *Quarterly Journal of Economics*, **47**, 493–503.

Lewis, W. A. (1969) *Aspects of Tropical Trade 1883–1965*, Alquist and Wicksell, Stockholm.

List, F. (1841) *Das Nationale System der Politischen Oekonomie*,

Der internationale Handel, die Handelspolitik und der deutsche zollverein. Publisher J. G. Colta, Scher verlag, Stuttgart.

Metzler, L. A. (1949) Tariffs the terms of trade and the distribution of national income. *Journal of Political Economy*, **57**, 1-29.

Morgan, T. (1959) The long run terms of trade between agriculture and manufacturing. *Economic Development and Cultural Change*, **8**(1), 1-23.

Myint, H. (Reprint 1964) (1963) Infant industry arguments for assistance to industries in the setting of dynamic trade theory, in *International Theory in a Developing World*, (eds R. F. Harrod and T. D. C. Hague), Macmillan, London, pp. 173-93. (Pages same for reprint as original).

Pincus, J. J. (1975) Pressure groups and the pattern of tariffs. *Journal of Political Economy*, **83**(4), 757-78.

Prebish, R. (1950) *The Economic Development of Latin America and its Principal Problems*, UN Department of Economic Affairs, New York.

Ricardo, D. (1951) *On the Principles of Political Economy and Taxation*, in *The Works and Correspondence of David Ricardo*, (ed. P. Sraffa), Cambridge University Press, Cambridge.

Smith, A. (1961) *An Inquiry into the Nature and Causes of the Wealth of Nations*, (ed. E. Cannan), reprinted by Methuen, London.

Winters, A. (1990) The national security argument for protection. *The World Economy*, **13**(2), 170-90.

Yarrow, Y. (1987) Economic aspects of anti-dumping. *Oxford Review of Economic Policy*, **3**(1), 66-79.

Summary of Part Two

The economic analysis carried out in this section showed that by adopting a policy of free trade, countries and, hence, the world economy in general can maximize its welfare. Our analysis also showed that any opening up from complete autarky will lead to an improvement in national welfare. This improvement, however, will not be costless. Some room is therefore left for political forces to influence the extent to which an economy exposes itself to the rigours of world trade. The openness or closedness of the world economy, hence, depends on the political power of protectionist forces in all countries. This power can be considerable because competition leads to both gainers and losers. Given the rigidities that exist in all economies, the losers may not be absorbed quickly into the expanding industries and, hence, have a greater incentive to mobilize opposition to changes that they see as potentially detrimental to their interests. Being a more homogeneous group than the gainers, they will find it easier to organize and press for the reversal of any opening up of the economy or to seek protection from foreign competition.

The arguments for protection are numerous and varied but can usually be split into those that demand continuous protection, i.e. the static variety, and those that involve temporary measures, i.e. the dynamic set. Examining the static arguments, such as rigidities in the commodity and factor markets, balance of payments problems and unemployment led to the conclusion that protection via the imposition of tariffs and quotas may not be the best policy. Subsidies and improvements to the workings of market mechanisms are better policies to follow. The use of revenue raising tariffs is also questionable and improving the basis on which public finance is raised is again a better policy. The only justifiable argument for the imposition of tariffs is the optimal tariff argument but this can be counter productive and lead to a general decline in world trade if other countries retaliate.

The dynamic reasons for protection are more subtle in that they are proposed for only a limited period until some improvement has been gained. Hence, arguments for protection against dumping or to help infant and senile firms and economies can be very appealing. Again one may question whether protectionist policies are the most appropriate with, perhaps, the exception of dumping. The possibility that temporary measures may become permanent is a strong one. More appropriate policies might be those that attack root causes, which in turn might be deeply embedded in the country's economy and society. The factors affecting competitiveness identified in Chapter 2 tend to be long run forces. Trade restrictions may bring short run relief from the adverse effects of changes in these factors. Improving competitiveness has no quick fix. It is, however, the key to long-term prosperity. The conflict between the interests of those who seek a more open and those who seek a more closed trading system are very powerful. Politicians have tried to channel these forces by setting up institutions to defuse potential conflicts. These institutions are examined in detail in Part Three.

PART 3
The international trading system

Introduction to Part Three

In Part Two we described why trade takes place between countries and why an open trading system is preferable to one that is closed. We also outlined the reasons why vested interests might well pursuade governments to modify free trade policies. In this section we will examine the institutional framework within which trade takes place. We will examine in greater depth the role of the nation state in the determination of the international trading structure and its role in determining the nature of international economic relations. In particular we will look at the development of bilateral and multilateral agreements, and the reasons behind the growth of regional trade associations. The types of measures that countries can use to restrict trade are examined as well as the international controls which attempt to limit their use.

The search for an orderly system for trade 4

THE NATION STATE AND ECONOMIC SOVEREIGNTY

Firms which engage in international commerce desire a degree of order for their international undertakings. Without order, business planning becomes impossible. The risks associated with conducting business in distant markets with different business ethics and cultures is difficult enough without having to worry about the unpredictable actions of individual country's governments. Governments, on the other hand, do not wish to give up the right to act swiftly to protect their national interests – including business interests. They may, however, want other country's governments to agree to limit their powers. The international trading system which has evolved represents a compromise between these two forces.

Despite the growth of international institutions, regional trade associations and transnational companies, the nation state is still the primary actor on the world economic stage. In the domestic arena it is the nation state, or rather its government, which has to arbitrate between the demands of interest groups, put forward compromises and formulate policies accordingly. On the international front, the nation state is faced with similar responsibilities. It has to promote the interests of its citizens while not upsetting its trading partners in such a way as to incur adverse reactions. As the international economy has become more integrated, the role of the nation state in inter-governmental bargaining or economic diplomacy has remained strong. With greater economic integration, national laws, regulations, and health and safety standards not only affect domestic producers but also, increasingly, foreign producers.

The nation state is not, however, simply a guardian of domestic economic interests. It has a wider and more direct role in seeing that both domestic and international economic policies aimed at expanding economic growth do not upset the country's internal stability or challenge its national security.

In many ways, the continued importance of the nation state is contrary to what one would expect. The rapid growth in world economic integration and the consequent transfer of economic decision making to supra-national bodies has reduced somewhat the economic and political sovereignty of nation states. Where this economic and political sovereignty has been conceded, particularly in the area of trade relations, the nation state still represents and promotes domestic national interests. Examples of this are clearly illustrated by the approach taken in multilateral trade negotiations by the US government in its pursuit of the interests of US farmers and also that of the French government for their farmers.

THE STATE AND THE STRUCTURE OF INTERNATIONAL TRADE

The role of the nation state, as it is portrayed in neo-classical economic theory, is confined to the maximization of the country's economic well being. In its approach to international trade the state should then stand against protectionism and join with other states in promoting an **open economic system** based on the principles of free trade. To do otherwise would not be rational and would reflect, at best, that governments and their advisors did not understand the most basic of economic principles or, at worst, were in league with those having a vested interest in protection from foreign competition.

The reality, of course, is somewhat different. The pursuit of maximizing economic welfare may be only one of several goals the nation state may wish to pursue. It has been said that the state tries to achieve four goals, i.e. to enhance its political power, maximize aggregate national income, enhance economic growth and maintain social stability (Krasner, 1976). Sometimes these goals are in harmony, while at other times they may conflict. They are affected, furthermore, by the degree of openness of the economy in question; by the relative size of the economy and its level of development.

How are these four goals related to trade structures? Conventional economic theory suggests that the greater the degree of openness, the greater the level of aggregate income, and that this applies equally to small or large states and to developed or under-developed countries. The static benefits of openness are, however, inversely related to size. For example, small states lacking the diversity in economic resources or the potential for economies of scale that are generally possessed by large states are able to gain more by specializing and trading than are large states.

The effect of openness on social stability may, however, be adverse. For example, as an economy is opened up to world competition some sectors will expand while others will contract, implying factor movements from declining to growing industries. As we saw in the previous chapter, those in the contracting sectors will oppose openness and change. Their opposition will lead to friction and social tensions. There is evidence to suggest that the adverse impact on social stability will be greater the smaller the state and the lower its level of economic development. Larger states have proportionately less of their resources tied up in the international market place while the higher levels of skills found in developed countries enables workers to move fairly easily between one sector and another. Social stability is thus inversely related to openness, although large economic size and a higher level of development reduce the worst consequences.

A country can also enhance its political power vis-à-vis other states by supporting an open trading structure if it knows that the adoption of a closed structure would have a significantly adverse effect on its trading partners. In other words, the higher the relative cost of closure the weaker the position of the partner states. As larger developed countries have lower direct income losses and lower adjustment costs than smaller countries when closed trading structures are adopted, their economic power is enhanced vis-à-vis smaller or less developed countries. Large countries will, therefore, prefer open trading systems since they can use their political power to achieve economic and non-economic goals.

As discussed in Chapter 3, there is some controversy as to whether an open or closed trading system promotes economic growth. Openness allows small states to produce for a world market which allows their industries to achieve the economies of scale that would be denied them under a closed system. Openness is also deemed to be in the interests of large, rich countries whose comparative advantage is in technologically advanced goods which also require large, growing markets to enhance their commercial success. Openness, however, may have adverse consequences for economic growth if a country begins to lose its competitive edge and lag significantly behind its rivals in the production of new and advanced products. With capital and technology free to move, these resources will leave declining economies in search of higher rewards in the relatively more expansive economies. It has been suggested that the US and Britain have experienced such periods of capital outflows and that their economic growth suffered as a result. Economists who study developing economies have also identified a similar phenomenon for poor countries. Which view is correct has not been finally decided. As noted in Chapter 3, those countries that tend to have open trading regimes seem to have higher levels of economic growth (Little *et al.*, 1993).

Given that states have more than one goal and that these are influenced by the degree of openness or closedness, what is the likelihood that a more open or closed trading structure or system will be adopted by the international community? We attempt to answer this question in the next section.

THE NATURE OF THE INTERNATIONAL TRADING SYSTEM

As states have a variety of goals, whose compatibility may well vary according to their size and stage of economic development, it is understandable that they will vary in their attitudes towards the degree of openness of the international trading system (Krasner, 1976). If the world was composed of a large number of small highly developed states, the probability would be that they would adopt an open trading system. The reason for this is that this system would increase the aggregate income of these countries and encourage their economic growth. Furthermore, the social instability envisaged from restructuring would be mitigated by the ease of factor mobility made possible by the high level of economic development of these countries. As the costs of closure fall symmetrically on all countries, there is no loss of political power to any state supporting this open system.

In a situation where a few large unequally developed states made up the world economy a **closed economic system** is likely to evolve. Why? True, each state could enhance its income by adopting an open system but the gains would be very small and would not appear worthwhile when compared to the social instability that would result. This is particularly true in developing economies. Given their rigid factor mobility, the relative costs associated with trade liberalization would be greater for developing economies. It would not, therefore, make sense to adopt or encourage the development of an open international trading system. The more advanced states might prefer an open system but, short of enforcing their will by military means, they would have to accept the position of the large less developed countries. One option available to the more developed countries is to open up trade between themselves by forming regional trade associations, an issue that will be discussed in Chapter 5.

In a system that is dominated by one large relatively more advanced country – the hegemonic state – an open economic system is again likely to result. This is the so-called **hegemonic system** and the reason for its openness is easy to see. An open system will give the hegemonic state higher aggregate income and increase its economic growth. This will be especially so when its industrial and technological base are in advance of the other countries. An open system will enhance the political power of the hedgemonic state since the opportunity cost of closure is less for it than for those that trade with it. The advanced nature of this state will mean that reallocation costs and social instability will be kept to manageable proportions given its low overall exposure to international trade.

The reaction towards this sort of system by other countries in the world would depend on their size relative to the hegemonic state. Small states are likely to accept an open system since the economic gains that will accrue to them are likely to be large relative to the costs. Their political power is unlikely to be adversely affected since, given their size, they are unlikely to have much anyway.

With medium sized states it is harder to predict their reaction. This will depend on how the dominant state chooses to use its economic resources. In the extreme, the hegemonic state could coerce them into adopting an open system by military means although this is unlikely since other more positive incentives can be offered. The hegemonic state, for example, can offer medium sized states and their industries, in particular, access to its large domestic market. Consumers in medium sized states would benefit from the hedgemonic states relatively cheap exports. As an alternative to these positive incentives, it can initiate negative ones that can damage the economic potential of medium sized countries. The large state, with its greater political power, can persuade smaller countries to discriminate in favour of its firms products and against those of the medium sized states. It can also withhold aid and support from less developed medium sized states and political and economic support from the more advanced. In this way, the hegemonic state can ensure that the world trading system is an open one.

The hegemony of one state, or its absence, means that international commerce is conducted at the whim of national states. The politicians in those states will have to balance the demands of the various parties with an interest in trade. Trade restrictions can be added (or removed) at will. Even if there is a hegemonic state, to ensure that other states acknowledge its position, the hegemonic state will periodically have to demonstrate its power. The use of economic power will likely mean that the rules of trade are changed. International commerce will be disrupted and the expectations of management dampened. Losses will arise and trade opportunities foregone. As a result, there has been a long search for a more orderly system for trade relations.

The scenarios developed in this chapter suggest that open trading systems are more likely to occur when there is a hegemonic state and one that is, more particularly, in the ascendancy. An open trading system is also likely to be the case when the world is made up of a large number of small advanced states. The opposite is likely to occur when the world economy is characterized by a few but relatively large unequally developed states. Evidence for these views can be seen in the development of the international trading system since the last century.

THE INTERNATIONAL TRADING SYSTEM THROUGH HISTORY

Before discussing the historical development of the international trading system it is important to define what is meant by an open trading system. Economists associate openness with three factors. Firstly, an assessment must be made of the height of trade barriers. The second measure of openness is the ratio of a country's trade to its national income. A period in which this ratio is increasing would suggest that the world trading system was open and expanding.

The third indicator is the extent to which international trade is concentrated within regions that are made up of countries at different levels of economic development. If trade is concentrated within regional groupings of countries – often called **blocs** – and trade outside the bloc is limited to a few states selected largely for political rather than economic reasons, then the conclusion one can draw is that the international trading system is tending towards the closed end of the spectrum.

An open economic system can therefore be defined as one in which trade barriers are falling, the ratios of trade to national incomes are rising and regional trade is becoming less concentrated. Using these criteria, six relatively distinct periods in world trade history can be identified. These periods have alternated between relatively more and relatively less open phases for the international trading system.

Excluding the times when major wars were being fought, the period from the 1820s to the late 1870s was characterized by openness. Tariff levels were reduced and trade ratios increased although there were some exceptions to this, e.g. the US increased its tariffs in the 1860s.

This was a period of British hegemony in both economics and international politics. As a result the international trading system was largely open. A major boost to openness came with the signing of the Anglo-French Treaty of 1860 and led to a large number of other trade agreements. By 1866, France had signed commercial treaties with Belgium, Italy, Switzerland, Sweden, Norway, Spain, the Netherlands, Austria and a trade association of German states known as the Zollverein. The principal European trading partners were thus linked by a whole series of trade agreements. Britain, in the meantime, adopted a unilateral free trade policy towards its trade partners. The nations with overseas empires brought their colonies into this trading system by ensuring that they adopted the tariff structures of their mother countries or at least lowered their tariff levels.

The period from the late 1870s to the end of the century contrasts with this relatively open era. Britain faced challenges to its economic supremacy and its influence began to wane. Economists, both in Europe and in the US, put forward theories proposing protectionism as an aid to economic development. The assumption that free trade was best also faced a serious intellectual challenge (List, 1904). This period was characterized by increases in tariff levels and a decline in trade ratios.

One of the major factors that led to this decline in openness was the competition that the agricultural sectors of 'western' Europe experienced from the emerging economies such as the US, Argentine, Brazil and Russia. The deterioration of the open trading system should not, however, be over exaggerated as real tariff rates remained relatively low up to the end of the century (Capie, 1983).

From the beginning of the 20th century up to World War I, openness began to reassert itself. This was due more to the increase in trade as a proportion of countries' national incomes and the decline in the concentration of regional trade than a reduction in tariffs. Tariffs remained near their original levels.

During the period between the two world wars, the international trading system entered a downward spiral of increasing trade restrictions on a massive scale. The onset of the world depression after 1929 led governments to attempt to isolate their economies from the effects of the depression by raising trade barriers. In a system without rules, when one country raised barriers other countries retaliated. This led to second and third round retaliations. Economists call these rounds of retaliation **beggar thy neighbour** policies. Beggar thy neighbour retaliations made matters worse and trade ratios fell dramatically. As countries only traded with those who provided them with essentials, or with whom they had political links, trade became highly concentrated.

The growing openness of the world trading system after 1945 can be attributed to the hegemony of the US and the acceptance of this by other advanced states, particularly those in western Europe. In the immediate post war period, western European countries needed to trade with the US in order to accumulate dollars to finance the reconstruction of their devastated economies. Later, these European countries viewed an open system as being beneficial. Their comparative advantage lay in sophisticated manufactures which required large markets if economies of scale were to be attained.

While the period was one of exceptional growth, it was also characterized by the growth of economic blocs – principally in Europe with the development of the predecessor of the EU (and the European Community), the European Economic Community (EEC) and the European Free Trade Area (EFTA). The development of these organizations is discussed in Chapter 5. Although these economic institutions led to trade being concentrated more heavily between their member states, the rapid growth in world trade did not damage the prospects of the industrial countries that lay outside these blocs. The US, for political reasons, wanted to see an economically strong western Europe acting as a bulwark against the perceived communist threat coming from the east. As a result, the US openly encouraged the closer integration of the western European economies.

There was a period in the 1970s and 1980s when the openness of the world economy looked under threat. The deep recessions brought about by the OPEC oil price shocks and the deflationary policy responses of the oil importing countries led to an increase in protectionist activity. During this period, however, no one country had the power or authority to dissuade others from imposing trade barriers. It was during this period that the US began to lose its hegemonic role in the world and began to have conflicts with its trade partners. These conflicts have been particularly acrimonious with Japan over cars, electronic goods and agriculture. There have also been conflicts with the EU, principally over agricultural products.

BILATERAL AND MULTILATERAL TRADING RELATIONSHIPS

Trade negotiations can either be carried out on a **bilateral** or **multilateral** basis. Two countries can either negotiate and agree on a framework within which trade can be carried out between out them, or a number of countries can negotiate collectively and apply equally to one another any agreements that are reached. The technical term used for the equal treatment of all the signatories of an agreement is the **most favoured nation (MFN)** principle. All this means is that no signatory will be treated any worse, or any better, than any other. It is a principle that became enshrined in the articles of the GATT (see Chapter 6).

What is the purpose of trade agreements? Their most important function is to provide rules for trade relationships so that firms have a basis upon which to plan their international commercial transactions. Principally, they provide mechanisms which help to increase trade by removing restrictions and to reduce the risks involved in trading across frontiers. Bilateral trade agreements usually have clauses incorporated in them which outline the procedures that should be used when difficulties arise. In this way, the risks become more transparent and business people are able to cover them through, for example, insurance markets. Bilateral agreements may also outline the dispute settlement procedures that must be followed, how the dispute mechanism is to function and which country's laws are to apply (see Chapter 16).

A problem with bilateral agreements is that they are subject to political erosion. Over time, the central tenets of the agreement may become eroded as domestic legislation in one or both countries supersedes them. Bilateral agreements are also prone to obsolescence in that they usually apply for only a specified period and then have to be re-negotiated. This makes them subject to attack from vested interests.

Further, although dispute settlement procedures may be agreed, it is possible that governments may be reluctant to allow them to operate fully if they perceive that their economic and political sovereignty is being challenged. As there is no objective measure of sovereignty, its interpretation depends very much on the political outlook of the government. It is to be expected that the more 'nationalistic' a government's credentials, the more likely it will be to resist restitution via the mechanisms laid down in the agreement.

Business people may well turn to their home governments for support but short of using military force it is difficult for them to do very much about broken agreements. They may attempt economic sanctions such as trade embargoes or the suspension of aid but the impact of such measures must be large enough to have the desired effect. There are also other issues to consider such as the adverse effect a policy may have on the population of the foreign country. A government may consider it best not to damage long-term relationships with a foreign country in order to support its business people in the short run. There have even been some examples of military action taken on behalf of home nationals. Usually, however, the process is more covert and involves diplomatic channels and negotiations.

The heyday of bilateral trading arrangements existed from the latter half of the 19th century up until the beginning of World War I. The previously mentioned Anglo-French treaty of 1860 and those that France concluded with Belgium, the German Zollverein, Italy, Switzerland, Sweden, Norway, Spain, the Netherlands and Austria were all conducted on a bilateral basis.

After World War I, bilateralism re-established itself, albeit in a more restricted form. While it could not be said that the bilateral system was to blame for the collapse of world trade in the 1930s, the deficiencies inherent in it contributed to its decline. For example, the limited duration of bilateral treaties made them vulnerable to attack from interest groups adversely affected by the depression of the 1930s. Many were simply not renewed. Further, bilateral treaties were broken as there was no real international control over states taking this course of action. It was not surprising then, that policy makers proposed that trade in the post World War II period should be based on multilateralism.

The multilateral system, as we shall see in Chapter 6, largely removed the tariffs and other discriminating devices that were imposed in the inter-war years. It also drew up rules which limited the use of quantitative restrictions, established procedures to settle trade disputes between countries and encouraged a series of trade negotiations that progressively liberalized world trade. There were deficiencies in the multilateral system, principally with regard to the dispute settlement and newer trade restrictions that fell outside its mandate. Nevertheless, it is a stronger system than that based on bilateral treaties.

While the international trading system since World War II was, and is, shaped by multilateralism, there is still a place for bilateral deals and negotiations. Trade relations with non-GATT members is largely carried out in this way. The trade deals between the EU and the former communist countries were negotiated bilaterally. Bilateral agreements are not confined to non-GATT member states, however, as they also exist between GATT members. Issues or instruments that fall outside GATT rules provide the *raison d'être* for such agreements. By conducting discussions and drawing up bilateral agreements, countries can further reduce and minimize potential areas of conflict between them.

There are many examples of these types of agreements. Only a few will be presented here. The first is the US–Canadian Automobile Agreement of 1965. The background to this agreement was that in the 1950s Canada was experiencing a balance of trade deficit with the US. The deficit was largely due to the latter country's successful exportation of cars, accessories and parts. The Canadian government responded by offering subsidies to its domestic car industry, which also included US subsidiaries. The objective was to increase the Canadian industry's competitiveness and switch consumption away from automobiles imported from the US. The policy was so successful that the deficit in cars, accessories and parts was not only eliminated but reversed. The US threatened to impose retaliatory tariffs to protect its industry. Before matters came to a head, both governments sat down and resolved the dispute. The experience gained by both parties in settling this dispute contributed to the establishment of the 1988 Canada–US Trade Agreement (CUSTA).

Our second example relates to the conflict between the US and Japan relating to a whole range of goods but principally agricultural commodities and electronics. Once again, the conflict is one centred on the balance of trade, with the US running a deficit with Japan.

In the area of agriculture, the US feels that Japanese protectionist policies prevented it from successfully exporting to the Japanese market. The US believes that it has a comparative advantage when it comes to agricultural production and its producers are being barred from entering the market. There are also cultural/culinary factors inhibiting exports some agricultural products to Japan but trade barriers remain an important explanation for the poor export performance of the US. Direct negotiation between the two countries led to the partial opening up of the Japanese agricultural sector, in particular the beef and citrus markets.

A similar story applies to the trade in electronics. Here the US, feeling that its conductor industry was under threat, reached an agreement with the Japanese government whereby the Japanese electronic industry would guarantee to purchase a proportion of its components from US firms. While none of these discussions were without acrimony, face to face negotiations prevented the situation from deteriorating into a trade war. It must be said, however, that US – Japanese trade relations cannot be classed as cordial and there are still several outstanding areas of conflict to be resolved.

Several bilateral agreements regulate aspects of EU – Japanese trade, in particular trade in automobiles. Some EU countries, fearing the competitiveness of Japanese automakers, attempted to negotiate voluntary agreements whereby the Japanese would limit automobile exports. So great was the fear of the Japanese that when they proposed circumventing these restrictions by establishing European subsidiaries, they were only allowed to do so if they agreed to source 60–80% of their components from local European companies.

Bilateral agreements also form the framework within which economic frontiers between countries are defined. For example, in the North Sea, the border between the British and Norwegian oil fields is set out in a bilateral agreement between the two countries.

Perhaps the most powerful example of a bilateral agreement is the decision by two or more trading partners to form an economic bloc. These regional trade associations are discussed in detail in Chapter 5.

REFERENCES

Capie, J. (1983) Tariff protection and economic performance in the nineteenth century, in *Policy and Performance in International Trade*, (eds J. Black and L. A. Winters), Macmillan, London, pp. 17–47.

Krasner, S. D. (1976) State power and the structure of international trade. *World Politics*, **28**, 317–47.

List, E. (1904) *The National System of Political Economy*, Longmans Green, New York.

Little, I. M. D., Cooper, R. N., Corden, W. M. and Sarath, R. (1993) *Boom, Crisis and Adjustment: The Macroeconomic Experience of Developing Countries*, Oxford University Press, New York.

Regional trade associations 5

ECONOMIC BLOCS AND REGIONAL ECONOMIC INTEGRATION

The formation of economic blocs is allowed under the broad umbrella of multilateral trade arrangements. The question still remains as to why a group of countries will eliminate trade barriers between themselves and not adopt unilateral free trade? There are several answers to this question. Firstly, the participants may feel that opening up their economies to a limited group of countries will bring some of the benefits of free trade but not all the adjustment costs. Secondly, while global free trade may be the economists' ideal, integrating an economy with its principal trading partners may be politically more desirable and feasible (Brada and Méndez, 1993). It will always be easier to negotiate agreements to liberalize trade when legal systems, business practices and cultures are similar. What forms can economic blocs take?

DEFINITIONS AND LEVELS OF ECONOMIC INTEGRATION

An economic bloc can be defined as a grouping of countries that mutually grant trading preferences to one another. Economists have identified four major types of economic bloc. They are now described, moving from the loosest to the tightest form of economic integration.

Free trade areas

In a free trade area trade restrictions between the member states are reduced to zero for either all or a set of goods agreed on by the member states. Each country is allowed to maintain its own trade/commercial policy towards countries which are not part of the free trade area. As a result, the level of trade barriers toward non-members will differ among members.

To prevent non-members from shipping their goods into the member state with the lowest restrictions and then transporting them tariff free to countries where restrictions are higher, the members of the bloc usually establish a common set of rules to prevent this form of behaviour. Within free trade areas, although the individual countries monitor their own trade policies, procedures exist for defusing potential conflicts between the member states. A central secretariat is usually created to deal with conflicts.

Customs unions

As a form of economic integration, customs unions are one step up from free trade areas. All members trade freely with one another but adopt a common external tariff against non-member countries. In trade negotiations they are, therefore, required to act as one and co-ordinate their policies, again usually via a central body.

Common markets

A common market is everything a customs union is plus the free movement of capital and labour. To work effectively, a common market requires that taxes are harmonized between the member states. If taxes are not harmonized then similar goods will vary in price across frontiers giving rise to 'false' trade flows. A further requirement is the co-ordination of health and safety regulations. Otherwise, the price of goods will vary and business people will complain that the commercial environment is not equal between countries – the 'playing field' is not level. The difficulties involved in co-ordinating this type of legislation leads very often to differences in interpretation between countries. The role of a central body to arbitrate and negotiate on such issues becomes even more important than in a customs union or free trade area.

Full economic union

The last form of economic bloc in our taxonomy is the economic union which incorporates all the aspects of a customs union but also includes the total harmonization of government spending/taxation policies and the operation of central banks. It does not, however, require the adoption of a single currency. The adoption of a single currency may be desirable for a number of reasons such as the elimination of currency conversion costs but most of the benefits of a common currency can be achieved by fixing the rate of exchange of one currency against another. Another requirement of an economic union is the elimination of national preference in the purchasing – or procurement – policies of member governments.

As countries progress through the forms of economic integration outlined above, they give up some of their economic sovereignty. It is sometimes argued that the eventual outcome of economic union is political union because governments have ceded most of their powers to a central authority or supernational body. This issue has led to major difficulties and conflicts for some governments in the EU. Despite the decline in national economic sovereignty, the economic power or sovereignty of the economic union will increase. In the economists'

Table 5.1 Trade creation and trade diversion

Exporters	Tariff rates	
	0%	*20%*
Americana	300 ECU	360 ECU
Iberia	320 ECU	384 ECU

language, therefore, there is a trade off between national sovereignty and that of the union.

Before we proceed to examine some real world examples of regional economic integration it is first necessary to consider in more detail the attraction of economic integration to the participating nations. For firms, economic blocs mean increased opportunities for exporting within the bloc (and also increased competition). Trade opportunities with firms in non-member countries may, however, have to be foregone.

THE THEORY OF REGIONAL ECONOMIC INTEGRATION

Economists have approached the study of economic integration from both a static and dynamic perspective. Static models will be dealt with first.

The static approach to trade blocs

The best way to evaluate the potential of an economic bloc is to examine the benefits and the costs that will arise from the mutual reduction of trade barriers between the participating countries (Viner, 1950). Benefits will result from the reduction in barriers as opportunities for new trade amongst the participants are created. Costs, however, will rise as more competitive producers remaining outside the block are discriminated against and consumption is diverted towards goods produced within the bloc. A numerical example will illustrate this point (see Table 5.1). Let us assume that Europa imports goods from two countries, Americana and Iberia, and that the goods produced by these countries can be sold at a price equal to their cost of production. If goods could enter Europa tariff free, Americana could sell its goods for 300 ECU (the currency adopted by Europa) while Iberia would charge 320 ECU. Suppose, however, that Europa imposed a 20% tariff. The price of these goods would increase subsequently to 360 and 384 ECU, respectively. Under a situation of free trade, and one where no tariff existed, Americana's goods would be cheaper than Iberia's and it would capture the market. Assume now that Europa and Iberia agree to form an economic bloc within which tariffs on member states goods are abolished. Tariffs on non-members such as Americana remain in place. The result of this is to reduce the price of Iberia's goods to 320 ECU

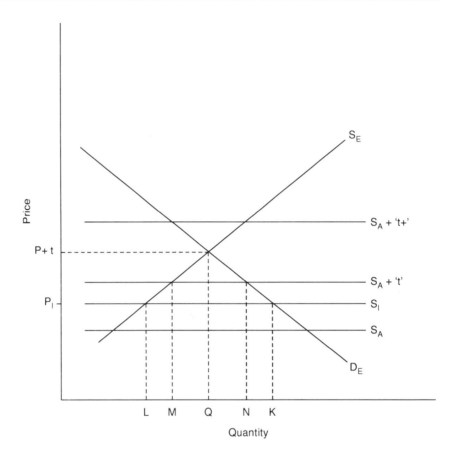

Figure 5.1 Trade creation and trade diversion.

which will now mean that it can under-cut Americana's price and capture Europa's market. In this example, trade has been created as Europa's consumers can now buy more goods at 320 ECU than at the original price of 360 ECU but trade has been diverted because consumers now buy from Iberia rather than from Americana. Hence, whereas trade creation is a positive move towards free trade since it lowers prices to consumers, trade diversion is negative as it moves consumption away from the low cost country with the comparative advantage and towards the higher cost producer.

This argument can also be illustrated by examining Figure 5.1. Europa's domestic demand and supply curves are denoted D_E and S_E for the good in question. Americana and Iberia's supply curves are S_A and S_I respectively. Their horizontal nature implies that they are both constant cost producers. The S_A supply curve being below S_I indicates that Americana is the lowest cost producer.

At price level P_E and above, Europa's demand is satisfied by home supply (i.e. Q). Applying a tariff of 't+' to both Americana's good and Iberia's good ensures that they were priced out of Europa's market.

Americana's supply curve would now become $S_A + 't+'$ while Iberia's would be above this although it is not shown in the diagram. Let us assume, however, that the tariff rate 't' is in operation and it is not prohibitive so that Americana's supply curve is denoted by $S_A + 't'$. This implies that demand in Europa's market is N of which M is supplied domestically while M–N is supplied by Americana. Why is this the case? The reason is that up to M, Europa's cost are lower than Americana's (as shown by the supply curves) so it can under-cut the competition but beyond quantity M the reverse is the case.

If Europa and Iberia now form an economic bloc which abolishes tariffs, Iberias supply curve will re-establish itself at its original position S_I. Hence, S_I is between the tariff free and with tariff position of Americana's supply curve. The result of the removal of the tariff is to lower the price of the good in Europa's domestic market to P_I thus expanding demand to K and reducing domestic supply to L. By reducing tariffs the formation of the economic bloc has created extra trade of the magnitude LM + NK. This is the **'trade creation'** effect. With the removal of the tariffs on Iberia's goods, it is able to under-cut Americana's good and capture its market. Americana's original supply of MN is now superseded by that of Iberia. In other words **'trade diversion'** has taken place. The economic bloc has thus increased the level of trade but it has transferred trade towards the higher cost producer.

The formation of the economic bloc can only be considered beneficial if the gains from trade creation outweigh the losses incurred from trade diversion. How can these gains and losses be measured? In Figure 5.2 (which is essentially Figure 5.1) the reduction in price from P_A to P_I brought about by the formation of the economic bloc has increased **consumers surplus** by area $(e + g + f + k)$. (Consumers surplus is the area between the demand curve and the price. It is considered a surplus due to the unique character of market prices whereby all consumers pay the same price. The demand curve indicates willingness to pay. As some consumers are willing to pay more than the market price they get a bonus or 'surplus' from the existence of a market price system. The surplus could be captured by sellers in a non-market price system such as haggling or bargaining where the price is the subject of negotiation. A smart seller would be able to get the consumer to pay closer to what he/she is willing to pay and, hence, capture part of the surplus.) The **producers surplus** accruing to domestic suppliers is reduced however by (e) as their sales are reduced to L. (Producers surplus is the area between the supply curve and the price. It is considered a surplus due to the unique character of market prices whereby all sellers receive the same price. The supply curve indicates willingness to sell. As some producers are willing to sell at a price less than the going market price they get a bonus or 'surplus' from the existence of a market price system. The surplus could be captured by buyers in a non-market price system such as haggling or bargaining where the price is the subject of negotiation. A smart buyer would be able to get the producer to charge closer to its supply price and, hence, capture part of the surplus.) The tariff

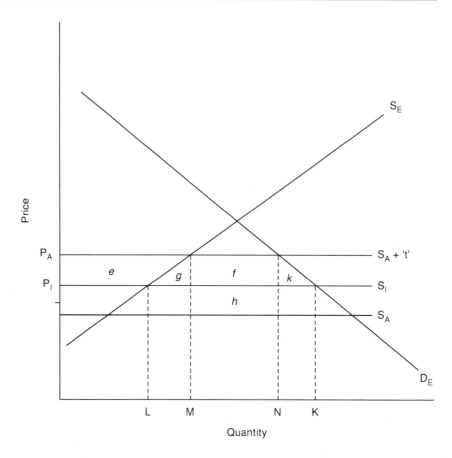

Figure 5.2 Costs and benefits of trade creation and trade diversion.

revenue that Europa previously collected on the volume of trade with Americana ($f + h$) is now lost as trade is diverted to tariff free Iberia. As long as the benefits ($e + f + h$) brought about from trade creation exceed the losses of ($e + f + h$) from trade diversion then the formation of the economic bloc will be beneficial to the parties involved.

Despite the work of some theoretical economists who have shown that there are exceptions to these conclusions (Cooper and Massell, 1965), the general conclusion remains roughly the same. It is, furthermore, possible to identify the conditions that will maximize trade creation and minimize trade diversion. This will improve the likelihood of a successful economic bloc being created.

The first set of conditions is the degree of overlap in the economies of the countries contemplating the formation of an economic bloc. The greater the overlap between the economies the greater the likelihood that the bloc will be a trade-creating one both in terms of inter-industry trade and intra-industry trade. It has been suggested that the growth in trade is likely to be of the intra-industry variety (Verdoorn, 1960). If economies do not overlap, as in the case when a basically agricultural producing country joins a mainly manufacturing country, then there is little scope for trade creation but a great deal for trade diversion.

The second group of conditions relates to the differences in production costs between the potential members in their overlapping industries. The greater the variation in these costs, the greater the potential for trade creation. Conversely if the differences in costs are small, so will be the gains.

The third set of conditions concerns the height of tariff rates prior to the amalgamation of the economies. The higher they are then the greater the gains from the associated tariff reductions. Hence, the greatest gains from the formation of an economic group can be achieved if:

1. The economic structure of the economies overlap.
2. The industries that are common to both have a wide variation in their costs.
3. The level of import tariffs placed by these countries on one another's goods is high prior to the formation of the bloc.

Dynamic factors and economic integration

Dynamic models of the process of regional economic integration do not give rise to one-off benefits but rather accumulate them through time, thus adding to the static benefits. Some economists have argued that these dynamic factors are more important than those discussed in static models.

The first dynamic effect to consider is the increased competition that emanates from the formation of an economic bloc. These are often seen as acting as a spur to greater efficiency by the participants industries. Stripped of their protection, to survive domestic firms have to find more efficient production methods which will in turn have the effect of lowering costs (Jacquemin, 1982).

The second dynamic factor is the impact that a larger market may have on the investment and output decisions of firms. The abolition of trade barriers means that the 'domestic' market has been expanded. As each firm expands its output to meet the new demand, they are able to reap the benefits of economies of scale. If the bloc not only allows the free movement of goods and services, but also the free movement of capital and labour, then these factors will gravitate to where their returns are highest thus increasing overall productivity.

The enhancement of economic and political power and credibility

While it is true to say that the economic integration of one economy with another, along with the adoption of common trade/economic policies, sharply reduces the individual economic sovereignty of the individual member states, it is also true to say that collective economic sovereignty is increased. As a result, small or medium sized states may find it beneficial to join or form economic blocs. The combined power of the bloc may enable the member countries to achieve objectives, say in trade negotiations, which would have been impossible had they tried to do so individually (Mundell, 1964).

A phenomenon that has emerged recently is the attempt by some countries to join a regional grouping when it would seem that their economies are not compatible (i.e. do not overlap) with existing member states. Usually this has been justified by the dynamic benefits to be gained from closer integration. It can also represent an attempt to gain credibility for domestic economic policies or political reforms recently undertaken. While the importance of the potential trade gains should not be overlooked, the recent move by Mexico to negotiate the NAFTA could be seen in this light.

In the European context the application and subsequent entry of Greece, Portugal and Spain to the EU was as much an attempt to secure democracy in those countries as it was to gain the benefits of economic integration. The more recent application of Turkey can also be viewed as one to gain credibility for its political structures and its new more liberal economic policies.

REGIONAL ECONOMIC BLOCS

To understand the operation and the problems associated with the development of economic blocs it is essential to examine some of those that currently exist. We begin by examining the development of economic integration in Europe. We will then look at the situation in North America and the Pacific rim. Finally we make some general comments about economic blocs in the rest of the world.

Europe

In Europe there have been three major economic groupings, the EU, the European Free Trade Area (EFTA) and the former Council for Mutual Economic Assistance (CMEA) which was also known as COMECON.

In western Europe, post World War II economic co-operation began with the establishment of the Organization for European Economic Co-operation (OEEC) in 1948. It was a body designed to administer US Marshall Plan aid on a Europe-wide basis and to ensure that scarce resources were not squandered. This body eventually evolved into the present day Organization for Economic Cooperation and Development (OECD).

Another aspect of the integration process began with the attempt by Belgium, France, West Germany, Italy, the Netherlands and Luxembourg to revitalize European coal and steel industries and make them internationally competitive. In 1952 these countries decided to establish the European Coal and Steel Community. Essentially, its aim was to create a free trade area in coal and steel. The success of this institution led these six countries to propose extending the community to cover other goods, principally manufactures and agricultural products, and to deepen their relationship by forming a customs union.

Economic matters were not the only determinant of integration. Political issues also played their part. There was a general consensus that European countries should not go to war again. The devastation of two world wars had caused enough economic and political turmoil and it was felt that should not happen again. This was particularly keenly felt in France having fought three wars with Germany since the 1870s. It was believed that by integrating the European economies closely, the possibility of a future war would be greatly diminished. While this argument galvanized much of the thinking behind the formation of the EEC, political factors also contributed to the formation of separate economic blocs, i.e. EFTA and CMEA. The development of these blocs will be discussed in greater detail; however, as a generalization, the countries that made up the former bloc either did not like the political implications of close economies ties or were debarred from joining on political grounds, while those that made up the latter grouping were suspicious of and ideologically opposed to the EEC.

The European Union

The EEC was established with the signing of the treaty of Rome in 1957 and was originally composed of West Germany, France, Italy, Holland, Belgium and Luxembourg – sometimes called 'the six'. The principal trade provisions of the treaty were as follows:

1. To establish a free trade area with the elimination of tariffs and other restrictions on the movement of goods.
2. To form a customs union by adopting a common external tariff that would be imposed on non-member countries but allowing some exceptions for former colonies.
3. To engender a common market by removing barriers to the free movement of capital and labour.
4. To devise a common agricultural policy that would co-ordinate farm policies between the member states and regulate agricultural trade with non-member states.

The history of what was to become the EU up to the mid-1980s is really one of the implementation and consolidation of these provisions. In the 1970s the 'six' were expanded by the accession of Britain, Denmark and Ireland. The so-called southern enlargement began in 1981 with Greece, a former associate member, achieving full status and was completed in 1986 with the entry of Spain and Portugal. As a result of these additions the 'six' became '12'.

Dissatisfied by low growth rates and ascribing these to internal factors, the member countries decided to embark on a further attempt to eliminate internal trade barriers and form a true common market (Commission EC, 1985). While it is likely that external factors, such as the lower rate of growth of the world economy, played their part, the continued existence of hundreds of restrictions on the free movement of goods, services, capital and labour were largely held responsible for the bloc's economic performance. For example, the continued border restrictions requiring the presentation of customs documentation at frontiers caused delays which increased the cost of transportation and raised the price of goods. Other examples that hindered the functioning of the common market were the mutual non-recognition of employees qualifications which impeded the movement of labour and various restrictions on the movement of capital – the latter were particularly relevant in France, Italy, Greece, Portugal and Spain. The activities of service industries such as banking and insurance were also impeded by a whole host of national regulations. Differing health and safety standards also played their part in raising costs and impeding trade (Cecchini, 1988).

Spurred on by estimates that the abolition of the remaining barriers to trade would lead to an increase in growth of 4–7%, the member states agreed to set a timetable for their elimination staring in 1987. This became known as the 1992 programme which was to be completed by the end of that year.

The main trade impediments were dealt with by opening up government procurement to competitive tendering, mutually recognizing one another's health and safety standards, and employee qualifications. New custom documentation and practices were also enforced which cut out waiting time at the borders. Regulations covering service industries were also harmonized. More problematical was the harmonization of taxation. The continued existence of variations in sales taxes and excise duties has led to some 'false' border trade. This has been particularly true in the area of alcoholic beverages between Britain and France, and petrol between Belgium, the Netherlands, Germany and France, where national taxes vary. Despite these discrepancies, their adverse impact is considered to be small.

The 1992 programme was looked upon by some of the EU's trading partners, in particular the US and Japan, with some suspicion. The process is sometimes characterized as a move towards developing a 'Fortress Europe'. The main concern was that as the EU reduced its internal barriers it would increase its external barriers (Brainard and Perry, 1989). What led to such a view? The principle evidence put forward was:

1. The EU's insistence that foreign producers should 'monitor' their exports in some sensitive industries for an undefined limited period after 1992 (e.g. US television programmes, Japanese cars, etc.).
2. The requirement that foreign companies setting up plants in the EU should guarantee a local input content of 60–80%.
3. The adoption of the so-called 'new trade policy instrument' which

allowed individual firms to appeal directly to the EU for the imposition of measures to counter unfair trade. Prior to this, firms had to appeal to their governments who were considered to be less willing than the EU to take up their case.
4. The tightening of the EU's anti-dumping measures.

This evidence, coupled with the general thrust of EU industrial policy which supported the electronic, aircraft and computer sectors, and its resistance to liberalization in cinematic products and agricultural commodities, confirmed many of the misgivings held by the trading partners.

There was another view of the 1992 programme which ran contrary to the protectionist interpretation. This suggested that the boost to economic growth, particularly in the long run, would benefit foreign just as much as EU companies. The uniformity in EU regulations would give all companies, not just domestic firms, cost advantages. Ease in transportation would allow firms, whether they be foreign or from the EU, to establish optimum sized plants in the most cost effective locations.

This contrary view also suggested that to become protectionist would not be in the EU's interests as it relied very heavily on exports and inward investment. The EU as a whole provided 25% of the world's exports. These exports accounted for 15% of its GDP. The EU also received 40% of all the foreign direct investment carried out by the developed countries.

Which view is correct is, of course, a moot point and depends on the position from which one views the process. The 1992 process will encourage further internal growth – trade creation – and will inevitably lead to some further trade diversion. This will have adverse effects on some companies who export directly to the EU but little on those that have subsidiaries operating within it. Certainly, a number of the companies from the EU's trading partners viewed the 1992 programme with suspicion and began to form joint ventures with EU companies, e.g. Saab–Renault. There was also a movement by the principal EFTA members to create a joint grouping with the EU and later to become full members.

The further deepening of the EU so that it becomes a true economic union – the **Maastricht** process – has not found favour with Britain and Denmark. Both these countries wish to resist the additional erosion of political and economic sovereignty that further integration implies. There are also misgivings, especially in Britain, regarding the economic impact of proposed EU social legislation. Britain's view is that it will add to the costs of industries and make them uncompetitive in world markets.

The elaborate legal structures that bind the EU together give plenty of scope for conflicts to arise between countries regarding the interpretation of EU legislation. To provide a framework for the defusing of conflicts, the European Court was established. Countries, individuals, firms and institutions can apply to this court for a ruling regarding the actions of other countries or individuals and companies. Most disputes of a trade nature are resolved between the states before the Court is brought into the picture.

The European Free Trade Area

The EFTA was established in 1960 by western European countries that either did not want to, or could not, join the then EEC. Austria, Finland, Sweden and Switzerland believed that to join the EEC, which was made up of NATO countries, would compromise their neutral status. Britain was also in a dilemma. Its trading policies since the 1930s had been based on Imperial Preference – relatively open access to products from its former colonies – and these ties and guaranteed markets would be threatened if it joined the EEC. It was also suspicious of the closer political links and loss of sovereignty that membership implied. Denmark also had reservations on this point. It also feared losing British markets for its goods if it joined the EEC and Britain failed to join. Portugal could not join as it had a totalitarian government. A country has to have a democratic government before it can join the EU. Forming a free trade area was, therefore, a way by which the benefits of closer economic integration could be achieved but without the closer political ties which would compromise neutrality and existing commercial policies.

Britain joined the EEC in 1972 followed by Denmark. The remaining EFTA countries realized that they had to come to some agreement with the EEC or suffer the consequences of trade diversion. A number of bilateral arrangements were negotiated which were aimed at abolishing tariffs on industrial goods by 1977. The process of tariff removal was not, however, completed until 1983.

With better access to a much larger market, EFTA gained more than the EU from these agreements. While, on the surface trade seemed free between the two groups, many barriers to trade remained (Herin, 1986).

The European Economic Area

The close trading links between the EU and EFTA made it inevitable that an even greater degree of economic integration would be sought by the participants. Discussions began in 1984 concerning the difficulties that had arisen between the two blocs. Areas covered included road and rail links, customs documentation and state aid to industries, to name but a few.

The onset of the 1992 single market programme in the EU was also a spur to the EFTA countries to seek a further accommodation with the EU (Norman, 1989). The EU agreed to extend the programme to include the EFTA countries and the European Economic Area (EEA) came into being on January 1, 1994. The EEA stretches from the Arctic to the Mediterranean and it is the largest economic bloc in the world, with a market of 372 million people. Not all the EFTA members are participants. Austria, Finland, Iceland, Norway and Sweden decided to join, while Liechtenstein and Switzerland remained outside.

While the EEA is a major move towards European integration Austria, Finland and Sweden see it as a step on the road to becoming full members of the EU. The political changes in Europe since the collapse of communism have rendered their neutral position unnecessary, while not being able to participate fully in the decision making bodies of their principle market places them at a disadvantage. For these countries, negotiations and agreements for them to become full members of the EU have already taken place. All that remains is ratification by the legislative bodies in the member-states. The EEA/EFTA framework has been proposed as a structure in which the former Soviet Union and eastern European countries could participate as a step to joining the EU.

The Council for Mutual Economic Assistance

The CMEA was made up of all those European states that constituted the former Soviet Bloc and included in later years Cuba, Mongolia and Vietnam. It was principally established to co-ordinate trade amongst these countries and to reap any benefits from harmonizing these countries' national economic plans.

The concentration on heavy industry by **command economies** and the pricing of goods with very little regard to their cost of production led to a pattern of trade that did not adhere to the principles of comparative advantage. By the mid–1980s, it became evident to the majority of participants that something was wrong with the workings of the CMEA (Smith, 1992). Certainly, the hegemonic Soviet Union believed that it was subsidizing the other members and demanded payment for its products in convertible currencies, principally US dollars.

The collapse of the Soviet Union led to the emergence of free central and eastern European states which wish to participate in the world economy. In particular, they want closer trade relations with the EU; however, the trade flows that were established under CMEA cannot be abandoned immediately. In a number of cases, the goods produced under the old centrally planned system are inferior in quality and would not find ready markets in the EU. As many of their industries are based on obsolete technology, it is unlikely that they could compete with those of the EU if they were opened up to full competition. The EU has suggested that the former command economies first join an institution like EEA as a half-way house before applying for full EU membership. In the case of Hungary, this view has been rejected and it has applied for full EU membership. Whether the former command economies will be allowed to join the EU will ultimately depend on their rate of progress towards market based economies and their subsequent economic performance. As with any attempt to join an economic bloc, the greater the differences between the economies, the more difficult the negotiations will be.

Economic integration and North America

As previously mentioned, the original catalyst for economic integration in North America was the series of discussion between the US and Canada regarding trade in the automobile industry. The experience gained in those negotiations led to the eventual signing of a free trade agreement between these two countries which came into effect on January 1, 1989.

The Canada-US Trade Agreement

The CUSTA brought into existence a market of approximately 272 million people with an average income per head of about US$17 400. These two countries were already the worlds largest trading partners and enjoyed zero or low tariffs on most goods. Sectoral trade agreements governed some other sectors. The agreement nevertheless envisaged the elimination, over a period of ten years, of the remaining trade restrictions and the opening up of Canada to direct US investment (Schott, 1988). To iron out difficulties that might arise in the operation of the agreement, very elaborate disputes settlement procedures were established.

The North American Free Trade Agreement

In 1991 negotiations on a North American Free Trade Agreement (NAFTA) began. The aim was the creation of a market of 364 million people. NAFTA is a series of bilateral agreements between Canada, the US and Mexico, building upon the CUSTA framework. The Mexican government believes that by integrating its economy with its northern neighbour it would not only gain economically but also politically. The mutual reduction in trade barriers would lead, given Mexico's comparative advantage, to an inflow of direct investment. The products that would be produced by these factories could then be exported duty free back into the US and Canada. This process would promote Mexican economic growth.

The benefits that are assumed will accrue to Mexico may, however, create problems for labour intensive industries in the US. Over a number of years, several of these industries have taken advantage of Mexican 'free trade zones' or **'maquiladoras'** and have moved some of their operations south of the boarder. This process is expected to accelerate and could cost the loss of 170 000 low skilled US jobs (*Business Week*, 1993). The potential losers are expected to be those working in the auto parts, furniture, glass and seafood industries, as well as producers of agricultural produce such as sugar, peanuts, citrus fruits and vegetables. As in the CUSTA, in order to settle the inevitable conflicts that are likely to arise, elaborate trade dispute procedures have been created.

Other countries in the western hemisphere

The creation of the NAFTA has had a dynamic effect on the area's trading partners in both the rest of Latin America and the Caribbean. There have been a number of past initiatives in these areas to promote integration and free trade but they have usually not been very successful. The reasons are many but very broadly are concerned with conflicting economic ideologies and disagreements regarding the distribution of the benefits among participating countries.

In South America, the Latin American Free Trade Area formed in 1961 largely foundered because the member states continued to pursue import substitution policies. Its replacement, the Latin American Integration Association, established in 1980, also suffered from this problem. Realizing that they needed to revitalize their economies by opening them up to greater international competition, two new regional groupings have been formed to encourage, as a first step, regional free trade. These are MERCOSUR which includes Argentina, Brazil, Paraguay and Uruguay and the Andean Common Market (ANCOM) comprising Bolivia, Colombia, Equador, Peru and Venezuela.

Initiatives for integration have also taken place in Central America with the establishment of the Central American Common Market (CACM) and the Caribbean Community and Common Market (CARICOM). The former, while successful in reducing trade restrictions amongst its members, has suffered not only from political conflicts in the area but disagreements between the states regarding the distribution of the benefits from trade liberalization. The latter grouping has had difficulties in trying to integrate the diverse and dispersed set of island economies that make up its membership.

The emergence of NAFTA led to some fears in Latin America regarding the future growth of their exports to the US. The Central American nations and the Caribbean economies in particular, have been affected by the loss of preferential status for exports which existed prior to NAFTA under the US Caribbean Basin Initiative. The US Enterprise for the Americas Initiative (EAI) was designed to alleviate some of these effects by extending incentives to those countries that encouraged capitalist development and trade liberalization. The long-term aim of the principal countries in the western Hemisphere is the formation of a free trade area encompassing North, Central and South America as well as the Caribbean island economies.

Economic regionalism and the Pacific rim

The rapid growth of trade between the countries bordering the Pacific ocean has led to growing interest in the formalization of economic relationships. These ideas are not new with Japan having suggested a

Greater East Asian Co-prosperity Sphere before World War II. In the late 1960s, the Association of South East Asian Nations (ASEAN) was formed, largely to counter a perceived communist threat. Its members are Malaysia, Thailand, Indonesia, The Philippines, Singapore and Brunei. By the late 1970s an economic dimension to this organization was developed, largely based on co-operative activities amongst the states and preferential trading arrangements (Suriyamongkol, 1988).

By the late 1980s it became evident to the majority of Pacific rim states that the growth of the EU and the development of NAFTA required a more formal response. This took place in 1989 with the formation of the Asia–Pacific Economies Co-operation forum (APEC) which was made up of the six ASEAN nations plus Australia, Canada, Japan, New Zealand, South Korea and the US. The group was enlarged in 1991 to include China, Hong Kong and Taiwan.

The main principle of the APEC grouping is the stimulation of the area's economic growth through the promotion of regional trade. Currently, it has concentrated on the removal of trade barriers and the establishment of dispute settlement mechanisms. In other words, it has concentrated on areas which do not necessarily damage the interest of nations or blocs outside the area (Kirkpatrick, 1994). A permanent secretariat has been established in Singapore to co-ordinate the activities of the working parties established to examine areas of mutual interest.

Absent from the APEC grouping are, of course, the Latin American countries that border the Pacific, although there are moves afoot to deal with this omission. As some of the most dynamic economies are members of APEC, it may be worth watching to see if it coalesces into a bloc in the future.

Economic blocs in the rest of the world

Having covered Europe, the Americas and the Asian/Pacific area, we are really left with Africa, the Middle East and the area surrounding the Indian sub-continent. In Africa there have been some limited successes such as the Economic Community of West Africa States (ECOWAS) and the East African Common Market. Low incomes and disputes, once again concerning the distribution of the benefits, coupled with largely protectionist national policies has limited success in trade expansion. The same is also true in the Middle East where many of the original initiatives to foster greater regional economic co-operation have not been fruitful (Fischer, 1992). One exception has been the Gulf Co-operation Council (GCC) which was established largely for political and strategic reasons but has achieved a measure of economic integration amongst the member states of Kuwait, Oman, Qatar, Saudi Arabia and the United Arab Emirates. Even here, however, with their limited economic base the benefits of trade creation must be regarded as small. India has followed a very protectionist import substitution policy. Some moves toward liberalization have, however, recently been made. Political problems between India and Pakistan will likely prevent further economic integration in the region.

ECONOMIC BLOCS AND THE NATION STATE

Despite the growth of regional institutions, international economic relations are still very much the purview of the nation state. The degree of openness of the international economic system depends very much on how the nation state perceives its interests. Nation states juggling a number of possibly conflicting goals may not wish to pursue a policy of unilateral free trade. Nation states, furthermore, exist in a world of nation states where power is not distributed equally amongst them and where freedom of action may well be constrained in the area of trade policy. The openness, or otherwise, of the world trading system has depended very much on how the leading trading nations view their interests.

In conducting international economic relations, a state can select either a bilateral or multilateral basis to pursue its aims. Most choose to use a combination of the two. The fragility of the set of alliances and treaties that formed the basis of trade in the last century was fully exposed during the depression of the 1930s. As a result, the architects of the post World War II economic order set the basis for trade on a multilateral footing.

One area where bilateral negotiations and agreements have dominated is in the formation of regional trade associations. As a result of the long-term success of the EU there has been a rapid expansion in the number of regional trade associations. Whether they will lead to the further expansion of world trade or whether they will begin to actively compete and lead to its contraction is not yet clear (de Melo and Panagariya, 1992). Currently, all the groupings that have taken place have been trade creating in that they have not sought to impose tariffs that are higher than those that applied prior to their formation. Time will tell.

REFERENCES

Brada, J. C. and Medez, J. A. (1993) Political and economic factors in regional economic integration. *Kyklos*, **46**, 183–201.

Brainard, W. C. and Perry, G. L. (1989) *Brookings Papers on Economic Activity No. 2*, Washington, DC.

Business Week (1993) A noose around Nafta. *Business Week*, February 22.

Cecchini, P. (1988) *The Costs of non Europe*, Wildwood House, London.

Cooper, R. N. and Massell B. F. (1965) A new look at customs union theory. *Economic Journal*, **75**, 742–7.

Commission EC (1985) *Completing the Internal Market: White Paper*, Office for Official Publications of the European Communities, Luxembourg.

de Melo, J. and Panagariya, A. (1992) *The New Regionalism in Trade Policy*, World Bank/CEPR Washington, DC.

Fischer, S. (1992) *Prospects for integration in the Middle East*, paper presented to the World Bank and CEPR conference on New Dimensions in Regional Integration, Washington, DC.

Herin, J. (1986) Rules of origin and differences between tariff levels in EFTA and the EEC. *EFTA Occasional Paper No. 3*.

Jacquemin, A. (1982) Imperfect market structure and international trade – some recent research. *Kyklos*, **35**, 75–93.

Kirkpatrick, C. (1994) Regionalization, regionalism and east Asian economic co-operation. *World Economy*, **17**, 191–202.

Mundell, R. A. (1964) Tariff preferences and the terms of trade. *Manchester School of Economic and Social Studies*, **32**, 1–13.

Norman, V. (1989) EFTA and the internal European market economic policy: a European forum, *EFTA Occasional Paper No. 20*.

Schott, J. (1988) *United States–Canada Free Trade: An Evaluation of the Agreement*, Institute for International Economics, Washington, DC.

Smith, A. H. (1992) Integration under communism and economic relations after communism in eastern Europe, in *The European Economy*, (ed. D. Dyker), Longman, London.

Suriyamongkol, M. L. (1988) *The Politics of ASEAN Economic Co-operation*, Oxford University Press, Oxford.

Verdoorn, P. (1960) The Intra Block Trade of Benelux, in *Economic Consequences of the Size of Nations*, (ed. E. A. G. Robinson), Macmillan, London.

Viner, J. (1950) *The Customs Union Issue*, Carnegie Endowment for International Peace, New York.

Institutions of the multilateral trading system 6

THE BASIS OF THE MULTILATERAL SYSTEM

Unfortunately, the world of international commerce is not governed by one set of rules by which the movement of goods between countries is to be conducted. Irrespective of the country in which it operates, a business which is involved in international commerce will deal with a wide variety of regulatory regimes. These sets of rules will vary, both with the individual countries with which business is being conducted and with the commodity traded. Making the investment in acquiring a good working knowledge of this myriad of rules and regulations can be very important for the development of business strategies. If these rules are understood and used strategically, they can enhance a firm's competitive advantage and, under the right conditions, simultaneously reduce the competitive position of one's rivals. Firms operating in the international sphere may also find it to their advantage to provide input into the process by which their government formulates both the domestic legislation governing the conduct of international business and the strategies to be used in trade negotiations with other countries. Hence, it is important for business people to understand both how the institutions operate and the array of trade regulations with which they are likely to be faced when undertaking commercial relations across international boundaries.

No multinational organization exists which is comprehensive in its coverage of international trade matters or to which all countries belong. An attempt to negotiate a comprehensive International Trade Organization was made at the end of World War II. Agreement could not be reached except on a limited subset of trade matters which had been negotiated in the GATT and a comprehensive organization was stillborn. The GATT, by default, subsequently became the principal multilateral organization regulating trade. A number of countries, for the most part current or former communist countries, chose to remain outside its structure. The GATT, however, had been negotiated in a period when much of the world was still colonized. While nations could join when they gained independence, there has been an ongoing general concern that the GATT has not adequately addressed the needs of these new, largely third world, nations. In 1965, the **United Nations Conference on Trade and Development (UNCTAD)** was organized to address problems of trade between developing and developed countries.

The GATT's original mandate was limited to trade in goods. In the absence of a more comprehensive international trade organization, nations attempted to extend the activities of the GATT to cover other areas of international commerce. International rules covering trade in services, protection of intellectual property, investment etc. were required. As the GATT's organizational structure was not designed for this wider role, negotiations undertaken under the auspices of the GATT resulted in an agreement in 1993 to establish a WTO. In 1995, the WTO came into being. It is the most comprehensive international trade organization to date as it is responsible not only for trade in goods but also trade in services and for the international protection of intellectual property rights. The GATT continues to operate under the wider WTO umbrella. These three institutions are the main multilateral trade organizations. Certainly, as discussed in Chapter 5, a large number of bilateral and regional trade organizations exist. Most of these, at least in theory, conform to the conventions of the WTO and/or UNCTAD.

THE WORLD TRADE ORGANIZATION

The agreement to establish the WTO was reached at the Uruguay Round (so-called because the decision to undertake the negotiations was made in Uruguay) of GATT negotiations. Members of the GATT automatically became WTO members. The WTO is responsible for administering all of the agreements arising from the Uruguay Round.

Unlike the GATT, the WTO is a permanent organization. It is guided by a regularly scheduled conference of ministers from all WTO members. The day-to-day administration of the WTO is the responsibility of the General Council. The WTO's General Council acts both as the body which settles disputes between members and which reviews, on a regular basis, the trade policies of members. At the conclusion of the Uruguay Round, as well as a new GATT agreement covering trade in goods, new agreements on trade in services – the General Agreement on Trade in Services (GATS) – and on the international protection of intellectual property – the Agreement on Trade-Related Aspects of Intellectual Property (TRIPS) – were reached. The WTO is responsible for implementing these agreements. It co-ordinates the work of three new institutions, the Goods Council, the Services Council and the Intellectual Property Council.

The Goods Council oversees the functioning of the GATT – which deals with tariffs – and 12 other sub-agreements negotiated at the Uruguay Round which relate to specialized aspects of trade in goods. The Services Council oversees the GATS and the Intellectual Property Council oversees the TRIPS agreement.

The WTO's trade policy review mechanism keeps members informed of changes in each other's trade policies. It can also require governments to explain their trade policies. The dispute settlement procedures given to the WTO are much more effective than those which were administered previously by the GATT. Further, a common set of dispute settlement procedures are used for trade in goods, for trade in services and for the protection of intellectual property.

THE UNITED NATIONS CONFERENCE ON TRADE AND DEVELOPMENT

The UNCTAD, in terms of the number of nations which take part, is the largest multinational trade organization as its membership embraces the market economy countries, the formerly communist countries of eastern Europe and developing countries including China. It deals with issues concerning trade relations between developing and developed countries and, hence, is narrow in focus. Its scope is very wide ranging, however, covering almost all topics of concern in international trade. The mandate of UNCTAD is to attempt to enhance third world countries' development prospects by improving their trade opportunities. Its effectiveness is limited and it remains primarily a forum for the presentation of ideas and the exchange of information on trade problems. It attempts to reform trade through the use of persuasive arguments based on ideas of obligation and responsibility – moral suasion. The major policy making forum of UNCTAD is international conferences convened every four years. These conferences are commonly referred to by their chronological orderings, e.g. UNCTAD VI. The major topics of concern at UNCTAD have been attempts to find mechanisms to stabilize and/or raise the prices of commodities exported from developing countries to developed countries, to improve market access for developing countries' manufactured goods in developed countries, to increase and improve the use of aid transfers, to facilitate the resolution of third world debt problems and to enhance technology transfer (UNCTAD, 1985).

The most notable achievements of UNCTAD have resulted from its attempts to bring 'orderly marketing' to the volatile markets of economically important commodities exported from the third world. Largely through the ability of UNCTAD to keep problems in the public eye and the moral suasion applied, a number of international commodity agreements have been negotiated – rubber, sugar, tin, coffee and cocoa. The success of the agreements in operation has varied considerably. The fact that these agreements have existed at all, and that solutions to market volatility are being sought through international co-operation, can largely be attributed to the work at UNCTAD.

Businesses conducting international trade in the commodities covered in an agreement can be affected by the agreement's rules. Hence, firms should be careful to monitor UNCTAD initiatives which attempt to extend similar agreements to additional commodities. Further, the deliberations of UNCTAD bear watching because they often provide a barometer for new issues which may become important for the conduct of international commerce. Finally, UNCTAD's extensive list of publications provides an excellent, sometimes the only, source of information on product movements, international market structures and trade problems.

THE GENERAL AGREEMENT ON TARIFFS AND TRADE

The GATT is often a frustrating institution for business people because it is seldom what one might expect it to be. This frustration and confusion arises primarily because one's normal frame of reference is national institutions whose regulations are backed by the force of law. Those who break domestic laws of commerce similar to those which the GATT oversees internationally are punished by the courts and compensation is often provided to the injured party. On the surface, the GATT appears to act as both the regulator and, through the dispute resolution mechanisms of the WTO, the adjudicator of the international trade in goods between nations. There is, however, no super-national legal authority and the GATT, through the WTO, must rely on the voluntary compliance of its members encouraged by the weight of international moral pressure. It is probably most useful to think of the GATT as an additional 'special interest' which must be considered by domestic politicians when they weigh trade issues. When a GATT member's domestic economy is showing solid growth and when trade tensions are low, the GATT's influence will grow. On the other hand, when a domestic economy falters and when trade tensions are high, GATT concerns will receive less weight.

The GATT, which came into being in January 1948, is the only truly multilateral body which lays down agreed rules for the international trade in goods. Approximately 120 countries currently subscribe to it and together they account for nearly 90% of world trade. The GATT's principal objective is to liberalize the international trade in goods and provide a secure environment under which trade can be conducted. It provides a set of rules by which contracting countries agree to conduct their trade relations.

Both the liberalization of trade and the ongoing development of rules for trade has been accomplished through successive rounds of negotiations which have become the buzz words of international trade – Annecy Round (1948), Torquay Round (1950–51), Dillon Round (1956; 1960–62), Kennedy Round (1964–67), Tokyo Round (1973–79) and the Uruguay Round (1986–1994). As the number of countries has expanded and the breadth of issues the GATT has attempted to resolve increased, so the lengths of the various Rounds have increased. Part of the problem arose because the GATT, as originally conceived, was only part of a package that was to have become a comprehensive international trade organization – that portion concerned with the reduction of tariffs. Until the

1993 agreement to establish the WTO, the GATT was forced to act in a much wider context than originally intended.

The framers of the 'new world order' that arose in the wake of World War II believed in trade liberalization both philosophically and by observation. They could remember the relatively smooth functioning system prior to the Great Depression and had observed at first hand the disastrous effects of the tariff wars of the 1930s. They set up the GATT with the single objective of removing trade barriers. At the time there was considerable discussion of the so-called 'spirit of the GATT' whereby any disputes that did arise could be handled by rational diplomats according to economic principles. Underlying the spirit of the GATT was a fundamental disdain for lawyers and a distrust for legalistic approaches to international rules of trade. Basically, the GATT was conceived as a club of around forty diplomats from countries with similar philosophical-cultural backgrounds where 'things could be worked out'. Life for 'club members' was made easy, however, because they did not have to deal with countries having alternative economic systems. The communist countries were not interested in joining and most of the third world was still under colonial administration. Further, it was an era when governments played a much smaller role in their national economies than is common today.

High tariffs had been erected in the beggar thy neighbour period of the 1930s and these were still in place at the end of World War II. These high tariffs acted to obscure a plethora of potential trade problems which would become visible as tariffs declined over time. When tariffs are the major barrier to trade, countries can put a large number of policies and regulations in place which would be considered trade inhibiting in the absence of the tariffs. In other words, behind high tariff walls countries can pursue domestically desirable policies without worrying about their trade effects.

Tariff reduction combined with **tariffication** are the major liberalizing mechanisms of the GATT. Tariffication is a process whereby alternative trade restricting practices are converted into tariffs which provide an equivalent degree of protection. When trade restrictions are in the form of tariffs they can be directly compared. As they can be compared, negotiating their removal is simplified. A major GATT principle is that once a country agrees to lower its tariff rates they become 'bound', i.e. cannot be raised, at that new level. The early rounds of GATT negotiations were very successful in reducing the high tariffs of the 1930s.

A second major principle of the GATT is non-discrimination – this means that tariff concessions given to any member must be extended to all members – the previously mentioned most favoured nation rate. Non-members can be charged any rate and, hence, an incentive is provided for non-members to join. Non-discrimination is also one of the major principles which enables the GATT system to function as it was intended. For example, a country might be faced with protectionist pressures to restrict the product of one country – say low cost electronics from South Korea. If the importing country was allowed to discriminate, it could impose tariffs only on South Korea electronics and suffer the retaliation of only the South Korean government. The next example of domestic protectionist pressure might be for the reduction of fish imports from Iceland. In this situation trade problems could be addressed one-by-one and the importing country would suffer only mild economic and political fallout each time. If nations cannot discriminate, the tariff restriction aimed at South Korea would have to be applied to electronics products from all countries and the restriction aimed at Iceland applied to fish imports from all countries. All trading partners are likely to complain and, under the GATT rules, have the option of imposing trade restrictions of equivalent value on the original country. Hence, non-discrimination makes acquiescence to domestic protectionist pressure more difficult for politicians by greatly increasing both the political and economic cost.

A third major principle of the GATT is transparency. Transparency means that any trade action taken by a country must be reported to all of the members of the WTO. Further, once informed, other countries can bring forward their concerns at the WTO. Basically, there can be no secret deals and, hence, transparency acts to strengthen non-discrimination.

Accepted retaliation is the GATT's fourth principle. As individual countries can ignore the trade rules established by the GATT in ways which could injure other countries, the injured countries have the right to retaliate up to an amount of equivalent value without fear of second round retaliation. There is a fundamental acceptance of the fact that there may be overwhelming domestic priorities which require countries to renege on their GATT commitments and that those instances should not lead to beggar thy neighbour retaliations.

As the GATT was not conceived as a legal entity, its formal mechanisms for settling disputes were weak. The dispute mechanisms agreed to at the Uruguay Round and administered by the WTO are much stronger. Adjudication by GATT 'Panels', however, centred on legal interpretations of GATT Articles. This is because GATT Panels were only initiated when the 'club of reasonable men' approach failed. The process was cumbersome. Having a GATT Panel hear a dispute depended on the agreement of all participants, including the contending parties. The new rules administered by the WTO allow a Panel to be called when only one party requests it. The GATT's Articles have proven difficult to interpret and narrow legal interpretations have, for the most part, not been successfully translated into reasonable economic solutions which were in keeping with the 'spirit of the GATT'.

As the organization grew to include a large number of countries with a variety of economic systems at various stages of development, the 'club' became too big and philosophically diverse. As a result, the consensus on what is reasonable was eroded, leading to a greater reliance on legal approaches to trade disputes. This weakened the organization's effectiveness (Wolf, 1986). With the erosion of the principles associated with a 'club of reasonable men', the stronger dispute mechanisms of the WTO are needed to help enforce increasingly legal interpretations.

Further, as tariffs came down with successive GATT rounds, many domestic economic policies have been exposed as considerable barriers to trade. As a result, nations wishing to maintain their domestic systems have found other means to limit trade. The rapid pace of technological change and the rising proportion which services comprise of national economic activity has meant that the basis of international commerce has broadened beyond trade in goods. As a result, starting with the Tokyo Round, there was an attempt to extend the GATT into new areas – non-tariff barriers, trade in services, protection of intellectual property, rules for international investment and a number of other topics. The attempt to expand the scope of the GATT was only partially successful and it became clear that the organization was not sufficiently robust to deal with the changes expected of it (Jackson, 1978). The WTO was established to provide a more comprehensive organization. The GATT remains the organization responsible for trade in goods while the new GATS and TRIPS agreements are responsible for other areas of international economic activity. The GATT rules regarding trade in goods are dealt with in greater detail in the remainder of Part Three.

REFERENCES

Jackson, J. H. (1978) The crumbling institutions of the liberal trade system. *Journal of World Trade Law*, **12**(2), 93–106.

UNCTAD (1985) *The History of UNCTAD 1964–1984*, United Nations, New York.

Wolf, M. (1986) Fiddling while the GATT burns. *World Economy*, **9**(1), 1–18.

7 Orderly markets

WHY ORDERLY MARKETS ARE DESIRED

Many international trade problems can be attributed to rapidly changing markets. Rapidly changing markets arise primarily from volatile supply conditions or rapid rates of technological change which cannot be used to equal effect in all countries. Instability may cause economic hardship for some market participants. Further, in some nations the economic 'outcome' which some or all markets provide may be considered politically unacceptable and alternative non-market allocation mechanisms put in place. Under these conditions, nations may wish to co-operate to regulate the international movement of goods through non-market means. The stated rationale is bringing 'order' to the international trading system. Three mechanisms which attempt to provide 'orderly markets' are examined in this chapter – international commodity agreements, voluntary export restraints and countertrade.

INTERNATIONAL COMMODITY AGREEMENTS

An international commodity agreement can take many forms but they usually involve a single commodity or a group of closely related products. The major supplying nations, and often the important importing coutries as well, negotiate an agreement to intervene in the market to stabilize and/or support prices. A number of international commodity and product agreements currently exist or have existed in the recent past. Some have been initiated under GATT auspices – the Multifibre Agreement (textiles and clothing), the Arrangement Regarding Bovine Meat (beef) and the International Dairy Arrangement. Other agreements have been fostered by UNCTAD – for tin, natural rubber, sugar, cocoa, jute and tropical timber. The agreements are commodity specific and the provisions negotiated are tailored to the particular problems associated with the commodity. The range of powers agreed to in the negotiations vary greatly, from the Arrangement on Bovine Meat, which attempts to help nations anticipate problems by providing better information on a multilateral basis, to the Multifibre Agreement with explicit and complicated restrictions on product movements. All, however, have been put in place to prevent rapid changes in international market prices. There is a perception that by fostering orderly markets both importers and exporters will benefit from the resulting stability. Many of the benefits are expected to arise from being better able to plan business investments whether they be in tin mines in developing countries or in textile plants in developed countries.

In some cases, instability arises from rapid technological change taking place at different times in different countries. Technological change lowers costs and, as a result, the nation undergoing the most rapid technological change will become more competitive. A country unable to effectively use the new technology may find that the rates of adjustment imposed on its domestic suppliers by competitively priced imports are unacceptable. It may wish to slow the process of adjustment to an acceptable rate by imposing some form of import restriction. Exporters, faced with the spectre of decreased import markets and, as a result, fiercer competition from other exporters for remaining markets, may opt to co-operate with importing nations in return for a guarantee of market share. This was the essence of the Multifibre Agreement prior to an agreement reached at the Uruguay Round to phase it out (Das, 1985). Once an exporting firm received its share of the total imports that were negotiated by its government, it had a relatively secure market. This type of arrangement often specifies rates of growth for imports so that firms can better plan their investments. Firms in importing countries are assured that they will not have to compete with imports for a portion of the domestic market and the future rate of growth in imports is known. Investments can then be made in technology to improve efficiency without the fear of volatile and/or falling prices arising from uncontrolled imports. These agreements may, however, become 'too successful'. They can create a vested interest in perpetuating the agreement in both importing and exporting countries.

It is vitally important for firms who wish to begin exporting to know whether such an arrangement exists for their product. Unless the firm has secured a portion of its nation's share of the importing country's market, exports will not be possible. The WTO is unlikely to allow these types of agreements in the future and existing arrangements are to be phased out over a number of years.

In markets where there can be large changes in supply, either due to the vicissitudes of the weather – a reduction of the Brazilian coffee harvest due to frost – or rapid entry and exit of producers in response to price changes, attempts are often made to stabilize prices. Prices will be particularly volatile if the demand curve has a steep slope – where a small change in supply leads to a large change in price. This is the type of demand curve many tropical products face.

The usual mechanism used to stabilize prices is the strategic use of storage. The agreement establishes price bands and storage is used to keep prices between the maximum and minimum prices specified for the band. When prices are low the commodity is removed from the international market by storing it. On the other hand, when prices approach the top of the band, stocks are released into the market to slow the price rise.

A number of issues must be settled before the agreement can come into force. Who will pay the cost of storage – exporters, importers or will the costs be shared? The width of the price band must be negotiated. The wider the band, the less will have to be stored, the narrower the band the larger the proportion of the crop which must be stored. Hence, who pays the storage cost becomes vitally important. Some long-term mechanism must also be included to adjust the price bands over time. If the minimum price is set too high, then stocks will simply grow over time making the scheme unviable. In an attempt to increase their incomes, exporters have sometimes negotiated a minimum price which is set too high and an agreement has become unviable. This certainly was the major contributing factor to the collapse of the sixth International Tin Agreement in 1985. While most agreements have provisions for lowering the minimum price, they are not automatic. To lower price requires the agreement of most, if not all, of the sellers. In practice, a price reduction has proved difficult to secure. Further, any agreement must include the major players in the market or those excluded will be able to act opportunistically making the scheme unviable over time (Gilbert, 1987).

It is important for firms who deal in commodities covered by such agreements to take an interest in the agreement's long-term viability. If an agreement is not structured on a sound basis it will eventually collapse and the markets will return to their previous volatility. Investments made on the basis of the stable prices when the agreement was in operation may not yield the expected returns if prices change.

VOLUNTARY EXPORT RESTRAINTS

Voluntary export restraints (VERs) are bilateral arrangements whereby a country voluntarily agrees to restrict its exports at the suggestion of an importer. The question immediately arises as to why a country would 'voluntarily' agree to such a suggestion. Of course they would not. The agreement is only 'voluntary' in the sense that a country chooses this course of action in the face of a threat by the importing country to impose a more costly trade restriction.

It should always be remembered that, given sufficient domestic pressure for protection, any country can slip outside the GATT rules and impose restrictions on imports as long as it does not discriminate among exporters. The country may suffer economically from retaliation up to a level of equivalent value on a mix of its exports but the benefits to the protected importers may be perceived as exceeding the costs imposed on the country's exporters. Of course, the importer will not wish to suffer the retaliation of all trading partners and may request that they agree to restrict their exports instead.

An exporter, faced with this choice, may wish to exercise the option to voluntarily restrict its exports. Firstly, retaliation to the level of equivalent value may impose considerable additional costs on the exporter's economy. To retaliate it will have to restrict imports from the other country. This will increase the cost of the trading partner's goods. If few alternative suppliers are available, detrimental increases in input costs and consumer prices will result.

Secondly, if the protectionist country imposes a tariff, it collects a duty when the product crosses the border and increases government revenue. The exporting country sells less at the same or lower price. If, on the other hand, the country restricts its own exports, the effect is to reduce the supply to the protectionist country, driving up the market price. The exporter's firms could ship the same quantity of goods as would be the case with the tariff in place but receive the higher price. Hence, while there may be a loss in the volume of trade, at least firms in the exporting country benefit from high prices on their remaining sales to the importing country. Thirdly, by 'voluntarily' agreeing to co-operate with the importing country's request, an exporting country may be able to secure a better deal than if tariffs are unilaterally imposed. This might come in the form of a less severe restriction on the commodity in question or trade concessions on other commodities.

When a country agrees to restrict its exports to a specified quantity, it must then allocate the agreed amount among its exporting firms. If it wants firms to receive the benefit, it will use some non-price allocation mechanism. It is extremely important that these opportunities be watched closely by firms producing the commodity. Even if a firm has not previously been exporting to the protectionist country, the new higher price expected for the commodity may justify the effort required to obtain an allocation. As the remaining exports are more valuable, existing exporting firms will have to work hard to ensure that they obtain as large a portion of the allocation as possible. Competition among current and potential exporters is likely to be fierce.

If the government in the exporting country wishes to capture the revenue arising from the difference between the cost at which firms in the exporting country are willing to supply the commodity and the price in the importing country, then it can auction the rights to export. It becomes very important that exporting firms estimate the long-term value of these rights so that they do not pay more for them than they are worth. Of course, once an allocation is secured by a firm, it will have an incentive to ensure that the VER continues.

In the 1980s, voluntary export restraints became the preferred method for circumventing the 'spirit of the GATT'. While often seen as a means for more powerful countries to discriminate against weaker trading partners, VERs were also used by major trading powers to defuse politically sensitive trade issues among themselves. Japan 'voluntarily' restricted its automobile exports to the US and video recorder exports to the EU.

The proliferation of VERs led to a considerable degree of concern, especially among the middle sized trading nations, and the issue of

VERs was included in the Uruguay Round negotiations. Under the terms of the Uruguay Round agreement, WTO members will not initiate any new VERs and must phase out all but one of their VERs within 4 years after the establishment of the WTO. This single exception must be phased out by the end of the century. Hence, the importance of VERs as trade instruments will decrease over time. It is still possible for countries to negotiate VERs with nations which are not members of the WTO.

Firms should be particularly wary of purchasing exporting rights belonging to another exporter. While these were valuable in the past, they will have no value when a VER is phased out. Firms should monitor existing VERs closely because their demise may provide considerable new export opportunities.

COUNTERTRADE

Countertrade is international trade conducted on a barter basis – goods for goods. Over 20% of world trade may be conducted on a countertrade basis. This share is declining due to the liberalization of the former communist economies – who were heavily involved in countertrade – and the movement toward less government intervention in developing countries. Countertrade, however, remains an important aspect of trade and can be particularly important to individual firms in market economies because of the size of individual countertrade deals. Countertrade transactions take place in the absence of transparent market prices although there may be non-comparable (and hence, useless) accounting prices available. The absence of market prices significantly increases the costs associated with conducting international commerce – costs economists generally refer to as transactions costs.

Why would a country wish to undertake international trade without the use of money? Countertrade arises when a country has a currency which is not freely convertible into other nations' currencies or when access to foreign exchange is rationed. Typically, the countries which have initiated countertrade programs have been command – or centrally planned economies or developing countries who are maintaining their currency at an overvalued and fixed international exchange rate.

Centrally planned economies resort to countertrade because market forces are not used to determine the prices of goods in their domestic markets. As a result, the relative prices of goods may not reflect their true value in international markets. For political and ideological reasons, the domestic prices of goods may be kept artificially low. If foreign buyers were allowed to pay the 'official' domestic price they would, in fact, receive a subsidy from the exporting nation. If the 'official' price of the good is too high, on the other hand, foreign buyers may be deterred from purchases. As a result, it may be better to ignore the 'official' domestic prices and attempt to arrange value-for-value exchanges of goods.

Centrally planned economies, as well as some countries in the third world, have followed the practice of not allowing the relative value of their currencies to be determined on international money markets. Typically, the 'official' exchange rate overvalues the domestic currency. In some cases the currency is overvalued to keep down the prices of vital imports. Whatever the reason for following this practice, the effect is to make foreign goods appear cheap to prospective importers. As the currency is overvalued, more foreign goods can be purchased for each unit of domestic currency. Given that foreign goods appear inexpensive, there will be an excess demand for them at the official rate of exchange. The government then must find some means of priorizing access to the foreign exchange needed to pay for imports. This means that the government decides which imports have priority and allocates the available foreign exchange to those imports. Further, it makes the country's exports appear expensive and, hence, unattractive to foreign buyers. To get around this dual problem, value-for-value exchanges of goods are promoted. In this case, countertrade is an attempt to obtain non-priority imports in exchange for what otherwise would be unattractively priced exports.

Why do the transactions costs increase for firms which may wish to export to or import from countries with countertrade programmes? Freely convertible currencies, combined with domestic prices determined by market forces, provide an extremely low cost method for importing firms to determine the value of the goods they are purchasing. All of this inexpensive information disappears with countertrade. All contracts become goods for goods swaps. This means that the value of the commodity received in trade in the importer's market must be determined in the absence of meaningful price information. Unless the market is already well developed, the price consumers will be willing to pay for an unknown product may be extremely hard to determine. Before a deal is struck, experts may have to be hired to evaluate the value of the products offered in payment.

Costs will increase as each transaction will require a one-on-one matching of buyer and seller. A counterpart must be found, meaning a larger number of sales staff. In the case of a firm wishing to import, a bundle of commodities which is acceptable to the agency with export goods on offer will have to be identified and acquired. As every transaction becomes a one-on-one negotiation regarding the exchangeability of two different goods, the negotiations are often protracted and costly in terms of staff time and expenses. Finally, it is often difficult for personnel who are used to prices as a measure of value to deal in situations where prices are meaningless and any referral to 'official' prices can be dangerous. Personnel involved in countertrade will need special training and extensive briefings (Kosticki, 1987). Profitable deals are available from countertrade but the cost of identifying those deals can be considerable. The problems which firms face in countertrade transactions are discussed in greater detail in Chapter 12.

The GATT, with its orientation towards market based trade, has never been able to deal adequately with countertrade activities. Most communist countries did not belong to the GATT and those that did belong were tolerated because the amounts traded were small (Jackson, 1992). The GATT more or less turns a blind eye to bilateral countertrade arrangements between countries.

REFERENCES

Das, D. K. (1985) Dismantling the multifibre arrangement. *Journal of World Trade Law*, **19**, 67-80.

Gilbert, C. L. (1987) International commodity agreements: design and performance. *World Development*, **15**(5), 519-616.

Jackson, J. H. (1992) *The World Trading System*, MIT Press, Cambridge, MA.

Kosticki, M. (1987) Should one countertrade? *Journal of World Trade Law*, **21**(2), 7-9.

How countries restrict trade 8

UNILATERAL ACTION BY COUNTRIES

When countries can find no means to co-operate with other countries to mitigate the effects of adverse external market forces on their economy or on a particular industry, they may wish to resort to unilaterally imposed trade measures. If the unilateral action affects a country which is also a member of WTO, then the country imposing the trade restriction should expect to face retaliation up to a level of equivalent value. However, the GATT rules on many trade-restricting practices other than tariffs and import quotas are extremely weak and easily circumvented. While the GATT discourages any attempts to initiate unilateral trade-restricting actions, it also recognizes that there may be situations where domestic political pressure requires a country to take such action.

TRADE RESTRICTING MEASURES

In theory, tariffs are the only trade-restricting measure which should be used by GATT members to restrict the movement of goods from other GATT countries. Of course, any trade-restricting measure can be used against a non-member. Trade barriers can affect international commerce in a multitude of ways and it is important for firms to identify the measures which are in place and anticipate their ramifications.

Tariffs

A **tariff** is a tax on goods collected when they pass through an importing country's customs. Tariffs are pre-announced at a fixed level and may be either a set monetary amount per unit of import (flat rate) or calculated as a percentage of the imported good's value. The latter are known by the Latin term ***ad valorem***. Hence, tariffs are narrowly defined and should not be confused with other border taxes which can be varied at the discretion of the importer. It is the fixed and pre-announced nature of tariffs which make them the GATT's preferred measure to restrict trade. Tariffs are the least distortionary trade restriction for a given level of protection because when tariffs are applied to exporting countries in a non-discriminatory fashion, foreign suppliers are chosen on the basis of the relative prices of their goods. In other words, while a tariff provides protection to an importer's industry, as the price at which the commodity becomes available in the importer's country is determined on the basis of exporter's price plus a fixed tax, the lowest cost foreign supplier will be the most competitive.

Ad valorem tariffs tend to discriminate in favour of trade in raw materials and against trade in goods with a high degree of processing or manufacturing. As the value of processing is included in the price, the absolute size of the tariff increases given that its calculation is based on a percentage of the price. Hence, *ad valorem* tariffs encourage a greater proportion of the economic activity associated with processing to be undertaken in the importing country. On the other hand, *ad valorem* tariffs are open to manipulation by importers and exporters as the real price (as opposed to the price reported on the shipments manifest) may be difficult for customs officials to determine. Flat rate tariffs based on the quantity of imports are, hence, less costly to monitor.

It is important that importing firms add in the cost of tariffs when determining their expected selling price. *Ad valorem* tariffs can be calculated on different base prices. For example, they can be calculated on a price which includes the 'cost, insurance and freight' (**c.i.f.**) associated with moving the good to the importer's port of entry. They can also be based on the 'free on board' (**f.o.b.**) price, which is the price of the good once it is loaded onto the ship, plane, train or truck in the exporter's country. When tariffs are calculated on an *ad valorem* basis and an expensive transportation mode such as air freight is used, the cost of the tariff will be considerably higher when it is calculated on a c.i.f. basis.

Import quotas

While strictly a non-tariff barrier, **import quotas** probably deserve to be in a category all of their own. This is because, historically, they have been the major trade-restricting policy alternative to tariffs. They are, however, a more distortionary measure than tariffs and can be easily administered in a fashion that violates the major GATT principle of non-discrimination. The official GATT position on import quotas is that they should be transformed into tariffs which give the importing country an equivalent degree of protection. Once tariffication takes place, then tariff reduction can be negotiated under the auspices of the GATT.

An import quota is a pre-announced numerical limit on the number of units of a product which can be imported over a specified period of time – normally one year. The effect of a quota is to limit the total supply in the importer's market to the sum of the quantity which domestic firms wish to supply plus the quantity of imports specified in the quota. The reduction in total supply available in the domestic market increases the price of the good.

Import quotas have a major advantage over tariffs when international prices are volatile. A tariff, with its fixed rate, simply adds a constant to the exporters price. If the international market price fluctuates, that volatility is passed through to the domestic market. An import quota, on the other hand, simply fixes the total supply in the domestic economy regardless of the international price.

Quotas are bureaucratic in nature. Once the importing country determines the total quantity which is to be allowed into the country, this quota must be apportioned among the countries wishing to export. This apportioning becomes a political process involving bilateral negotiations and is virtually impossible to administer in a fashion which appears non-discriminatory. Further, even if some simple rule is used to apportion import quotas, such as each exporting nation receiving a share of the total quota equal to its previous market share, over time distortions will increase. If the relative costs in supplying nations change then, to minimize the trade distortion, their proportion of the quota should also be altered to reflect this change. In practice, both identifying cost changes and re-negotiating the quotas will be very difficult. Further, new countries who wish to export must be given a portion of the quota. This raises the issues of what size this allocation should be and whose allocation should be reduced to accommodate the new exporter? These questions can only be resolved through political negotiations. It is very important for exporting firms to monitor such developments and ensure that their government negotiators are informed of the potential benefits from acquiring a share of the import quota.

An import quota system can be very lucrative for importing firms. The imported product can be acquired at the low international price and sold at the higher domestic price. Governments must monitor the rate at which imports enter the country to ensure that the quota is not exceeded. Often, to facilitate this monitoring, the government issues domestic firms with import licences. Without an import licence it is impossible for a firm to import. This creates a vested interest in the quota system for firms having import licences. New firms who wish to import must get the 'ear of government' to ensure that they acquire a licence, while those who have licences will attempt to have them extended. Firms with licences will lobby hard to keep the import quota system in place and will lobby against tariffication where the government instead of the firm collects the difference between the international and domestic price.

While many import quotas have been changed to tariffs, the guaranteed levels of access which countries must provide to agricultural products and textiles as a result of the Uruguay Round are essentially quotas by a different name. The import levels which the EU has negotiated with the former communist countries is another example.

Non-tariff barriers

As formal barriers to trade such as tariffs and import quotas have been progressively reduced through GATT, non-tariff barriers to the international movement of commodities have become much more common. This is for two reasons. Firstly, nations put into place a large number of domestic policies and regulations when their markets were protected. With the removal of tariff protection, many of these now act to restrict trade. Often, new domestic regulations are introduced without full (or any) consideration of trade ramifications. Further, they are most often put in place to address a genuine domestic concern. As a result, negotiating their removal can be very difficult.

Secondly, the GATT had no effective means to deal with non-tariff barriers until the conclusion of the Uruguay Round. Hence, nations under domestic pressure to provide protection put non-tariff barriers in place rather than new tariffs. By doing so they avoided GATT sanctioned retaliation. The Uruguay Round eliminated the use of some non-tariff barriers and put additional restrictions on the use of others. Their very complexity, however, makes their elimination extremely difficult. The form and shape of non-tariff barriers is only constrained by the inventiveness of bureaucrats and providing a comprehensive list is not possible. As a result, only a selection of the major non-tariff barriers is discussed.

Variable levies

Variable levies are a tax on goods collected when they pass through an importing country's customs but, unlike tariffs, they are not pre-set at a fixed level. They are used to keep the domestic price isolated from changes in the world price. As the international price falls the size of the levy increases and as the world price rises, the size of the levy decreases. In effect, variable levies have the same stabilizing effect on domestic price as an import quota without the bureaucratic problems associated with quota allocations. Distortions are minimized because imports will come from the least cost supplier.

The most contentious use of variable levies was by the EU. They were applied on agricultural imports (where, prior to the conclusion of the Uruguay Round, GATT disciplines were particularly weak) into the EU and were an adjunct to the Common Agricultural Policy (CAP). While variable levies provided a high and stable price for farmers in the EU, all of the international price instability was borne by exporting nations. In fact, variable levies acted to increase exporters' price variability. Hence, the use of variable levies proved to be a very contentious trade issue. Many of the world's suppliers of agricultural commodities are third world countries which require an increased degree of stability to foster their economic development. In the Uruguay Round, the EU agreed to change its variable levies into import tariffs. This is expected to have a stabilizing effect on world agricultural prices.

Export restrictions

While most trade-restricting measures relate to the protection of an importing country's markets from changes in international markets, there are circumstances where exporting countries wish to restrict the movement of commodities or products out of the country. While, at first glance, such behaviour may not appear as if it should be of international concern, both the short-run and long-run effects of such actions may be detrimental to the international trading environment and, ironically, to the interests of the exporting country.

Nations will want to restrict exports in situations where world supplies of the commodity are declining and, as a result, export revenues are rising. This may seem perverse behaviour. However, if the commodity in question is a significant input into major domestic industries or a food staple, then the exporter may wish to limit supplies leaving the country so that domestic prices can be kept low. Exports can be reduced by using export taxes or quantitative restrictions.

The short-run consequences of limiting the supply going to international markets further increases the price of the commodity in importing nations. For importers, this increases the hardship created by the shortage. The long-run effect is to increase protectionist pressures in importing countries. Firstly, as the importer's security of supply is threatened by the actions of the exporter, subsidies or protectionist measures may be put in place by the importer to foster increased domestic supplies.

Secondly, the high short-run prices in the importer's country may encourage firms to invest in facilities to provide the product domestically. When the export restriction is removed at a later date, those who invested in the new facilities can be expected to lobby vigorously for protection. There can be little doubt that the failure of the Japanese to liberalize their agricultural trade can, in no small part, be attributed to the US soybean – a major input to livestock production – embargo on exports in the early 1970s. Clearly, once the international shortage passes, the exporter may face reduced access to its traditional import markets.

Health, sanitary and phytosanitary regulations

These non-tariff barriers encompass a wide range of measures which relate to the physical condition of products when they enter a country. Every nation has regulations in place to ensure that products coming from abroad do not carry diseases which could be hazardous to the environment or to the health of humans, animals and plants. Further, regulations are put in place to ensure that domestic products are handled in a sanitary fashion to protect human health and that they are grown under conditions – *phyto* is a Greek term referring to plants – which are not hazardous to individuals or the food chain. Bans on the use of DDT provide an example of the latter. Exporters should expect to conform to importing countries' regulations. Regulations of this type are primarily applied to agricultural imports.

As these regulations address legitimate domestic concerns, they have proved extremely difficult to deal with on an international basis. There is no doubt that protecting domestic livestock herds from 'foot and mouth' disease in countries where it has been eradicated is a legitimate action by an importing country. It cannot be denied, however, that the ban on imports of livestock from countries such as Argentina, where the disease persists, has considerable economic impact given the country's potential as an exporter.

The major problem with health, sanitary and phytosanitary regulations is that they may unnecessarily restrict imports. As standards in different countries are developed independently, they may become barriers to trade unintentionally. They can also be used opportunistically to restrict imports.

The major reason that differences in regulations become barriers to trade is that they can significantly increase transactions costs for exporters. For example, an exporter of meat products will have to comply with domestic sanitary standards by putting certain procedures in place which are then monitored by government inspectors. If the country to which the firm wishes to export requires different procedures – even if the eventual standard of health is the same – then both sets of procedures will have to be followed, resulting in increased costs. In some cases, scientific procedures may simply be incompatible and a potential exporter must choose between the domestic or export market. It may be impossible, for example, to design a slaughterhouse which can satisfy the regulations of both the domestic and a foreign market. This means that exporters must have separate 'dedicated' export facilities. Of course, the transactions costs may be cumulative if an exporter wishes to supply more than one country.

The tests needed to monitor compliance with the regulations have a scientific basis and require qualified personnel to undertake them. Problems may arise regarding the international equivalence of scientific testing facilities and the training of personnel. As a result, exporters may be required to pay to have inspection personnel trained and certified in the importer's country. The exporter may have to pay to have domestic laboratories inspected by foreign personnel and be required to bear any costs of modifying the facility. It may be that the importer requires the tests to be undertaken in specified facilities within its own country. The facilities specified might not have sufficient capacity to handle the volume of imports. The lack of facilities will have the same effect as an import quota. If the specified facilities in the importer's country are owned by the government, the charge for undertaking the procedures may be set artificially high. The effect is the same as a tariff.

Further, even if all the regulations can be met by the exporter, by simply altering the regulations frequently, the importer can significantly increase transactions costs for the exporter. Facilities will have to be re-inspected, staff training upgraded and testing facilities modified.

It should be clear that there is a wide scope for these types of regulations to be used opportunistically as trade barriers. Exporting firms shipping products covered by such regulations should take great pains to ensure that the importer's regulations are met because refused loads may deteriorate in transit or may not be suitable for sale when returned to the domestic market. Further, exporting firms should monitor any proposed regulations so that a presentation can be made to the importer's government if the changes are likely to have trade inhibiting effects.

Consumer protection legislation

As with health regulations, consumer protection legislation can become a barrier to trade because nations develop their standards and procedures independently. Exporters will incur increased costs if they must comply with multiple regulations. This increase in transactions costs may be sufficiently high so as to totally inhibit trade. While much consumer protection legislation acts only as an unintentional barrier to trade, it can also be used strategically to limit trade. As consumer protection legislation does address legitimate domestic concerns, it often becomes difficult to argue for their removal on international trade grounds.

Transactions costs can increase for an exporter as a result of simple differences in regulations such as labelling requirements. If the exporter's domestic market and export market have different labelling requirements, a shut-down of the production line may be required so that the changeover can be affected. This reduces the length of production runs thereby increasing per unit cost. It also adds to the firm's down time. For a firm which exports to 20 different markets, these additions to cost may prove to be significant.

In some cases, extensive modifications may have to be made to the final product or the entire product redesigned. The safety features of automobiles provide one such example. Even small regulatory differences in the spacing of lights can require entirely new metal stamping dyes for the export market. Some European cars imported into California must have very expensive modifications to meet pollution and safety standards – the modifications can sometimes increase the landed cost of the car by 30–50%.

Increased transactions costs can arise in a number of ways. In response to consumer concerns, the EU banned the production and sale of meat from animals which had been treated with growth hormones. This ban was extended to imports. Canadian and US exporters wished to continue to use growth hormones in production destined for their domestic markets. They could not find a cost-effective procedure to identify hormone-free cattle which would satisfy the EU and exports ceased.

As with the case of health regulations, exporting firms should monitor proposed changes in consumer protection legislation in countries where they have export markets. If the proposed changes will increase the transactions costs associated with exporting, then concern should be expressed to the proper authorities both in the importing country and with international trade policy officials in the exporting country's government.

Rules of origin requirements

Rules of origin requirements are imposed for two reasons: to directly restrict imports and to prevent tariff circumvention. The former normally arise when countries are attempting to foster industrialization. The case where a nation is attempting to prevent tariff circumvention arises when an importing nation is a member of a free trade area. As explained in Chapter 5, countries belonging to free trade areas are not required to have the same levels of external tariffs. Goods can move freely between members of the free trade area but goods may be imported at different rates of tariff from countries which do not belong to the free trade area. This creates a situation whereby high tariff countries can have their tariffs circumvented. For example, country A in a free trade area may have a 30% tariff on automobiles from country C which is not a member of the free trade area. Country B, who is also a member of the free trade area, may have only a 5% tariff on country C's automobiles. As goods can move tariff-free between countries B and A it becomes profitable to import country C's cars into country B, paying the 5% tariff, and then tranship them to country A and pay no additional tariff. The cost of C's automobiles including the 5% tariff, the additional transportation fees and the transactions costs associated with transhipment may be considerably less than the landed cost of directly shipping automobiles from C to A and paying the 30% tariff. As a result, the protection A has sought by imposing the 30% tariff has been circumvented. To overcome this problem, the high tariff member of the free trade area will negotiate a rules of origin agreement whereby goods moving from its trading partner must have a certain proportion of the value of the good added in the partner country.

Rules of origin requirements, whose primary purpose is to foster industrialization, are simply regulations specifying that a certain proportion of the value of a good sold in the country must have been added within the country. For example, the government in an importing country may require that 30% of the value of any automobile sold in the country be added within the country. Typically, this might mean that a car can be imported as parts and local labour used to assemble it. Sometimes a certain proportion of the vehicle's components – maybe the engine – must be sourced in the importing country. This type of rules of origin requirements are a means to capture additional value-added for the importing country. Third world countries have justified their use of these measures as being part of their overall industrialization strategies. The specific aim is to allow their industrial managers and labour force to become proficient at manufacturing.

Carrier of origin requirements

Carrier of origin requirements can be of two forms. An importing country may require that goods moving to its shores must be transported on ships registered in the that country (a flag-carrier) or on the importing country's national airline. On the other hand, an exporting country may specify similar requirements whereby goods exported must be moved on its flag-carriers or airlines.

In the export case, these requirements are often tied to countertrade arrangements or goods moving under foreign aid programs. It is a means for the exporting country to capture some of the benefits arising from the international transaction. It also provides a means for fostering domestic shipping interests in high cost countries or indirectly supporting a national airline.

In the case of importers, flag-carrier or national airline stipulations can act as a significant barrier to trade. Of course, it is also a means to capture additional benefits from international transactions. Specifying that goods must move by the importer's carrier may make it impossible for the exporter to access transport. If an importing country wishes to act strategically to protect certain industries, it may simply inform the exporter that no transport is available during the period when the exporter's goods need to be moved. The effect is the same as an import quota. If the carrier is a nationalized firm then the importing government may set the shipping/air freight rates prohibitively high. The effect is the same as a tariff.

Restrictions on government procurement

Over the period since the GATT was established in 1948, the governments of most countries have come to assume a much larger role in their economies. Most developed market economies have become mixed economies with certain sectors controlled directly by the government – health care, electricity generation, communications systems, automobile manufacture – although the degree of government involvement and the activities undertaken by government vary considerably. In addition, the concept of the 'welfare state' has been extended from the Scandinavian countries to a greater or lesser degree in all developed economies. To support these activities, government bureaucracies have grown apace. As a result, in many countries the government share of GDP can exceed 40%.

Many of the developing countries which received their independence since the formation of the GATT opted to follow a socialist path to development. This has meant that the government proportion of the modern sectors of their economies tends to be quite large.

When goods and services are purchased from the private sector by government, it is usually accomplished through procurement contracts. In many cases, these contracts are allocated using a competitive bidding process. Whatever the means of letting contracts to supply the government, the application process is often restricted by legislation to firms owned by citizens of that country. When governments constitute such large proportions of total economic activity, these restrictions become major barriers to trade.

In certain circumstances, there may be legitimate reasons for restricting access to procurement contracts to the country's nationals. In particular, it may be desirable to have national defence contracts restricted. This protects the country from disruptions to weapons supplies and spare parts in time of war. Further, there may be some strategic industries where one does not wish to be dependent on foreign suppliers as this might make the country vulnerable to economic blackmail or even international sanctions in times of political disagreements with supplying nations.

For the great majority of goods and services purchased by government, no such national security case can be made. Restricting procurement contracts to nationals simply becomes a means of protecting domestic firms from international competition.

In parallel with, but not part of, the Uruguay Round, an Agreement on Government Procurement was reached. It will constitute part of the WTO. Only about a dozen developed countries – with the EU signing as one – are party to the agreement. The EU has eliminated restrictions on government procurement within the Union and the CUSTA reduced the barriers to trade arising from government procurement contracts. The difficulties associated with removing barriers to foreign firms in government procurement contracts are discussed further in Chapter 18.

Control of the use of trade barriers 9

THE NEED FOR MULTILATERAL CONTROLS

As governments will, at times, be forced to give in to domestic political pressure for protection, international agreements attempt to mitigate against the effect of trade restrictions through a variety of control measures. While these control measures must be voluntarily agreed to in an international forum, once in force they become difficult to ignore and, hence, can be a major influence on domestic decision makers. Obtaining a multinational consensus on control measures has proved very illusive and, as a result, many of the previous GATT provisions for control were weak. An attempt at considerably improving the effectiveness of control measures was made during the Uruguay Round. Their true effectiveness will only become clear as they are operationalized and tested in the WTO. Far greater success has been achieved by regional trading agreements. As members of regional economic groupings are likely to have more homogeneous economies and a smaller number of participants, controls are more readily agreed to. This can be a two-edged sword as, while regional agreements tend to reduce the total number of trade barriers, it may become more difficult to reach agreement among regional groupings.

MEASURES TO CONTROL THE USE OF TRADE RESTRICTIONS

As trade restrictions take many forms and affect imports in a variety of ways, no single method of control can be totally effective. As a result, a variety of measures form the multilateral basis for control of trade barriers.

Tariffication

The process of tariffication has been the main and preferred instrument of control at the GATT. Tariffication is the conversion of all non-tariff barriers, including import quotas, into tariffs which provide an equivalent degree of protection. Once tariffication of a non-tariff barrier has taken place, then the tariff becomes subject to the GATT tariff reduction negotiations at the WTO. Given the success of the

GATT tariff reduction rounds, tariffication has proven to be an effective strategy for reducing barriers to trade.

The GATT chose tariffication as its primary control measure for five reasons. Firstly, it allows direct comparison of different nation's levels of protection. Attempts by economists to calculate the rates of protection which non-tariff barriers and subsidies provide – their tariff equivalents – has only led to acrimonious debates over methodology and the technical competence of experts (Pinder, 1988). Tariffs are simple and easily understood. Secondly, tariffs are transparent. Transparent means that the degree of protection is readily observable and, hence, exporting firms can easily take them into account in their business calculations. Thirdly, they cannot be used to discriminate amongst exporting countries without explicitly charging individual countries different rates. Most non-tariff barriers have sufficient administrative leeway to allow importing nations to discriminate. Fourthly, as they cannot be used in a discriminatory fashion, the trade which remains will be undertaken on the basis of international efficiency. Fifthly, tariffication provides easily compared measures of protection when trade barrier reductions are negotiated. This greatly simplifies the process as it prevents 'apples versus oranges' arguments at the negotiations.

Beyond nations' reluctance to move to tariffication because they wish to retain the opaqueness and opportunities for discrimination which non-tariff barriers provide, it may also be difficult to agree upon the tariff rate which provides an equivalent degree of protection to the non-tariff barriers they replace. Since non-tariff barriers, such as import quotas, provide different levels of protection as the international price rises and falls, determining the size of a tariff of equivalent value becomes a topic for negotiation and clearly a matter of timing.

Harmonization

For many non-tariff barriers, tariffication does not provide a practical means by which trade restricting effects can be removed. As different regulatory regimes pertaining to health, sanitary, and phytosanitary matters or consumer protection act as unintentional barriers to trade, an alternative means to control their trade-restricting effects must be found. In other words, nations need regulatory regimes in place to protect their citizens and they cannot simply be removed and converted to a tariff. Since it is the differences in regulations which cause trade distortions, one means of removing their trade-distorting effect is to remove the differences in regulations. This is the process of **harmonization**.

Harmonization means that nations agree to negotiate a redrafting of their individual regulations into one common set of regulations. They must also collaborate when drafting all new regulations. For example, both the 1992 initiatives in the EU and the CUSTA have commitments to harmonize technical standards. A number of Uruguay Round

Agreements have harmonization provisions. In the Agreement on Sanitary and Phytosanitary Measures, for example, while harmonization is encouraged, nations are still effectively allowed to set their own standards. The Agreement on Technical Barriers to Trade, in a similar fashion, encourages countries to establish international standards for testing and certification procedures. In the Agreement on Rules of Origin, WTO members agreed to set up a harmonization program which must be completed within a fixed period of time.

Harmonization requires long and arduous sets of negotiations. As many of the regulations are very technical in nature, the negotiations are often left to scientific and technical experts. Domestic firms trading internationally should monitor and provide input to the negotiations because the changes which will inevitably arise as harmonization takes place may require significant alterations to existing procedures and/or new capital expenditures. In some cases, meeting the new common standards may prove to be prohibitively expensive even for firms who only sell in the domestic market. Firms should attempt to ensure that harmonization is accomplished in the least costly manner – something that the technical personnel conducting the negotiations may not always take into account.

Harmonization of new regulations has often proved cumbersome and, hence, slowed the introduction of new regulations. Further, the process is often complicated by political systems which have multiple levels of government. Sub-national governments may have no direct role in the harmonization process and, hence, introduce regulations without understanding their international ramifications.

Regulatory harmonization can prove difficult and ultimately costly even when economies are at similar levels of development. When economies are at different levels of development, it may be beyond the budgetary and technical ability of developing nations to raise their levels sufficiently to conform to those of the developed country. As food safety and consumer protection are likely to be important to consumers, lowering of developed countries standards cannot be expected in negotiations. As a result, harmonizing multilaterally may have to wait until considerable economic development takes place. Unfortunately, in some cases the absence of regulatory harmonization may be a major inhibitor of trade-led economic development.

National treatment

When non-tariff barriers act to inhibit trade and where harmonization may not be appropriate or is prohibitively expensive, the extension of **national treatment** may provide an alternative. National treatment means that citizens and firms from the country to which it is to be extended will, as far as commercial purposes are concerned, be treated as nationals of the country extending the treatment. Reciprocal extensions of national treatment are normal.

National treatment might be extended in the case where a country has 'carrier of origin' requirements in place. As part of a regional trade agreement, a country could extend national treatment to the carriers of other countries with which the agreement was concluded. This would mean that the carriers of partner countries could act as the means of transport for all goods that had been previously restricted to carriers of the extending country's flag.

In a similar fashion, national treatment can be extended to the bidding process for government procurement contracts. This would mean that a foreign firm bidding for the government contract would be treated no differently than a domestic firm. In a similar fashion, if countries have restrictions on foreign access to defence contracts or investment in sensitive sectors of the economy – energy, banking, utilities – national treatment can be extended to other members of customs unions or free trade areas.

It is important that potential exporters monitor the negotiation of bilateral or regional trading agreements to ensure that national treatment is extended to their activities. Agreements to remove tariffs and harmonize technical barriers to trade will not be sufficient to ensure access to all sectors of the trading partner's economy when legislation exists restricting those sectors or activities to the country's nationals.

Equivalence

The mutual granting of **equivalence** provides an alternative to harmonization when regulatory differences exist which inhibit trade. The granting of equivalence means that the standards used by foreign trading partners will be considered equivalent to those imposed on domestic firms. For example, it may be that automobile safety standards in two countries provide equal degrees of consumer protection but are met through different means. Harmonization might impose considerable capital costs on automobile manufacturers who would have to alter their processes to meet new common standards. The changes would, however, provide little gain to consumers. Granting equivalence to domestic regulations for cars manufactured to the trading partner's standards may be a cost effective means of removing trade barriers. It may be even more important in the case of testing facilities and professional certification. Harmonizing testing facilities built under different regulatory regimes may prove prohibitively expensive. Further, harmonizing the professional certification of individuals involved in scientific testing may require reform of the entire education system and individuals trained prior to harmonization may have to undergo expensive and long-term retraining. The granting of equivalence will reduce these costs.

The granting of equivalence will, however, require a process whereby the different regulatory standards and procedures are evaluated to ensure that the protection provided to a nation's citizens is not reduced. Further, in the absence of an agreement to harmonize future regulations, all new regulations established in one country would have to be judged as to the equivalence of their effect. Facilities and procedures which are granted equivalence have to be monitored over time by the granting country to ensure that standards are being maintained.

While, in the short run, the granting of equivalence for some activities may prove more cost effective, in the long run harmonization will reduce monitoring and evaluation costs. An optimal solution may be to grant equivalence for some current activities while at the same time making a commitment to harmonization over the long run. Firms should take particular care that the granting of equivalence for foreign procedures does not extend an economic advantage to competitors from another country. In other words, the cost for foreign firms to conform to their regulations may be less than it cost domestic firms to conform to their own country's regulations. Firms should lobby for the acceptance of these foreign procedures for use in their own domestic industry.

Safeguards

The safeguard procedures which are included in the GATT act like a steam pressure release valve by allowing countries to escape from their GATT commitments when domestic protectionism becomes too strong for them to ignore. Safeguards also act as a containment vessel. While countries are allowed relief from imminent political problems, their actions do not lead to harmful beggar thy neighbour free-for-alls or force them to leave the GATT entirely. The level at which this pressure release valve is triggered was raised at the Uruguay Round negotiations.

A GATT member is allowed to take a 'safeguard action' to protect a specific domestic industry from an unforeseen increase in imports which is causing, or which is likely to cause, serious injury to the industry. The Uruguay Round agreement sets out the criteria for determining serious injury. The trade restrictions put in place when the criteria for the existence of serious injury have been met can only be applied in a manner which will mitigate the effects of a serious injury. Given that domestic political pressure for protection can be intense when there is an unanticipated surge of imports and that the procedures for determining serious injury are time consuming, safeguard provisions allow for a preliminary finding of serious injury. Any trade restriction imposed on the basis of a preliminary finding can only remain in place for 200 days.

Tariffs, as the least distortionary trade restricting measure, are the protectionist policy which GATT members are encouraged to use in safeguard actions. Import quotas are allowed but shares of the total import quota must be allocated to exporters on the basis of their past market shares. This is an attempt to uphold the principle of non-discrimination and to prevent an individual country's exports being targeted by an importing country. A safeguard committee operates under the auspices of the WTO and, if it decides that there are exceptional circumstances, then the shares of import quotas can be allocated in a manner which is different from that based on historical shares.

In terms of containment, safeguard trade restrictions can only be in place for a maximum of 8 years, and then only if there is evidence that the protected industry is attempting to become more competitive with imports. Otherwise, safeguard restrictions can only be in place for 4 years. Once a safeguard trade restriction has expired, or been withdrawn, then the importing country must wait 2 years before beginning proceedings to re-impose the safeguards. Furthermore, an additional period of time equal to the duration of the previous safeguard action must elapse before trade restrictions can be re-imposed.

A 1 year waiting period is imposed if the previous safeguard trade restriction had been applied for less than 180 days. Further, re-imposition is only allowed if the restriction had not been applied to the product more than twice in the previous 5 years.

The clear intent of safeguard procedures is to allow politicians a means to defuse protectionist pressure and to provide an incentive for the importing country to encourage their industry to adjust. An attempt is made to eliminate the strategic use of safeguards to forestall the need for adjustment by domestic industries. Politicians, in replying to protectionist pressures, can use the argument that uncompetitive firms have had their chance to change.

If the importing country adheres to the safeguard provisions when imposing a trade restriction, then other WTO members cannot ask for compensation for 3 years. The exporters adversely affected can negotiate with the importing country to receive compensation after that period. If agreement is not reached on compensation, then the exporter can impose trade restrictions of equivalent value on the exports of the original importer. No further beggar thy neighbour retaliation is allowed.

Safeguard actions pose a threat both to firms in the exporting country and the importing country. The former is more direct. The agreement on safeguards requires countries considering a safeguard action to announce their intentions and give public notice for hearings and other avenues for interested parties to present evidence. Firms involved in exporting should monitor the situation in their major markets closely and be prepared to take part in safeguard hearings. Otherwise, only the point of view of importing firms will be heard. Further, exporting firms should make sure that their governments are aware of pending foreign safeguard hearings and lobbied to take part in the proceedings.

Firms which export different products from the country imposing an import restriction under a safeguard action may also suffer a loss of markets. This can occur in the case when the original exporting country exercises its right to retaliate when compensation cannot be agreed. It is likely that retaliation will be taken either to maximize the impact on the country which initiated the safeguard action or to reduce protectionist pressure at home. Firms should realize when they are in industries which are likely candidates for retaliation. They should encourage their government to provide compensation for the original safeguard action. If this strategy fails, they should be prepared to lobby the retaliating government against the imposition of restrictions on their product.

Adjudication

As with any system of rules, the rules agreed upon by nations to regulate the international movement of commodities will be subject to differences in interpretation and may require clarification from time to time. When nations cannot agree on the meaning of what has been agreed to or on whether their actions conform to the existing rules of trade, then some form of adjudication is required to ensure the continuance of the arrangement. In some sense, the need for adjudication can be seen as a breakdown of the 'spirit of the GATT'. The result is, to a greater or lesser degree, a retreat to legalistic mechanisms.

The establishment of effective dispute mechanisms has proven to be one of the more difficult tasks associated with institution building in international trade. This is because it requires nations to agree to give up a measure of their sovereignty to some supra-national institution. Restrictions on national sovereignty have been stoutly resisted by most politicians of almost any stripe, no matter what the country. Further, as the individuals who must constitute the adjudication authority remain citizens of some nation state, ensuring that those individuals act (and appear to act) in a non-partisan fashion can prove very difficult.

Prior to the WTO, the establishment of GATT panels to adjudicate disputes and the acceptance of the recommendations of the panels relied primarily upon the principle of consensus, including the acquiescence of the accused party. Hence, dispute settlement was dependent on the power of moral suasion, both for getting a dispute to the panel stage and for ensuring compliance. The entire GATT dispute procedure was long and cumbersome with the onus on the contending parties to find a satisfactory solution bilaterally. Only as a last resort were they to apply to have a panel struck. While panels were charged with the responsibility to work quickly, and most did, the process whereby countries reach the point where a panel could be asked for was often very long and drawn out. As the imposition of many trade-restricting measures arises from short-term strategic considerations rather than fundamental structural differences between economies, the slowness of the GATT dispute settlement mechanism could not prevent opportunistic imposition of trade-restricting measures when relief from trade problems was sought. The slowness of the procedures also allowed them to be subsequently abandoned when a GATT panel's judgement appeared imminent. In many cases, countries did not bother to refer disputes to the GATT. A nation imposing trade-restricting measures could use the weakness of the dispute procedures to achieve its short-term goals.

Frustration with the GATT dispute mechanism was one of the major reasons for the establishment of bilateral and regional trade associations. These agreements usually have much stronger dispute settlement mechanisms. As discussed in Chapter 5, the EU has followed a judicial or legal approach to dispute settlement. Trade disputes among member countries are first expected to go through national courts. Appeals can then be made to the European Court. As a result, the entire process is cumbersome, costly and time consuming. The major problem with the EU system, however, is that the European Court must rely on national courts and governments to ensure compliance with its judgements. In a number of cases this support has not been forthcoming, or only forthcoming very slowly. The CUSTA took a non-legal approach. The dispute mechanism agreed to relies on arbitration rather than a judicial approach and on strict timetables for the arbitration process (Apuzzo and Kerr, 1988). Procedures are explicitly set out for the selection of individuals for the arbitration panels so that biased arbitrators can be rejected.

The WTO has taken over responsibility for the adjudication of disputes from the GATT. A common set of dispute settlement procedures is applied to all areas of WTO responsibility including trade in goods. The Uruguay Round Understanding on Rules and Procedures Governing the Settlement of Disputes (DSU) follows, to a considerable degree, the arbitration model set out in the CUSTA. Adjudication of disputes is administered by the Disputes Settlements Body (DSB) of the WTO.

The DSU has two major aspects which are common in arbitration – as opposed to judicial – procedures: the use of neutral adjudicators and strict timetables for proceedings. In addition, a panel can be established on the basis of a complaint from only one party to the dispute. This removes one of the major weaknesses of the previous GATT dispute settlement procedures which required the consent of all parties to the dispute before a panel could be set up.

Panels have three members who are not citizens of the countries in dispute. They are drawn from a list maintained by the WTO of people of appropriate background and experience. Appeals to panel rulings can be made to an Appellate Body composed of seven members, three of whom will hear any individual case. Countries can only appeal on the grounds that panels have not acted appropriately or on the basis of legal interpretations made by the panels. The actual case is not heard by the Appellate Body. The appeals procedure, which is new in the WTO, adds a legal element to dispute settlement but the use of experts on panels is consistent with the original GATT concept of settlements based on economic rather than legal criteria.

As protectionist pressures tend to build and then tend to ebb away, it was in the interest of politicians to break a GATT commitment and then attempt the strategic use of delaying tactics to prevent an adverse decision being brought down by a dispute panel. As a result, the DSU provides for rigid timetables for all aspects of dispute settlement from the point in time when one party notifies the WTO of its intentions, right through to compliance with a panel's ruling. The first step is a request for consultations with the other country. Consultations must begin in 30 days or the complaining country can ask for a panel. When consultations are agreed to, if after 60 days no resolution is reached, a panel can be requested. The two countries in dispute have 20 days to find mutually agreeable members for the panel. If they do not, the DSB will appoint the panel. Panels have 3 or 6 months to complete their work. After a panel issues its report, a maximum of 60 days is allowed before it must be accepted or rejected by the DSB. If one party wishes to appeal, the appeal must be made within this 60 day period. Appeals can take a maximum of 60 days. The parties must accept the panel report within 30 days of the release of the verdict on the appeal. If the judgement goes against the accused, then there must be a mutual agreement on implementation of the panel's recommendations in 45 days, or in 90 days if arbitration is required to determine the procedures for implementation.

The entire procedure should take no more than 600 days. This is less than 2 years and, compared to the past experience in the GATT, where disputes dragged on for years, exceptionally short. The WTO dispute mechanisms are new, however, and an assessment of how well they operate in practice will only be possible after a number of cases have been heard. The precedents set by the WTO panels will no doubt be monitored closely by firms engaging in international commerce.

REFERENCES

Apuzzo, A. M. and Kerr, W. A. (1988) International arbitration – the dispute settlement procedures chosen for the Canada–US Free Trade Agreement. *Journal of International Arbitration*, **5**(4), 7–15.

Pinder, J. (1988) Country intervention indexes. *Choices*, Fourth Quarter, 28–9.

10 'Fair' trade

CONTINGENT PROTECTION

Contingent protection measures are used by governments in importing countries when they feel that firms in exporting countries are conducting their international commerce in a manner which is 'unfair' to their domestic firms. The idea of 'fair' trade defies a workable definition in economics but remains a conceptual notion upon which many countries base their contingent protection. 'Fair' trade is often discussed in the context of the equally indefensible concept of the level playing field. Tariffs are applied to the goods of the exporter at rates which mitigate the perceived economic damage and their removal is contingent upon the 'unfair' practices being halted. Contingent protection measures are applied in two cases – when dumping occurs and when trade-distorting subsidies are used by an exporting country.

DUMPING

In theory, dumping is the international equivalent of certain business practices which are considered unacceptable even when firms sell only in their domestic market. The primary unacceptable business practice which anti-dumping measures attempt to address is the international equivalent of **predatory pricing**. Predatory pricing is selling below cost to gain a strategic market advantage. As selling below cost on an international basis has been difficult to prove, alternative tests which are supposed to provide a simpler means of identifying predatory pricing have been devised. These tests, while they may provide evidence of predatory pricing, do not necessarily do so and, hence, anti-dumping duties may be applied in situations which are not defensible in economic theory. Having anti-dumping duties imposed when predatory pricing is not taking place, however, serves the interests of firms seeking protection.

International predatory pricing might be practised by an exporting firm to gain market shares or even market domination in an importing country. It could sell below cost in the importing country and sustain this practice by cross-subsidizing with profits from sales in its domestic market. This may be the tactic followed when the importing country has restrictions on foreign investment which prevent the less expensive strategy of acquiring market share by purchase or merger (McGee, 1958). Clearly, predatory pricing is detrimental to competing firms in an importing nation and in many countries the practice would not be allowed if the predatory firm were a domestic competitor.

The definition of predatory pricing used in dumping cases is selling at a price below the full cost of production. Determining the full cost of production has, however, proved illusive. Firms seldom produce only one output with many inputs, machinery and facilities used in the production of a variety of outputs. Attempting to allocate a portion of the joint costs to the product which is suspected of being dumped is not a useful exercise. As there are no generally accepted international accounting rules, it only leads to debates between groups of accountants. Further, securing the required cost information from a firm in a different country may be difficult, if not impossible. As a result of the difficulties associated with the estimation of the 'full cost of production', alternative criteria for dumping cases have been developed.

One of the tests which is often applied is whether or not the price in the importing country, allowing for transportation costs, is less than the price at which the commodity is marketed in the exporting country. In certain cases this could be evidence of predatory pricing. However, predatory pricing is not the only explanation for this 'evidence'. It is well-known that a monopolist with the ability to keep markets separate, will practice price discrimination (Schmitz *et al.*, 1981). International boundaries provide an excellent means of keeping consumers apart. As a result, it may be the case that the optimum pricing strategy of the firm will be to charge a lower price in the importer's market. The lower price charged, however, will still exceed the full cost of production. The importing country should not care if foreign firms wish to monopoly price – charge higher than their true supply price – as this simply makes the importer's firms more competitive. In fact, if the exporting firm were forced to set the price at its cost of production, it would lower its price. The lower price would be detrimental to firms in the importing country. However, it may be to the advantage of firms in the importer's country to accuse the exporter of dumping. The tariff applied under anti-dumping provisions increases the price of imports to that which is charged in the exporter's domestic market.

Clearly, the tests for dumping are flawed. When accusations of dumping are made they may simply represent opportunistic behaviour by importing firms rather than a true need for relief from predatory pricing. Firms who are exporting should carefully assess the risks associated with pricing strategies which could be construed as dumping. Further, companies facing import competition should monitor the pricing of foreign products. Prices of imports as well as those of the same product in the exporter's home market should be tracked. If the evidence suggests dumping, the information should be provided to the relevant government agency.

COUNTERVAIL

Countervailing duties are the contingency protection measure used in the case of 'unfair' subsidies. The definition of what constitutes unfair is well established. In the GATT, a countervailable subsidy is one which is, firstly, trade distorting and, secondly, has caused material injury to a domestic industry in the importing country. Trade-distorting subsidies are specifically disallowed but there has been a long debate surrounding the difficult problem of defining a trade-distorting subsidy. It has never been seriously contemplated within the GATT that countervail should prevent governments from subsidizing. The requirement is only that the subsidies not be trade distorting.

Three kinds of trade-distorting subsidies can be identified:

1. Direct export subsidies.
2. Domestic subsidies which enhance a country's export performance.
3. Domestic subsidies which reduce or prevent the substitution of imported goods for domestically produced goods.

It is the latter two cases where difficulties with definitions have arisen. Theoretical attention has focused on devising subsidies which will not elicit a supply response from domestic firms which either increases exports or reduces imports. The term used for subsidies which would be acceptable, i.e. non-trade distorting, is decoupled. Decoupled means that the level of subsidy is independent (decoupled) from the firm's level of output. Finding subsidies which are not trade distorting has proved illusive (Kerr, 1988). At the GATT negotiations, a more pragmatic approach has been taken. Subsidies have been divided among agreed categories based on whether they are considered countervailable or not. There is general agreement that subsidies which are not specific to a product or an individual firm are acceptable (or 'non-actionable'). Subsidies on research and development which are broad based, education subsidies, interest subsidies, assistance to disadvantaged regions and payments for upgrading facilities to meet new environmental standards are all considered non-actionable.

Prohibited subsidies are those that depend upon the value or quantity of the goods exported or upon the firm receiving the subsidy having to purchase domestic goods rather than foreign goods. For example, to receive a subsidy, a US firm might have to agree to purchase only American steel. If a subsidy is judged to be in the prohibited category it must be withdrawn immediately. Some exceptions have, however, been negotiated for agricultural commodities and for developing countries. If a prohibited subsidy is not withdrawn, the complaining country can impose countervailing duties.

The third category ('actionable' subsidies) are more complex. The agreement reached at the Uruguay Round stipulates that no member country should, through the use of its subsidies, cause injury to the domestic industry of another member country. For example, a subsidy paid to all smelters might lower the price of copper production sufficiently to allow significant quantities of copper to be exported to another country. Further, subsidies should not reduce the market access expected by a country as a result of a reduction of tariffs. For example, as part of its GATT commitments a country might agree to reduce its tariffs on coal. Firms in exporting countries could expect an increase in their coal sales. The country which reduces its tariffs, however, might introduce a subsidy on the transport of domestic coal that would just offset the effect of the tariff reduction. Hence, the increase in sales expected by the exporter would be nullified.

As any subsidy is likely to have some effect on trade volumes, to prevent nuisance suits over trivial trade distortions, the concept of **serious prejudice** has been introduced. Serious prejudice is presumed to exist when a subsidy exceeds 5% of the subsidized product's value. When the subsidy level exceeds 5%, if a country complains to the WTO, it is then up to the subsidizing country to prove that the subsidy does not cause serious prejudice to the complaining member. Serious prejudice may prove difficult to define and, hence, easy to disprove in the case of an individual importing country. Whether the concept of serious prejudice will prove any easier to operationalize than the infamous 'more than an equitable share of the world market' previously used in the case of agricultural subsidies will have to wait until it is tested in the WTO's Dispute Settlement Body. At least having the onus of proof now placed on the subsidizing party will be an improvement over the pre-Uruguay Round procedures. If a subsidy is proved to be actionable, the subsidizing country must withdraw the subsidy or remove the adverse effects. If it does not, countervailing duties can be imposed by the injured country.

It is important for firms in importing countries to monitor the initiation of, or changes to, subsidies in the home countries of their major competitors. If the use of a prohibited or actionable subsidy is suspected, a representation can be made to the appropriate body in their own country. In a similar fashion, it is important that exporting firms work closely with domestic policy makers to ensure that new or altered subsidy programmes are not structured in ways which will lead to a request for countervailing duties from competing firms in their export markets.

REFERENCES

Kerr, W. A. (1988) The Canada–United States Free Trade Agreement and the livestock sector: the second stage negotiations. *Canadian Journal of Agricultural Economics*, **36**, 895–903.

McGee, J. S. (1958) Predatory price cutting: the Standard Oil (N.J.) case. *Journal of Law and Economics*, **1**, 137–69.

Schmitz, A., Firsh, R. S. and Hillman, J. S. (1981) Agricultural export dumping: the case of Mexican winter vegetables in the US market. *American Journal of Agricultural Economics*, **63**(4), 645–54.

Summary of Part Three

While the institutions which attempt to provide rules under which international trade can be conducted may be badly flawed and open to opportunistic manipulation, they have proved both durable and relatively effective. Their effectiveness is not based on their formal legal status but rather on their very existence. Firms which act to blatantly disobey the rules will likely face increased transactions costs as the eye of international scrutiny is focused on them. Time and resources will be required to justify their actions and to provide information to domestic and/or international bodies. Governments which attempt to ignore their voluntarily agreed to international commitments also face increased costs in terms of reduced international credibility and reputation. Further, concessions in other areas of economic or political interest may be more difficult to secure from trading partners. The threat of these increased costs is sufficient to keep most international players within the 'spirit' of the agreed rules of trade.

There is a general consensus that rules for trade are needed. The lesson of the economic disaster of the 1930s are not lost on contemporary trade policy makers. The tug of war between a county's desire for sovereignty and the need for an orderly system for trade will continue. As the world economy becomes increasingly integrated, however, more and more vested interests are created in the continuation of the orderly conduct of international trade.

PART 4

The economic actors who conduct international trade

Introduction to Part Four

The relative economic conditions in two or more countries create opportunities for engaging in international commercial transactions. The general rules within which international trade can be conducted are established under multilateral agreements or bilaterally between nation states. In addition, each individual country imposes laws and regulations relating to the conduct and administration of its international trade. In combination, this set of constraints represents the commercial environment within which international business activities can be undertaken. It is up to individual 'economic actors', however, to identify and act upon the opportunities for international trade which exist. These economic actors may be either private firms or government organizations. International transactions can take place between two private firms, between a private firm and a government organization or between two government organizations. These distinctions are important because government organizations may have different objectives and operate under a different set of constrains than private firms. Depending upon the constraints faced by the individual economic actors, some opportunities for trade may be enhanced while others may be reduced or eliminated. Even if a firm is not directly involved in international business, the international activities of firms and government organizations can alter its competitive position domestically. Hence, it is important to understand the economic actors which initiate and carry out international transactions.

International business must be approached from a very wide perspective. The traditional view of trade transactions being the exchange of goods between two firms located in different countries – commodity exports/imports – is far too narrow to encompass the range of activities which constitute international commerce. Some firms operate in more than one country – transnationals or multinationals. Expanding the definition of what is being traded to include (1) intellectual property, (2) goodwill (or reputation) and (3) services (particularly managerial services) helps to explain the activities of transnational firms. A foreign subsidiary run by a manager sent by the parent firm may simply be the export of managerial services from a nation where a particular form of managerial expertise is relatively abundant to a nation where it is relatively scarce. A transnational firm that manufactures new products or uses new processes in one country which were invented in its Research and Development division in another country is simply importing the output (intellectual property) of its research program. Expanding the definition of exports/imports, however, does not help to explain why transnational firms exist.

As an alternative to setting up an operation in a second country, any firm which perceives an export opportunity has the option of simply operating in one country and selling to a firm in another country. Companies 'rent out' managerial services to independent firms in foreign countries. Patented processes are sold outright to foreign firms. Further, simply extending the definition of what is being traded does not explain the existence of the large number of intermediate forms of organizing international commercial activity which exist in between market transactions by national (those that choose to operate in only one country) firms in two countries and exchanges among the operations of a transnational firm. These intermediate forms of business organization include international joint ventures, licensing arrangements, franchising and long-term contracts. In Chapter 11, the types of considerations which influence a firm's choice for the organizational form which it will use to exploit perceived international business opportunities will be examined in detail.

An additional choice faces national firms that have identified a profitable international business opportunity. They can choose either to export their products directly to foreign customers or they can choose to sell to companies that specialize in arranging international transactions. These 'trading houses' can operate in the exporting country, the importing country or they may be transnationals. They may be large trading conglomerates like those which have long been associated with Hong Kong (such as Jardine, Matheson and Co.) and Japan (such as Mitsubishi) or they may simply be small import/export businesses. There are national firms primarily concerned with the production of goods that undertake international transactions themselves and there are others that choose to sell to intermediaries. What factors influence that choice?

The undertaking of international business is extremely complex, and will vary with the nations involved, with what is being transacted, with the size of the market and with the partners to the transaction. As a result, a business must consider each transaction on its own merit. There are no fixed rules which can provide 'cookbook answers'. This section, however, provides a guide to some of the complex decisions facing business people wishing to engage in international commerce.

National firms and transnational firms 11

DO TRANSNATIONALS MAKE SENSE?

In the early 1990s there were approximately 37 000 transnational corporations, a fivefold increase in two decades. They had 170 000 foreign affiliates. About one third of the US$4 trillion in world exports of goods and services is intra firm trade between parents and affiliates (UNCTAD, 1993).

The question of how international transactions are actually organized has not been an important concern of most economists who have been in the forefront of developing the theory of international trade. They have been interested in understanding the economic forces which create opportunities for trade and which can alter the international competitiveness of industries. Whether a trade opportunity is acted upon by a British firm selling to a French firm or by a British firm transferring some of its output to a subsidiary in France, the trade flow is the same. Relative profitability should determine whether a British firm sells directly to a French firm or sets up a subsidiary. The alternative means by which international transactions can be organized will differ in their costs and these costs will be an important factor in determining the organizational form which is chosen by firms. Trade theorists of the neo-classical school, who are not concerned with the organizational form under which trade is conducted, simply assume that these 'transactions' costs are small enough to safely ignore. For most of the questions they wish to explore, little is lost in making this assumption. Transactions costs cannot be ignored, however, if questions concerning the organization of international commerce are to be answered.

THE COST OF ORGANIZING INTERNATIONAL TRANSACTIONS

The relationship between the costs of organizing international transactions and the types of institutions, e.g. bilateral contracts between national firms in different countries, transnational firms, joint ventures, international licensing agreements, etc., which actually co-ordinate those transactions is part of the more general question concerning whether firms co-ordinate economic activities or whether markets are used to co-ordinate economic activities. This approach to understanding the organization of economic activity has its roots in the work of Nobel Prize winner Ronald Coase (1937) who asked the question; What determines the size of a firm? – where size is taken to mean the number of activities which come under the direction of a firm's management. Turning this question around, it becomes; 'At what stage will markets – or some other mechanism – replace within-firm managerial orders as the means of moving products through the production and distribution system' (Gaisford et al., 1994). A new 'school' of economic thought known as 'transactions cost economics' or 'new institutional economics' has arisen which attempts to answer these and other related questions. Some of the major authors identified with new institutional economics are Armen Alchian, Yoram Barzel, Stephen Cheung, Paul Joskow, Benjamin Klein and Oliver Williamson. A readable discussion of new institutional economics can be found in Cheung (1992).

All of the methods which can be used to accomplish the process of moving products through production and distribution – **vertical co-ordination** – require a commitment of resources and, hence, impose costs on a firm. When markets are used to organize vertical co-ordination, it is prices which provide the incentives for firms to sell products or to purchase inputs. Changes in prices force firms to re-evaluate their decisions. The constant re-evaluation of selling and buying decisions allows for the identification of the mix of business activities which will maximize profits. Firms using markets, however, must expend resources to acquire information on prices, to negotiate a deal with the selected suppliers or customers and to ensure that the deal is honoured. Such activities come under the general headings of information, negotiation and enforcement costs.

Let us use the example of a car manufacturer to illustrate this point. Assume the manufacturer purchases the brake pads that are subsequently incorporated in its new vehicles. To select a supplier, purchasing personnel must first phone around to various potential suppliers to get rough price quotes – information costs. These price quotes must be evaluated. When a number of likely suppliers are identified, executives must spend time in preliminary discussions with those firms. Once a deal is struck in principle with a supplier, lawyers must be brought in to draw up the legal contract of exchange – all of these are considered negotiating costs. It may then be necessary for the car manufacturer to institute a program of testing the brake pads supplied to ensure that they meet its specifications before they are installed in the new cars – enforcement cost. Testing is necessary because the quality of brake pads cannot be determined through simple visual observation. If the seller used inferior metal then the pads would wear out too quickly and the car manufacturer would be forced to replace customers' brakes or lose them as future customers. Testing the brake pads before they are installed will be much cheaper than either of these alternatives. Still, resources must be expended on testing. If the quality of brake pads could be determined without cost then the buyer would simply not pay the stipulated price for them. They could only be sold at a lower price which reflected their inferior quality. As the price system does not work perfectly and costlessly, the seller may choose to act opportunistically and use inferior materials to increase his profits. To prevent the seller from exercising this option, the buyer must incur the costs associated with testing.

As an alternative to using the price system to acquire the brake pads, and incurring the costs associated with using it, the car manufacturer could simply purchase the brake pad supplier. Its own managers could then ensure that brake pads of the correct quality specification were supplied to the car assembly division. This would save the cost associated with acquiring and assessing competitive prices. No negotiations would be required and no legal fees incurred as there would be no need for a contract. Quality standards would be specified as part of the car manufacturer's internal quality control system. Vertical co-ordination would be accomplished through managerial orders given to employees.

If managerial orders were always a less costly way of accomplishing the tasks associated with vertical co-ordination, then firms would tend to expand until they were vertically integrated along the entire production and distribution chain. While this sometimes happens, it is clearly not the case for the majority of firms. This suggests that internally managing vertical co-ordination also has costs associated with it.

Managers charged with co-ordinating production or distribution activities within a firm require information upon which to base their decisions. This information is generated by the internal accounting system. Managers must ensure that this information is checked and verified. Further, employees have to be supervised to ensure that they efficiently undertake the tasks assigned by managerial orders. Without supervision, employees can exercise opportunities to 'shirk'. A manager may order that a truck load of brake pads be loaded for delivery to the assembly plant on Friday afternoon to meet a Monday morning automobile production deadline. Unless there is adequate supervision the workers may leave before the job is completed or work slowly knowing that they will be retained and receive overtime pay to ensure that the Monday delivery can be met. Clearly a system of managerial orders also has costs associated with it.

Transactions cost theory suggests that when it is more profitable to use a system of managerial orders to co-ordinate a production or distribution activity, then the firm will vertically integrate to internalize the activity. If markets can be used at a lower cost then the activity will not be internalized. Of course, in some cases both methods will be too costly and the activity will not take place.

A firm that decides to vertically integrate across international boundaries becomes a transnational firm. A firm's goodwill, management skills and the use of its intellectual property as well as the movement of goods can be co-ordinated internally across international boundaries. Conducting business across international boundaries, however, can both alter the relative size of transactions costs and presents firms with an array of new transactions costs which are not present when business operations are confined to one country. There are the obvious costs of currency conversion and of meeting the requirements of the importer's customs regulations. The latter can add considerably to the costs and risks associated with doing business, particularly when overzealous scrutiny of paperwork, tedious border inspections and capricious refusals of entry for cargoes are used as non-tariff barriers to trade. For a discussion of one example of how the cost of these activities can affect firms' decisions to trade see Bruce and Kerr (1986).

Each country has its own consumer protection legislation which can force firms to alter production processes or to entirely redesign products. Foreign consumers may have different tastes which must be catered to. For example, most beef consumers in North America and Europe prefer lean meat. In Japan, for a variety of religious and culinary reasons, consumers prefer beef which has a very high degree of internal fat (Kerr *et al.*, 1994). To successfully export to this lucrative Japanese niche market requires firms in beef exporting countries to alter their beef processing procedures, livestock production systems and even the genetics of the animals used in production. Meat plants wishing to supply Islamic countries must employ mullahs to conduct Halal slaughter rituals. In Britain and Japan, cars are driven on the left hand side of the road while in western Europe and North America they are driven on the right. Successful exporters in Japan and Britain had to design and engineer their cars to accommodate both right and left hand drives. (Car manufacturers in the US have not designed their cars for right hand drive mechanisms which may explain better than any other reason their failure to export to the Japanese market. Of course, some US manufacturers solved this problem in the UK by establishing subsidiaries.)

Tax regimes differ among countries such that time and resources must be spent to determine the correct mix of activities to be undertaken in each country. Tariffs may have to be paid. International shipments may require sturdier packaging. Executives may have to be given training in foreign business practices, and they and their families familiarized with a foreign culture.

European transnational oil companies operating in the Middle East provide intensive orientation programs for their executives and their families before they move abroad. Expensive leave, travel and emergency health care packages must be offered to executives and professional personnel sent to many foreign postings. While the numerous additional costs of doing business internationally can be identified and factored into business decisions, the important question is how these costs affect the way in which a firm chooses to conduct its international activities.

CAPTURING THE RETURNS TO RESEARCH AND DEVELOPMENT

Some firms spend considerable resources on researching and developing new products and production processes. To re-coup these costs, including the costs of failed research projects, companies must be able to reap the benefits. Otherwise, they will not be willing to invest in these activities. In the developed countries, where most of the world's research and development takes place, governments have recognized that ensuring that firms can expect to receive the returns to their research and development activities is important for the process of economic growth. It does not matter how a firm captures the return on investment – by producing the new product or employing the new process in its own factories, by leasing the knowledge to another firm or by selling the knowledge outright. However, the ability to lease, sell or prevent others from benefiting from industrial espionage requires that the companies who do the research and development receive the property rights to the product or process. One method of assigning the rights to intellectual property is through the use of patents.

The success of patents as a means of providing firms with intellectual property rights depends upon the willingness of governments to enforce those rights. Intellectual property can be sold or leased. When a foreign government rigorously enforces patents, firms can be assured that they will receive the benefits from the use of their knowledge in the foreign market. When property rights are not rigorously enforced by foreign governments, firms have an incentive to vertically integrate their operations into the foreign country so that they can maintain control of their property. (The term horizontal integration is often used to describe foreign branch plant operations which produce the same product as that which is produced by the firm in the home country. As we are expanding the definition of export/imports to include intellectual property, goodwill and management services, branch plant operations are simply an alternative way of vertically co-ordinating exports and to be consistent we will use the term vertical integration.) Of course, the poor enforcement of property rights means that firms operating transnationally must expend resources to prevent industrial espionage in their foreign operation. This is often accomplished in subtle ways. For example, it may mean sending engineers or technicians from the home country to run the operation in the foreign country. If the knowledge is carried in their heads, possibilities for stealing copies of specifications and formulations are reduced. Further, individuals operating in a foreign environment may be less open to selling their knowledge – either through covert activities or by simply being hired away – than foreign nationals. If the knowledge is so complex that written records of specifications and procedures must be kept, or that they are simple enough to be acquired by observation, transnational firms will tend to hire and train local foreign personnel. Managers sent from the home country may be more diligent at preventing industrial espionage than local managers.

While the intellectual property of domestic firms may be well protected, foreign held patents and foreign operations may not receive the full measure of protection from the police and courts. Hence, the system of justice has a national bias. Some companies spread a single industrial process among a number of countries so that no complete set of information on a process exists in any one country. This strategy reduces the incentive for industrial espionage or even confiscation of intellectual property through nationalization. Of course, each company must assess the loss of returns associated with selling or leasing its knowledge to firms in countries with poor enforcement of property rights against the extra cost of active measures to prevent industrial espionage. Clearly, firms may choose to become transnationals to increase the returns to the intellectual property which they own. Evidence of firms acting upon these types of incentives can be found in Buckley and Prescott (1989) and Davidson and McFetridge (1982).

Protection of intellectual property rights has been particularly poor in a number of developing countries. In some countries, allowing local firms to treat the intellectual property of foreign firms as fair game has had the implicit, if not explicit, approval of the government. In many cases, however, the local government does not have the resources or capacity to enforce its laws relating to patents. To maintain their property rights, large numbers of transnational firms operate in these countries. Little research and development work is, however, carried out in developing countries. In some cases this has led to transnationals becoming a focal point for nationalist discontent and policies have been put in place to restrict the activities of transnational corporations (Kerr and Anderson, 1992). One of the major problems associated with the liberalization of the former command economies of eastern Europe, Russia and the rest of the former Soviet Union has been the absence of both a tradition of commercial law and the will to enforce newly proclaimed systems of commercial law.

USING GOODWILL TO INTERNATIONAL ADVANTAGE

A firm's goodwill relates to its reputation regarding the quality of the goods produced, the quality of the service provided or the trustworthiness with which it conducts its business affairs. One manifestation of goodwill is the firm's trademark. Firms wishing to capitalize on their trademark internationally, i.e. export their goodwill, have three forms of organization to choose from. They can export their products and prominently display the trademark on the products. They can also vertically integrate by setting up operations in the foreign country. Finally, they can rent their trademark to a firm in the other country through a franchise operation. Of course, in industries like fast food the first option does not exist because the perishability of the product precludes its direct export. The decision regarding how to enter a foreign market will depend on the degree of protection given to trademarks and the costs of monitoring activities in foreign countries.

Low quality counterfeits dissipate the firm's goodwill with consumers. If the laws restricting counterfeiting are poorly drafted or enforced, then a firm may choose to operate transnationally by establishing its own distribution system. By directly controlling distribution, substandard counterfeits cannot be passed off as trademark products. This has been the strategy followed by at least one major blue jean manufacturer.

Franchises will be used when it is easy to monitor the quality of the product. If the holder of a franchise can cheat on quality, say by using substandard parts in electrical goods or lowering service standards in a franchised fast food chain, they can lower costs and enhance their profits in the short run. The firm selling the franchise loses goodwill over time as customers become less and less satisfied. Having the foreign operation run by a salaried employee reduces the temptation to cheat on quality. Some major fast food chains prefer direct ownership to franchises. Where quality may be difficult to measure, such as in banking or for engineering consultants, direct ownership is more likely to be used.

PROTECTING VULNERABLE ASSETS

An incentive can be created for firms to integrate transnationally in cases where a large degree of **asset specificity** exists in a good which is to be traded across borders. The incentive also exists when investment in production processes dedicated to individual foreign markets is required. Asset specificity arises when investments are made by one party which, once made, are limited in alternative uses. After the investment is made, the other party to the transaction may be able to 're-negotiate' the terms of the transaction to their advantage (Klein *et al.*, 1978). Formally, this purposeful re-negotiating of an agreement for economic gain is known as **post-contractual-opportunistic-behaviour (PCOB)** or **opportunistic recontracting**. For example, suppose a firm in an exporting country could negotiate a contract to supply a guidance system suitable only for installation in one particular type of aircraft made by a firm in another country. To produce this guidance system, however, the exporting firm might have to make a considerable investment in a production line which would have few alternative uses. Prior to making the investment, the firm would have to negotiate a price for the guidance system which would cover its production costs and at least a competitive return on investment. Once the investment is made, however, the buying firm has the opportunity to attempt PCOB. It has an incentive to re-negotiate the price it pays for the guidance system because the selling firm has no other market in which to sell its guidance system. As long as the buyer will pay a price sufficient to cover the production cost of the guidance system and to contribute something to a return on capital, the selling firm will be better off than if it is forced to cease production. Refusing to produce the guidance system unless it gets the original agreed price would mean higher losses because the exporter would receive no contribution to return on capital. While it may be possible to attempt to seek enforcement of the original contract price in the courts, legal costs may be large, and litigation long and drawn out. When legal recourse must be sought across international boundaries, enforcement may be difficult and the legal process may suffer from national bias. Teece (1976) discusses a number of examples of opportunistic recontracting.

Firms in exporting countries, however, may well be cognizant of the risks of PCOB and build extra premiums into the prices they are willing to negotiate. The buying firm, on the other hand, by integrating backward into the exporting country can set up its own production facility and avoid these price premiums. Transnational operations in mining and other resource based industries can be explained in this way. Specificity can also be present in consumer products. Special goods may be produced to satisfy a unique foreign taste and, hence, can only be sold at a discount in the country where production takes place. For example, the very fat beef preferred by Japanese consumers can only be sold at a considerable discount to consumers in exporting countries like the US, Canada and Australia (Hobbs and Kerr, 1991).

If product quality is costly to determine, buyers are faced with the possibility that sellers are either unable to deliver the required quality or may cheat on quality. Buyers may build in price discounts to their offer prices which reflect their perceived risks. At these prices, sellers may not realize sufficient profits and, hence, will not sell high quality merchandise. As a result, no international trade will take place in high quality products. If the buying firm decides to operate transnationally by purchasing the operation in the exporting country, then it can eliminate this risk by setting up a quality control system run by its own managers. Japanese importers complain that quality control is lax in both beef production and processing in exporting countries. Shipments are often refused. Negotiating a mutually acceptable contract price with risk-averse beef exporters has proved almost impossible. Some Japanese firms have purchased ranches and processing facilities in Australia and the US (Anderson *et al.*, 1992). Exporting firms are likely to integrate forward and operate transnationally when the distribution of their product requires specific investments or if their product is subject to deterioration if improperly handled during distribution.

EXERCISING MARKET POWER

If international **cartels** are outlawed, or if the cost of enforcing cartel arrangements is too high, then there may be an incentive to operate transnationally so that the full benefits arising from the exercise of market power can be realized (Casson, 1985). For example, if separate firms in a number of countries are producing and selling very similar products under monopoly conditions, each individual firm may have an incentive to attempt to increase its market by exporting to another country. In other words, the individual national monopolies would be broken by competition from imports. The resulting competition reduces total profits. Hence, there is an incentive for firms to co-operate to maintain their individual national monopolies. In many countries, however, joining a cartel is illegal. Even if cartels are legal, there may be large incentives for individual members to cheat. If detection of cheating is difficult, total profits of the cartel will be reduced. If production comes under the ownership of one firm operating transnationally, then it can order its individual national subsidiaries not to export. Since the total potential profits of the transnational firm are larger than the sum of the potential profits of the individual firms, the transnational can afford to purchase the individual national firms. When circumvention of market sharing agreements is easy to identify and police by the firms involved, cartels will be the preferred form of industrial organization. Cartels may also be preferred when the purchase of national firms is prohibited. This is the case for international air flights where government owned airlines predominate.

STRATEGIC USE OF TRANSFER PRICES

Firms operating transnationally may be able to increase their profits by taking advantage of differences in tax rates among countries. Strategic use of internal **transfer pricing** across national boundaries can reduce a company's tax bill. Internal transfer prices are the reported accounting prices at which goods or services are transferred between different divisions of a company. Assume that an importing country taxes profits at a higher rate than the country where the exports originate. Increasing the reported price at which the exporting division transfers the product to a subsidiary in the importing country decreases the pre-tax profits made by the division in the importing country. At the same time, the high transfer price increases the pre-tax profits in the exporting division. These increased pre-tax profits are taxed at a lower rate resulting in higher net profits for the firm. This will give the transnational corporation an advantage over separate firms engaging in transactions at the market price. Abuse of transfer pricing, whether real or imagined, has been one of the major criticisms of transnational corporations and has led to considerable friction with national governments.

Some countries have elaborate customs regulations which require firms to provide detailed information. Complying with these regulations is costly for firms. Even if the transfer of goods is undertaken at the prices that would prevail in the market, the transnational corporation may be able to charge a high price for management fees or other services whose true value may be extremely difficult to estimate by tax departments.

LONG-TERM CONTRACTS

Long-term contracts can be used as an alternative to both transnational operations and arms length export sales at spot market prices. Contracts may be less costly than operating transnationally when the importer's legal system is well enforced, relatively inexpensive and does not have a bias toward national firms. Contracts work well when the relationship between the exporting and importing countries is harmonious, the prices of the traded goods are not volatile and the market environment is sufficiently well understood so that the contract can be specified to account for most contingencies. Compensation for breach of contract should be included in the contract. Long-term contracts are less costly than one-off export sales when guarantees of ongoing sales are required to justify investments in scale-based cost saving technology. When fraud is easy to detect but hard to prove in court, problems with opportunistic breach of contract can be eliminated by choosing to produce the required commodity through a transnational operation. When exchange rates are unstable or markets unpredictable, it will be difficult to specify all contingencies in a contract. As a result, greater reliance will be placed on one-off export sales.

JOINT VENTURES

International **joint ventures** arise when capital or expertise from firms in different countries are combined to mutual advantage. In equity joint ventures, both parties contribute capital. When one firm contributes only expertise, it is a technical joint venture. In both cases, profits are shared on the basis of the contribution of the partners. Joint ventures differ from licensing arrangements or franchises in that any profits are shared whereas the holder of the licence/franchise can keep all profits once the fee is paid.

By drawing on two sets of expertise, costs can be reduced. Business practices and customs differ among countries. A firm with an opportunity to sell its product in another country could choose to integrate forward by operating transnationally but would then have to make a considerable investment in learning local business practices and customs. Mistakes can be costly. Many examples exist of attempts to transfer advertising campaigns to foreign markets where they have, at best, had no impact and, at worse, have greatly offended local consumers. Western businessmen who are used to writing complex contracts have had great difficulty adjusting to Japanese business relationships based primarily on trust built up over a long period of time. Of course, the problems encountered by Japanese automobile firms when they attempted to transplant their personnel management practices to the US and Europe have been the subject of a number of movie comedies. Having a joint venture partner can eliminate these costly learning periods. Further, governments may be more predisposed to provide grants and subsidies when a local partner is involved in a venture.

Joint ventures are distinct from mergers in that they are set up with a specific task in mind. When the task is accomplished, or the venture is no longer mutually advantageous, it can be terminated without the difficulties associated with dividing the assets of fully integrated firms. Both parties share in the profits and, therefore, each has less of an incentive to act opportunistically than if they were separate firms. The incentive to cheat is not, however, totally eliminated. This means that time and resources must be expended to monitor the activities of partners. Further, while the cost of learning how to conduct business in the foreign economy is eliminated, managers seconded to the joint venture may have to learn to work with partners who have very different business practices. These cultural differences can often endanger the success of joint ventures. The fact that many governments have forced foreign firms into joint ventures suggests that these transactions costs are not trivial.

Joint ventures may be terminated because the objectives of firms change over time. By observing their joint venture partners, the exporting firm may learn enough about the local market to feel sufficiently confident to undertake the distribution of its product directly. On the other hand, if the joint venture involves production, the local partner may learn a sufficient amount about the process to set up its own production facility. Hence, joint ventures carry the risk that future competitors will be created. The relative cost of a direct transnational operation will have to be weighed against the risk of creating future competition.

Due to the ease with which they can be dissolved, joint ventures represent a means by which the transactions costs associated with abandoning international operations can be reduced. If a transnational firm makes it known that it wishes to shut down its operations in a country, the local government may attempt to prevent the loss of economic activity by restricting capital repatriation or threatening confiscation. If entry into a foreign market is perceived as risky, it may be prudent to enter the market via a joint venture operation. If the foreign joint venture proves to be not worthwhile, it may be sold at a discount to the local partner. There is less likely to be a problem with capital repatriation after a sale to a local partner.

If partners in the host country are considered too untrustworthy, the economy of the host country is considered too unpredictable or the host government restricts repatriation of capital, equity joint ventures may not be advisable (Middleton *et al.*, 1993). There may still be scope for technical joint ventures where the host country partner puts up the capital and the exporting partner provides technical or managerial expertise through seconded staff. Profits are shared on a pre-agreed formula. A commitment of staff is made but they can be easily withdrawn if the venture proves to be untenable.

GREENFIELD INVESTMENTS VERSUS ACQUISITIONS

Firms will likely incur additional organizational costs when they choose to operate transnationally. Providing correct incentives and monitoring employees to prevent shirking may prove more difficult, and hence more costly, as cultural differences increase (Davidson and McFetridge, 1985). As a result, transnational operations may be more efficient when cultural differences are small. A firm wishing to enter a foreign market must also consider whether it wishes to enter the market by acquiring a firm in the host country or setting up an entirely new subsidiary – a **'greenfield' investment**. If the latter alternative is chosen, more mistakes are likely and learning the foreign market will take longer. If the former method of market entry is chosen, then the firm inherits a local corporate culture which may not mesh well with its own.

LIMITS ON FOREIGN DIRECT INVESTMENTS

As transnational corporations may have a competitive advantage over domestic firms, governments may wish to limit their activities (Kerr and Anderson, 1992). These restrictions act to limit FDI as discussed in Chapter 1. If firms decide to organize themselves as transnationals it suggests that this is the most profitable means of conducting their international commerce. Restrictions on FDI have similar trade limiting effects to direct limits on the movements of goods and services. These restrictions can take many forms. There may be limits on the total amount of FDI. Foreign direct investment may be restricted to certain sectors of the economy. Joint ventures with local firms may be required. Limits on the repatriation of profits can be imposed. These **trade related investment measures (TRIMS)** have been addressed both in bilateral negotiations and at the GATT.

For a number of years, Canada required all FDI proposals over a certain value to be vetted by its Foreign Investment Review Agency. The agency seldom, if ever, used its powers to deny an application. However, the paperwork required for the review process imposed additional costs on potential investors and the process caused delays. Its public nature also informed Canadian firms of potentially profitable business ventures. Foreign firms, particularly in the US, felt that these procedures caused them to lose profitable opportunities. Canada agreed to significantly reduce its powers of scrutiny in the CUSTA.

The Uruguay Round also addressed the issue of TRIMS. The WTO will oversee the Agreement on Trade Related Investment Measures. Regulations requiring transnationals to purchase local inputs or that restrict the volume or value of imported inputs they can purchase must be eliminated over fixed periods of time. The agreement, however, is weak as it fails to deal with direct restrictions on investment and domestic regulations which may limit the business strategies of transnationals.

Clearly, the choice of organizational structure which firms use to expand into foreign markets depends upon a large number of factors which each carry different costs. The continued existence of a wide range of international commercial arrangements suggests than no single type of arrangement offers consistent advantage. Further, how firms conduct international commerce evolves over time. Hence, it is important that firms engaging in international business should be willing to consider alternative organizational structures. Regular evaluations of these alternatives should be carried out.

REFERENCES

Anderson, C. L., Hobbs, J. E. and Kerr, W. A. (1992) Transactions costs and the benefits of trade: liberalizing the Japanese importing system for beef. *Asian Economic Journal*, **6**(3), 289–301.

Bruce, C. J. and Kerr, W. A. (1986) A proposed arbitration system to ensure free trade in livestock products. *Canadian Journal of Agricultural Economics*, **34**(3), 347–60.

Buckley, P. and Prescott, K. (1989) The structure of British industry sales in foreign markets. *Managerial and Decision Economics*, **10**, 189–208.

Casson, M. (1985) Multinational monopolies and international cartels, in *The Economic Theory of the Multinational Enterprize: Selected Papers*, (eds P. J. Buckley and M. Casson), Macmillan, London, pp. 60–97.

Cheung, S. N. S. (1992) On the new institutional economics, in *Contract Economics*, (eds L. Werin and H. Wijkander), Blackwell, Oxford, pp. 48–65.

Coase, R. H. (1937) The nature of the firm. *Economica*, new series, **4**, 386–405.

Davidson, W. H. and McFetridge, D. (1982) *International Technology Transactions and the Theory of the Firm*, Working Paper No. 106, Ames Tuck School of Business Administration.

Davidson, W. H. and McFetridge, D. (1985) International technology transfer mode. *Journal of International Business Studies*, summer, 5–21.

Gaisford, J. D., Kerr, W. A. and Hobbs, J. E. (1994) Non-cooperative bilateral monopoly problems in liberalizing command economies. *Economic Systems*, **18**(3), 265–79.

Hobbs, J. E. and Kerr, W. A. (1991) Japanese beef importing system changes may be less useful than first appeared. *Journal of Agricultural Taxation and Law*, **13**(3), 236–57.

Kerr, W. A. and Anderson, C. L. (1992) Multinational corporations, local enterprises and the political economy of development – some basic dynamics. *Journal of Economic Development*, **10**(1), 105–24.

Kerr, W. A., Klein, K. K., Hobbs, J. E. and Kagatsume, M. (1994) *Marketing Beef in Japan*, The Haworth Press, New York.

Klein, B., Crawford, R. G. and Alchian, A. (1978) Vertical integration, appropriable rents, and the competitive contracting process. *Journal of Law and Economics*, **28**(2), 297–36.

Middleton, J., Hobbs, J. E. and Kerr, W. A. (1993) Poland's evolving food distribution system: joint venture opportunities for British agribusiness. *Journal of European Business Education*, **3**(1), 35–45.

Teece, D. J. (1976) *Vertical Integration and Divestiture in the US Oil Industry; Economic Analysis and Policy Implications*, Institute for Energy Studies, Stanford University.

UNCTAD (1993) *World Investment Report 1993: Transnational Corporations and Integrated International Production*, United Nations, New York.

12 Private firms and state trading agencies

GOVERNMENT INVOLVEMENT IN INTERNATIONAL COMMERCE

In many countries the conduct of international commerce has, to some degree, been removed from the private sector and placed in the hands of the government. State trading agencies are often set up. Sometimes these agencies are broad based, handling a large number of products. More often, they are specialized to a limited range of commodities. Their degree of autonomy from the international trade ministry, or other government departments with an interest in international commerce, varies considerably. In some cases, they operate almost as profit maximizing private firms while in other cases they are instruments of government policy. Dealing with state trading agencies can present special problems for private firms wishing to import from, or export to, countries where they operate. Even where state trading agencies do not have a monopoly on a nation's commerce, they can alter the profitability of a transaction organized between private firms by granting concessionary trade terms to competitors. Further, transactions between state trading agencies in two different countries may not take place on a commercial basis and, hence, may affect the profitability of privately organized international transactions. Even if a private firm does not deal directly with state trading agencies, it is important to understand the motivations of these agencies and the parameters which determine their operating practices.

State trading agencies have been established to achieve a variety of political objectives. These objectives determine, in part, how state trading agencies interact with foreign firms and how they influence the international trading environment.

STATE TRADING AGENCIES IN COMMAND ECONOMIES

In the command economies which were established in Russia and its empire after the communist revolution, and subsequently in eastern Europe, Asian communist states and Cuba, all international trade was in the hands of **state trading agencies**. International commerce was an arm of state foreign policy. State trading agencies, however, simply reflected the organization of communist economies where all but the smallest of private enterprises were banned.

Vertical co-ordination in command economies is accomplished by two types of non-market direction. Within 'socialist enterprises' managers directed economic activity but had no choice regarding their input suppliers, who they sold to, what labour they would use or what equipment they would have to work with. These decisions were made in the planning ministry. The movement of goods between socialist enterprises was also directed by bureaucrats in the planning ministry.

State trading agencies acted as intermediaries between socialist enterprises and foreign firms. At times, national self reliance was the emphasis of government policy and international trade was severely restricted even when mutually advantageous trading opportunities were available. While the recent changes in what was the 'communist bloc' has led to a degree of liberalization in what are now termed 'former command economies', full liberalization is likely to be a long process. State trading agencies are likely to remain heavily involved in international trade. Further, when former 'socialist enterprises' are allowed to trade directly, their conduct of international business may still be affected by the market distortions resulting from the former command system.

The major problem for command economies wishing to enter into international commercial relations is the absence of a meaningful domestic price system. Prices are arbitrarily set by the planning ministry and do not reflect the economic value of outputs or inputs (Mises, 1981). Once all prices are arbitrarily set by the state, there is no means of determining the relative worth of export sales versus domestic sales or foreign obtained inputs versus inputs produced domestically. If arbitrary domestic prices are set too low, then export sales simply subsidize foreign consumers to the detriment of the national economy. At low relative prices, socialist enterprises have an incentive to export. As a result their activities require the supervision of a state trading agency. Advantageous trading opportunities are forgone if domestic prices are set too high. If domestic input prices are set too low, then less costly foreign imports are discriminated against. National welfare is not maximized. While state trading agencies in command economies have no means of establishing accurate relative prices, they are still needed as an intermediary between the two price systems.

Even those communist states which believed most fervently in self-reliance could not achieve autarky and hence had to trade. International trade, however, is very difficult to accommodate within the planning process of command economies. Pre-specified quantities of foreign inputs or consumer goods can be allowed for in the plan. For the plan to be fulfilled, however, that quantity of inputs must be acquired. As command economies operate with non-convertible currencies and fixed exchange rate regimes, it means that to acquire the foreign exchange necessary to finance the purchase of foreign goods, export sales of equal value have to be generated. As the international market prices of products tend to fluctuate, planning offsetting quantities of exports becomes very difficult.

A rise in the international price of planned imports requires that additional exports have to be drawn from other areas of the plan. If the additional exports were to be inputs to other domestic processes, the plan is further disrupted. It is, hence, easier to alter the plan at the final economic interface – sales to consumers. As a result, state trading agencies in command economies usually attempt to sell consumer goods and buy intermediate inputs.

Foreign firms negotiating sales of consumer goods to these state trading agencies often find that the deal is called off at the last minute. This simply reflects the state trading agency's need to conserve foreign exchange as a result of an international price increase in some unrelated input market. At other times, large quantities of consumer goods may be offered at concessionary prices if the state trading agency urgently needs to acquire additional quantities of foreign exchange to attain the level of imports set out in the country's national plan. State trading agencies are responsible for balancing imports with exports. To ensure that the planning targets for foreign inputs can be met, state trading agencies tend to be more concerned with ensuring supplies than with price. Long-term contracts are used to lock in future supplies. Joint ventures between socialist enterprises and partners in non-command economies tend to stipulate that the socialist enterprise's return is specified as a proportion of output at fixed prices (Henderson and Kerr, 1984/85). Typically, they attempt to negotiate countertrade transactions where quantities or values of imports are directly tied to offsetting quantities or values of exports.

Private firms who must deal with state trading agencies in command economies have little information upon which to base negotiations. As state trading agencies are concerned with satisfying objectives which may have little to do with the actual transaction being negotiated, private firms may find themselves faced with unusual requests, be able to obtain concessions which seem to make little sense when judged on commercial criteria and find that the emphasis of discussions changes over time. As the prices at which transactions can be negotiated bear little relation to the value of the product, competitors may be able to negotiate deals with state trading agencies which considerably enhance their position in the market. As there is no way to assess true costs of production in command economies, recourse to anti-dumping remedies is limited. This is one of the major reasons why command economies are not compatible with the GATT accords.

While considerable changes have taken place in the former command economies, for certain segments of industry, particularly large-scale enterprises, prices have not been fully liberalized. Further, even where market prices now prevail, the state often gives these enterprises large subsidies which maintains the distortion of prices by artificially lowering costs. These artificial domestic prices give false signals to international markets. As a result, even after the abandonment of formal state planning the country's currency may not be fully convertible and state trading agencies will still be used to interface between domestic and international markets. They still have an important role in rationing foreign exchange.

STATE TRADING AGENCIES IN MIXED ECONOMIES

Many countries, whose economies are not based on central planning and vertical co-ordination based on command, put at least a portion of their international trade in the hands of state trading agencies. Many developing countries established state trading agencies to replace the transnational corporations which controlled their international commerce. These transnationals were often able to exploit their market power to the detriment of local producers. State trading agencies may also have been established to provide local exporters with a degree of market power in international markets. The Canadian Wheat Board, which is responsible for Canadian grain exports, was established with this objective. If they are run on a strictly commercial basis, state trading agencies may simply be extremely hard bargainers. Dealing with them will be similar to what might be expected from a private firm in a monopoly position.

In other cases, state trading agencies may be more closely linked to the diverse goals of government policy and, hence, may not make their decisions on strictly commercial criteria. This is particularly true for state agencies dealing in arms, munitions and strategic materials. The success or failure of negotiations between a state trading agency and a private firm in another country may well depend on such diverse criteria as the firm's employment practices, its environmental record, its investment portfolio, the countries with which it has commercial relations or the politics of the country where its head office is located. It is important that firms dealing with state trading agencies understand these non-commercial criteria. Otherwise, a great deal of negotiation time and effort may be expended to no avail. Firms may have to assess whether the potential profits from the transaction would justify altering their practices. To achieve political ends, governments may also be willing to accept lower rates of return or to subsidize the losses of state trading agencies. As a result, private firms competing with state trading agencies in international markets may face prices or other conditions offered by a state trading agency which they cannot compete with.

State trading agencies may also be established when a country's demand for foreign exchange chronically exceeds the supply at the official exchange rate. In such cases, foreign exchange will have to be rationed. A government may feel that by establishing a state trading agency it can, through direct control over the composition of imports which the agency can provide, use its limited foreign exchange to the best advantage. Often, this means giving priority to capital goods rather than consumer goods or the import of food staples rather than luxuries. Dealing with these types of state trading agencies may be a long drawn out process as the demands for foreign exchange required for the particular transaction must be weighed by the agency against all other transactions. What appears to be a mutually advantageous international transaction when judged on commercial criteria may not be concluded because it fails to qualify under the criteria the agency uses to priorise the use of foreign exchange.

Private firms should be willing to commit larger amounts of resources to the negotiation process than may typically be necessary in a transaction with another private firm. The state trading agency may simply be attempting to keep the negotiations going until sufficient reserves of foreign exchange are available for the transaction to qualify for funds. Further, because its negotiation costs are high, the state trading agency may only be interested in negotiating large-scale deals. Small firms may be effectively shut out of the market, a point that may not be obvious at the outset of discussions. Small firms should be careful not to put too much effort into a proposal until they are sure that the state trading agency is sufficiently interested to seriously pursue negotiations.

PAYMENT IN KIND

When a state trading agency is only responsible for a few commodities or it is not directly involved in the allocation of foreign exchange reserves, its officials may not be able to acquire sufficient foreign exchange to finance the agency's import requirements. As a result, they may be encouraged to arrange international exchanges which do not require formal commitments of foreign exchange. These are usually some form of 'countertrade' arrangement whereby the exporter agrees to import a specified quantity or value of product from the state trading agency's country as payment. These payment in kind arrangements do not require foreign exchange.

Private firms considering entering into a countertrade arrangement may be faced with considerable transactions costs. The costs associated with breaching contracts may also increase considerably. For example, an exporter may contract to design a factory and supply production engineering services in a foreign country. The host country may fear that if the firm were to be paid in cash it could behave opportunistically and under-engineer the facility. Only sub-quality goods could then be produced. On the other hand, if as part of the contract the exporter agreed to accept a proportion of the factory's output as payment, it will have an incentive to ensure that high engineering standards are adhered to. Many countertrade agreements are based on this type of reciprocity and can be seen primarily as an aid to enforcing contracts (Williamson, 1985; Hennart, 1989).

Countertrade accounted for approximately 20% of the international exchange of goods and services prior to the liberalization of the economies of eastern Europe and the former Soviet Union. While this proportion will fall as the process of liberalization progresses, state trading agencies are likely to continue to play a considerable role in the former command economies as they do in both developed and developing economies. Hence, private firms interested in international commerce may forgo profitable opportunities if they refuse to consider countertrade arrangements. They must, however, be very careful to assess the transactions costs which will arise in the process of arranging and fulfilling the commitments made. These costs must be considered in the firm's decision making process.

There are three basic types of countertrade agreements:

1. Barter: goods for goods.
2. Buy-backs: agreeing to purchase a portion of the output resulting from the goods or service inputs provided to an importer.
3. Counter-purchase: where an equivalent value of unrelated goods must be purchased in return for securing the export order.

Each of these types of agreement will impose different transactions costs on the private firm entering into an agreement with a state trading agency.

Barter

If the countertrade arrangement is a **barter** agreement, whereby a specified set of goods and/or services is exchanged for another specified set of goods and/or services, the original exporting firm will have a number of new tasks to undertake. First, it must assess the market value of the goods offered in exchange. In some cases this may be relatively straightforward. If the goods on offer are already present in the home market of the firm which will receive the goods (or some other third market which can be assessed), then valuation can be determined from market prices. However, if the goods on offer are not present in the firm's home market then valuation may be difficult. Official prices in the supplying country are not likely to provide a reliable guide as they may be determined by a planning authority. Prices will not reflect market forces but instead foreign exchange distortions or subsidized costs. To determine value, quality must be verified. In some cases, samples offered by state trading agencies cannot be relied upon to provide a true representation of production quality. Until a reasonably accurate valuation is made, negotiations on the quantity to be exchanged cannot be concluded.

The receiving firm in the West may not have had any experience in marketing the product on offer – western heavy engineering firms having to find markets for eastern European aspirin. Once an agreement is concluded, the firm which has agreed to accept the return products offered in a barter agreement must make arrangements to take delivery. This may involve arranging transport. Further, the original exporting firm may have no experience with importing and additional expertise may have to be hired. The firm may then be faced with finding a market for the goods, incurring market entry costs and possibly establishing a distribution network. The goods may not arrive in convenient quantities and may therefore have to be stored until they can be sold over time. They may have to be re-packaged or further processed to meet the requirements of local consumers.

Of course, the firm receiving the goods in exchange may not wish to undertake these activities itself, particularly if the product line is not one with which it is familiar. In this case the product may be sold to another firm but at a discount. Barter arrangements appear to be the least popular form of countertrade. The associated transactions costs are sufficient in magnitude to make such arrangements unattractive (Banks, 1983). Stories of firms desperate to make an export sale who were subsequently lumbered with shoddily produced and unreliable televisions or unpalatable canned meat are sufficiently common to suggest that firms should be extremely careful when considering entering into a barter arrangement with a state trading agency.

Buy-back agreements

Buy-back arrangements usually entail the exporter supplying capital equipment and/or technical expertise for use in a new or upgraded production facility. A share in the future output from the facility is taken in payment. Raw material inputs may also be provided with repayment taken in the form of a portion of the output produced.

Buy-back agreements can also involve considerable hidden or unanticipated transactions costs. In some cases, the output produced may fit well within the exporting firm's activities and, hence, transactions costs are low. A steel producer who provides technical expertise to a new steel mill under a buy-back arrangement may well be able to integrate the additional steel received into its existing distribution system without much difficulty. On the other hand, a firm which produces paper making machinery may have no experience with the marketing of paper. Arranging for the disposal of the output received in payment may require considerable additional expenditure. It is likely that the buy-back arrangement was suggested by the state trading agency in the first place because it did not have a ready market for the paper.

Even if the product received as payment in a buy-back arrangement fits well within the exporting firm's operation, there still may be problems with scheduling deliveries. This can be a significant problem if the product received in return is an input into further production. If the facility in the other country cannot keep to its agreed production schedule then alternative supplies may have to be arranged, often at higher costs. If the output is specialized to the production of the receiving firm – suggesting high switching costs – production may be disrupted. For example, if a car manufacturer provided engine making machinery and expertise to produce engines for a particular line of its vehicles, no suitable alternative engine may be available if production in the engine plant is disrupted or the rate of production fails to meet a priori expectations.

If these problems were encountered in normal business transactions between private firms, the purchaser of the engines would have a number of alternatives. If management at the engine plant was perceived as the problem, then the car manufacturer could buy up the engine manufacturer and install its own management. This may not be possible when the deal is made with a state trading agency. Even if an alternative supply can be found in the case of a disruption in production, the firm is still bound to take the pre-specified quantity of output. A mismatch between the now available supply of the input and orders for the final output could be the result. Further, if the firm receiving the inputs has overestimated demand for its final output, it may be forced to carry excessive inventories of the agreed input because of the fixed quantities in the agreement.

Even if the product received in return is not an input into the exporting firm's production, problems may arise if the product does not meet the originally specified quality standards. The firm can refuse to accept the resulting output but is then in the position of not having received payment for the goods or services originally provided. If the state trading agency chooses to dispute the firm's claims regarding quality, then redress will have to be sought in the courts. State trading agencies, however, may receive preferred treatment from national courts. This is particularly true when state trading agencies are an integral component of government economic policy and courts are not independent.

Counter-purchase arrangements

Counter-purchase arrangements consist of two cash transactions without the need for foreign exchange. The exporter receives payment in the importer's local currency or credits equal to the pre-agreed value of goods or services which the exporter provides. These must be spent within the state trading agency's country. As the firm is allowed to select the items it takes in return, counter-purchase arrangements are more flexible than barter or buy-back agreements. The firm, however, is still faced with identifying suitable products to purchase and with arranging for import and eventual disposal.

If international trade is entirely under the control of a country's state trading agencies, the payment portion of the counter-purchase agreement will also have to be arranged with a state trading agency. The agency may attempt to restrict the range of products to which the firm has access – possibly to goods which are in surplus or which it finds difficult to sell internationally due to poor quality. Further, the state trading agency will have full information on the amount that the exporting firm must spend. If the goods on offer do not have a transparent domestic market or prices are set by the state, the state trading agency may be able to manipulate prices to reduce the firm's expected returns.

Many of the problems faced by private firms in their dealings with state trading agencies relate to the agency acting opportunistically. There are a number of reasons why this type of behaviour is more prevalent in state trading agencies. Countertrade exchanges tend to be large-scale one-off arrangements. The most important inhibitor of opportunistic behaviour is the threat of loss of future business. This is not a major concern in the case of arrangements which are not to be repeated. Further, as state trading agencies are not necessarily motivated by profits, the threat of the loss of future profits will weigh less in the decision making process. As state trading agencies may be large, private firms may find themselves dealing with a different set of negotiators for each transaction. As a result, personal relationships and mutual trust may fail to develop.

Even if the official policy of the state trading agency is to not act opportunistically, the advancement of bureaucrats in state trading agencies may not be based on long-term results. Hence, they may have an incentive to act opportunistically to maximize their own personal satisfaction – a **principal-agent** problem. [Principal-agent problems relate to providing incentives for employees or other agents to act in ways which those setting the objectives – the principals – desire. In bureaucratic organizations like state trading agencies where measuring employees output (such as promoting repeat business over a number of years) is particularly difficult, opportunities for employees to act in ways different from those desired by the principals are likely to be numerous. For a discussion of principal-agent theory see Strong and Waterson (1987).] Further, state trading agencies in communist countries or those with strong socialist traditions may perceive private firms as socially undesirable and, hence, opportunistic behaviour towards them as being politically acceptable.

Firms should not be surprised when extra transactions costs arise from countertrade arrangements. Market determined prices, payment in money and a fully convertible currency are considered necessary conditions for efficient international trade. These conditions are seldom manifest when state trading agencies are party to international transactions. Firms should take particular care to plan for additional costs when dealing with state trading agencies.

REFERENCES

Banks, G. (1983) The economics and politics of countertrade. *World Economy*, **6**, 159–81.

Henderson, R. D. A. and Kerr, W. A. (1984/85) The theory and practice of economic relations between CMEA member states and African countries. *Journal of Contemporary African Studies*, **4**(1/2), 3–35.

Hennart, J. (1989) The transaction cost rationale for countertrade. *Journal of Law, Economics and Organization*, **5**(1), 127–53.

Mises, L. von (1981) *Socialism: An Economic and Sociological Analysis*, 3rd English edition, Liberty Classics, Indianapolis, IN.

Strong, N. and Waterson, M. (1987) Principals, agents and information, in *The Economics of the Firm*, (eds R. Clarke and T. McGuinness), Basil Blackwell, Oxford, pp. 18–41.

Williamson, O. E. (1985) *The Economic Institutions of Capitalism: Firms, Markets and Relational Contracting*, Free Press, New York.

Production firms and trading houses 13

WHAT IS A TRADING HOUSE?

Some firms specialize in organizing the international movement of goods. These import/export firms or **'trading houses'** act primarily as intermediaries between producers in exporting countries and users or distributors in importing countries. Trading houses may operate in one country or transnationally. If the trading house does not operate transnationally, it may deal exclusively with individual trading houses in other countries or a limited number of agents. In some cases, firms which started as trading houses have vertically integrated backward or forward into production or distribution activities and are virtually indistinguishable from transnational conglomerates. They may, however, still be referred to as trading houses. A producing firm which is thinking about expanding sales by entering a foreign market has a choice of directly exporting or using a trading house to expand its sales. Trading houses, however, should be distinguished from customs brokers or shipping agents which are only used by firms to facilitate the actual transnational movement of goods between countries.

The firm which is considering using a trading house may have the option of selling their product directly to the trading house or having the trading house act as their agent. This decision depends on the degree of control that the firm wishes to retain over its product in the marketing and distribution stages. In the case of the largest trading houses, a joint venture arrangement may be considered. As a result, the product expertise of the firm wishing to enter the foreign market can be directly combined with the trading house's knowledge of the local market. Importers can also be pro-active in using the trading house to aid in the search for foreign suppliers.

WHY USE A TRADING HOUSE?

Trading houses are a means to reduce the transactions costs associated with entering a foreign market. Their ability to reduce transactions costs will be determined by a number of factors including, the characteristics of the product which will be exported, the characteristics of the market to be entered, the characteristics of the firm wishing to enter the foreign market and the importance of the potential market to the exporting firm.

Trading houses act to reduce transactions costs by providing a convenient grouping of services. They may also be able to take advantage of economies of scale. Hence, they play a similar role to department stores or warehouse discounters in a domestic market. There are considerable costs associated with entry into a foreign market – costs of identifying potential customers from a distance, travel costs for personnel, verification of the potential customer's reputation, compliance with foreign government regulations, identification, and selection of foreign legal, banking, taxation and other business support services. Trading houses are able to spread these costs over a large number of transactions. Further, once a trading house has been in operation for a considerable period, it is not faced with the costs associated with learning by doing that a firm which decides to enter a foreign market directly will have to incur.

Product characteristics

Some products lend themselves better to being sold through a trading house than others. When a firm does not need to retain control of the product in the marketing and distribution stages a trading house may be cost effective. Generic products, which do not need any advertising support, can be sold to trading houses. It is then up to the trading house to locate a distribution system. When marketing a brand name is important to a product's success in a foreign market, the exporting firm may benefit from direct contact with the distributors. The experience which the exporting firm has gained in marketing its product's in the home market can be utilized to full advantage in this case. Of course, advertising and other promotion strategies may have to be tailored to the local market. Close co-operation may be required between the exporter and foreign distributors. When brand reputation is important, the firm may also wish to maintain control over distribution. Foreign distributors who do not properly care for, display or price the exporter's product to advantage can be dropped. For example, a firm may base its promotional activities on creating a quality image for its brand. The foreign distributor may try to capitalize on the quality image to its own advantage by selling the product at discounted prices. This will attract additional customers to its premises and add to the sales of the other products it carries. The process of discounting, however, may cheapen the image of the product with consumers and act against the interests of the exporting firm. Selling the product to a trading house means that this form of control is lost.

'Stand alone' or 'self-contained' products are more amenable to sale to a trading house than those which carry a large after-sales service component. After-sales services such as maintenance, repairs, spare parts, warranty work and replacement of defective units require specialized knowledge of the product which a trading house is unlikely to have and would find costly to invest in. As a result, firms wishing to export these types of products may well find it more efficient to set up their own transnational distribution organizations.

If the exporting firm perceives that the product it wishes to enter a foreign market with is 'risky' in terms of its possible acceptance in the market, then selling to a trading house may be a way to formally eliminate the risk. When approached, the trading house will contact its offices or agents in the target country to investigate the potential market. This should include an assessment of the risks associated with attempting to sell the product in that market. The trading house should be able to carry out the assessment at a lower cost than the producing firm because of its experience in the country. Risks can also be spread over the entire range of products that the trading house handles. Certainly, the trading house will take account of the risks when it determines the price it will pay for the product, but it does assume the risk. Of course, the problems which risk creates will be more important for producing firms who are small or where the foreign market is expected to be a large proportion of the firm's revenue.

When the producing firm is confident that its product will receive ready acceptance in the target market, then instead of selling the product to the trading house it may have the choice of using the trading house as an agent. This would mean that the producing firm will have access to the expertise of the trading house in the target market but will retain ownership of its product. The producing firm, however, assumes any risks associated with sales of its products. The trading house will simply charge a fee for its services. Of course, a producing firm's relationship with a trading house need not remain static. A producing firm may, at the initial stage of market entry when perceived risks are high, choose to sell directly to the trading house. If the market develops successfully and the risk level falls, the trading house can then be hired as an agent. At some point the market may become sufficiently developed that the producing firm may wish to consider direct sales to foreign distributors or to establish a transnational distribution operation. Hence, a trading house can be a useful stepping stone to full market entry over the long run.

Market characteristics

The characteristics of the market to be entered – or more correctly the degree of difference between the market targeted for entry and the markets with which the producing firm has experience – will be important in determining whether a trading house is used. If the target market's consumers are similar to those in the producing firm's home market, if business practices are similar, if there are no major language difficulties and if the interaction between business and government is undertaken under the same philosophical basis as in the home country, then it may be a simple matter to conduct business directly with foreign firms. The cost of learning how to deal with the 'foreignness' of the market will be low. Mistakes, and the losses associated with them, will be reduced. When these differences are large, however, trading houses become a much more cost-effective means of conducting international commerce.

For example, in the interface between east Asian businesses and western business, trading houses have taken a major role. In some cases they have come to dominate trade. This is particularly true in Japan where *Sogo Shosha* such as Mitsubishi and Mitsui are major forces in the national economy. The ten largest Japanese trading companies handle approximately 50% of Japan's exports and 60% of imports. The largest firms have in excess of 100 overseas offices. Further, due to their extensive international networks, these trading companies conduct a considerable proportion of their business by arranging commercial transactions between firms in third countries (e.g. between the Philippines and Peru). The major Japanese trading houses have developed a wider expertise which includes insurance, banking, distribution, marketing and management support plus air, ocean and land transport. They have extensive networks of subsidiaries and many business partners. They also have close relations with the Japanese government.

The Japanese trading companies arose, and still prosper, because business practices developed very differently in Japan and there is still a shortage of Japanese who understand and feel comfortable dealing with western business people. There are considerable differences between Japanese and western culture, in methods of conducting business and, in particular, business etiquette. While the study of Japanese business techniques has become popular since the spectacular Japanese success in the 1970s and 1980s, previously very little was known about Japan. Japanese education was very inward looking and foreigners were discouraged from living and working in Japan. The Japanese written language, which is based partially on characters rather than an alphabet, requires a very large investment in time for foreigners to learn. In the period when Japan was beginning to trade with the world, most European and American firms were unwilling to make the investment necessary to learn about the Japanese market. The task fell to the Japanese to develop trade links. Trading companies were the most efficient way to organize the limited quantity of Japanese people sufficiently versed in western methods to be of use in facilitating trade. Even today, there are few western firms who will spend the resources necessary to understand the Japanese market well enough to operate there directly.

Many western firms have lost lucrative export opportunities because they attempted to conduct business in Japan in the same fashion as in the west. In many cases the Japanese were offended, often in ways western firms were never able to comprehend. Many Japanese firms have had similar experiences when they attempt to enter western markets. For example, Japanese business relies much more heavily on building relationships based on trust and much less on contracts than their western counterparts. Japanese executives often feel pressured into concluding business deals before they feel they can trust western business people. On the other hand, western executives feel that the Japanese waste time and will not close a deal. Western firms are more hierarchical in their decision structure and, hence, are able to make decisions quickly. Japanese firms seek to make internal decisions by consensus, a much slower process.

Trading houses such as Jardine Matheson and Co. and Hutchison Whampoa developed in Hong Kong, primarily to facilitate western trade with China. They handled the problem of the cultural interface by internalizing it within the company's structure through the use of local Chinese *compradors*. These employees or exclusive agents were able to develop the personal relationships upon which most business in China is based. Any cultural conflicts were kept within the firms. The costs associated with misunderstandings were minimized through trust built up over long years of co-operation based on mutual benefit.

Keeping the cross-cultural relationships few and long standing meant that investment costs of cross cultural education were minimized for both the Europeans and the Chinese. In a similar fashion, the lifetime employment practices of Japanese firms made the considerable investment required of Japanese employers to train staff to deal with foreign firms more worthwhile than similar investments made by western firms for their more transient employees to learn about Japan.

The wider the cultural gulf between two countries, the larger the investment that will be required to directly trade successfully with the other country. A trading house can provide a cost advantage when this gulf is large. Identification of the right trading company to suit the particular requirements of the firm wishing to enter the foreign market may, however, require a considerable degree of investigation. Some trading houses are very specialized while others are broad based. Individual trading houses offer different ranges of services. Hence, there will be a matching process which may take considerable time to arrive at. Some trading companies act transnationally while others operate nationally. The latter may deal with a limited number of trusted agents in the foreign country. Again, the reason for the limited number of contacts is related to the investment time required to identify potential agents which can be trusted. Smaller or less well established trading companies may not have as effective or reliable foreign agents.

For some commodities, it may be virtually impossible not to use a trading house. This is because moving the commodity requires specialized handling equipment or because some industries' markets are relatively closed. The international transfer of grain, for example, is almost exclusively controlled by grain trading firms like Cargil or Continental Grain.

Characteristics of the exporting firm

Many of the costs associated with directly entering a foreign market, either through direct distribution or by trading with foreign firms without a trading house to act as an intermediary, can be considered indivisible or lumpy. This means that they are not related to the quantity of output sold. Business travel, negotiation time, business communications, paperwork, investments in machinery or other technology to comply with foreign customs regulations may be the same whether a 100 items or 50 000 items are sold. Clearly, the more units of output that are sold for export the lower the per unit costs of these activities. As a result, using a trading house may be much more cost effective for firms wishing to sell a small volume. If, over time, the market expands and develops, then a threshold may be reached where the firm may wish to consider dispensing with the use of a trading house.

Importance of the market

If a firm expects the market to be an important or long-term market for its product, it may wish to undertake the expense of direct market development from the outset. This is because using a trading house will mean that the firm will avoid the process of learning about the foreign market. In other words, it will become reliant on the services of the trading house and its contacts and agents. If the agents are closely tied to the trading house, then it may not be possible to deal with them independently when the producing firm decides that market volumes could justify dispensing with the services of the trading house. Even if retailers or other end users can be identified and contacted, they may not wish to damage their relationship with the trading house by dealing directly. Further, they may simply not trust the unknown producing firm even if they have direct experience with the commercial potential of the product itself. The production firm will be no further ahead than it was originally. The possible disruption to the normal distribution systems when the production firm subsequently attempts to enter the market independently may be costly.

QUESTIONS OF CULTURE

Clearly, the decision whether or not to use a trading house as the means to accomplish a firm's international ambitions is a complex one. Firms should not, however, underestimate the value of the services that a trading house can provide. Many production firms have not taken seriously the different ways business is conducted around the world. Even simple differences in language can cause loss of sales or ruin a major promotional launch. A car manufacturer spent considerable effort in inventing a catchy name – at least for the ears of an English speaker – for one of its new models. In the process it inadvertently picked a word which was suggestive of poor performance in Spanish – Nova translates as 'no go'. The launch of the car in Spain and Latin America was a disaster. Even when the same language is spoken, subtle differences in usage can thwart a marketing effort. The best salesman for a British manufacturer of writing materials and related products could not understand the cool reception and the lack of orders he received from a sales trip to visit the rather staid firms in the US stationary industry. It was not until he had been back in the UK for a while and was having a beer with an American friend that he discovered that the full range of rubbers he was offering US customers were taken to be condoms – the American term is eraser!

Business can involve a good deal of entertaining. The firm in a host country has a chance to trot out a range of culinary delicacies. Unprepared western executives in Asia have caused great offence by refusing oriental delicacies such as dog or live seafood. Eating with the left hand in Arab countries gives great offence. British firms have offered Muslim visitors ham and Hindu buyers beef. The results have been the same, offence, loss of a mutually beneficial transaction and the possibility of gaining a reputation which will have a detrimental effect on wider business prospects. There is no single culprit in these situations – both the buyer and the seller need to spend the resources to be better briefed. To understand when no offence was intended and that there are always ways to politely refuse is only efficient business practice.

Cross-cultural problems do not only arise in direct business dealings. Firms have sent employees with a fondness for alcohol to countries in the Middle East where consumption of alcohol is banned. The wives of western executives are often unprepared for the restraints put on women in some Muslim countries. Most problems can be avoided by careful preparation and screening of those who are to deal with foreign clients. The best salesperson in the local market may be the wrong person to send abroad. All of these screening and training activities add to the costs of organizing successful foreign transactions. As is often the case with advertising or other forms of marketing, these activities may be treated as a cost rather than a investment by company management. A company's international division may require considerably higher investments per sale, particularly in the early days of entering a new market. The division may have a difficult time justifying these investments to senior management who are only familiar with the types of activities required in the home market.

There are many means by which the transactions costs of entering or operating in a foreign market can be reduced if a firm decides not to use the services of a trading house. Firstly, it may be possible to hire personnel with valuable human capital. The children of immigrants from the country where market potential has been identified can often be particularly useful in helping to bridge the cultural gap. They are likely to have an appreciation of both cultures and be able to explain the obvious pitfalls or *faux-pas* to be avoided. Often they are bi-lingual and can be used for the direct conduct of negotiations. Even when they are not fully knowledgeable of their parent's former country, they are unlikely to require the same investment to 'get up to speed' as someone from an entirely different culture.

A firm should take care, however, before one hires the children of immigrants. For example, the children of Japanese who have immigrated to the US are often treated with suspicion by the Japanese. Similarly, while it may be an asset to have employees who are conversant in the language of the country to which exporting is to take place, this will not always be the case. It has been suggested that Japanese executives prefer to negotiate with foreign business people through a translator. The translation process allows them a longer time to formulate their responses.

Culture can often be used to advantage. Business people, particularly when they are new to a foreign environment, may be uneasy and unsure. A friendly face can get them relaxed or even leave them open to exploitation for commercial advantage. Japanese firms have been known to send one of their own employees, who was a native of the visitors country, to meet them at the airport on arrival. The task of the employee is to find out when the visitor has booked his flight home. Once this information is obtained from the 'friendly face', the firm's operation is co-ordinated so that the visitor is kept busy – touring the plant, meeting large numbers of apparently senior executives, wining and dining. A few preliminary negotiation sessions may be arranged but nothing substantive. All the while the clock is ticking and the visitor, who has an employer who has spent a lot of money on the trip and who will expect results, begins to politely ask when serious negotiations will begin. All manner of stalling tactics are used, unsettling the visitor even more. Finally, an hour or two before his plane leaves the Japanese make some form of offer. The visitor, out of time and with nothing to show will, it is expected, be willing to grant terms favourable to the hosts. Investing in the 'friendly face' can yield a high return.

THE COST OF IDENTIFYING NEW MARKETS

One of the major investments faced by a firm which chooses not to employ the services of a trading house is locating prospective buyers or suppliers in foreign countries. This **cost of search** is recognized as formidable by business organizations such as Chambers of Commerce and by governments. As a result, both provide a number of services aimed at lowering this transaction cost for individual firms. Trade shows and fairs provide a relatively low cost means of bringing large numbers of buyers and sellers together in one place. This lowers the cost of search for both parties. These gatherings, however, add a considerable element of competition. The buyer or seller is able to directly compare the firms they may wish to deal with. Chambers of Commerce provide a low cost means of identifying the dates, locations and the requirements of trade shows. Further, there are organizations which specialize in individual product lines, e.g. electronics, toys, wine, sporting goods, etc., which offer more focused gatherings.

Firms wishing to have an exhibit at an international show need to research both the expected clientele and the most effective means of communicating their message. A display that is considered very effective in the home market may fail to communicate in a foreign market. It may appear amateurish when compared with the sophisticated offerings of firms with considerable international experience.

Many governments have programmes aimed at helping firms wishing to enter foreign markets. The programmes attempt to lower the costs of searching out customers. Embassies in foreign countries have commercial attachés and other staff whose job it is to become familiar with the country's markets and commercial practices. They develop contacts with foreign business people. They can often be useful in identifying potential customers and getting an initial meeting organized. Governments also arrange formal visits for groups of business people where a large number of potential contacts are arranged. Often these trips are wholly or partially subsidized. Visits for potential foreign customers can be organized. Commercial attachés can often aid in the process of evaluating a potential customer. They may know the foreign firm's reputation or be able to suggest organizations in the foreign country which can provide an evaluation.

Banks which specialize in international transactions or which operate transnationally can often provide information which can aid in the evaluation of the reliability of potential foreign customers. They may also provide insights into business practices as well as assessments of political risk. They will be familiar with the regulations affecting the international transfer of funds.

Of course, the very wide range of services provided by Chambers of Commerce, governments and merchant banks are also provided in various forms by large trading houses. When one considers all of the activities which must be undertaken by each individual firm which chooses to organize its own international activities, it is not difficult to understand why trading houses have been so successful. As the world has effectively shrunk due to better communications and lower travel costs, the world business community has become more cosmopolitan. The widespread emulation of the American model of business education is reducing differences in business practices. International trading houses may find their competitive advantages eroded. The costs of organizing international transactions, however, are ever changing and the dynamics of world markets will continue to evolve. New markets and new technologies may arise where trading houses will be able to deliver their services at a cost advantage. Firms trading in other markets may no longer choose to employ their services. Firms engaging in international commerce will have to continue to consider whether or not trading houses provide the least cost means of accessing foreign markets.

Summary
Part Four

There is no one model of a successful international firm – one which has its product or service consumed in more than one country. Successful firms range from small one person import/export businesses run from an individual's home, to large conglomerates like Mitsubishi, to focused specialized firms like McDonalds, to government operations like the Canadian Wheat Board, to universities, to franchised dancing schools. The means by which they organize the vertical co-ordination required to accomplish international transactions is also extremely varied – spot markets, franchises, subsidiaries, agents, contracts, joint ventures, countertrade, licences. This continuing, and probably increasing, diversity suggests that firms, both those considering entering a foreign market for the first time and those who have been involved in international commerce for centuries, need to evaluate carefully the method that they will use to conduct international commerce. As with any business venture, long-term success will depend on the ability of the firm to adapt to new market opportunities and to changes in its costs.

International commerce has additional costs associated with both the identification of market opportunities and completion of transactions. Even if a firm does not directly organize its international commercial activities but rather employs an intermediary, it must still be cognizant of these costs to evaluate the services of its agent. The volume of international trade and commerce has been growing at a more rapid rate than most domestic economies. This suggests that foreign markets are worthy of more than a casual glance. Given the nature of the additional transactions costs involved, evaluations need to be done carefully.

The process of entering a new foreign market will be the most costly phase of international commerce. Once foreign markets are successfully entered, the special activities required will become familiar and routine. There will always be the additional costs associated with currency exchange, customs regulations and staff training. Products will have to be altered or modifications made to service activities to satisfy foreign tastes. Differences in business practices and cultures will always present a challenge. They need to be dealt with within the rational framework of expected returns on investment. The key is to realize that most 'problems' will arise because insufficient investments were made in investigating those practices which make foreign transactions different from those in the familiar home market.

Institutions that facilitate international trade

PART 5

Introduction to Part Five

Transactions between firms in two countries will almost always be more expensive than carrying out a similar transaction within one country. These international transactions costs can be sufficiently high that firms may seek out alternatives to directly exporting their products to firms located in other countries. The alternatives include joint ventures, licensing, franchises, vertically integrated transnational operations and selling to a trading house. Direct exporting, however, remains one of the most important methods of conducting international business. A number of institutions have developed over the long evolution of international commerce which act to reduce the transactions costs associated with organizing the movement of goods between firms located in different countries. These primarily private sector institutions charge a fee for their services. These fees must be taken into account when decisions regarding direct exporting are made. Direct exporting will be the mechanism used to undertake international business activities if the transactions costs associated with direct exporting are less than those associated with the alternatives.

A number of problems face the direct exporter once a tentative agreement has been negotiated with a foreign customer. It is important to stress that this is a point in time when only an agreement in principle regarding the transaction has been reached. Part of the final negotiations will relate to the specific institutional instruments which will be used to ensure that the transaction is completed to the satisfaction of both parties. Direct export opportunities, which appear to be mutually beneficial for both parties, often fail to take place because agreement cannot be reached on how to complete the transaction.

The three major problems facing a potential exporter are:

1. How is the transaction to be financed?
2. How are the goods to be physically moved from the exporting firm to the importing firm?
3. How are any disputes to be resolved?

These potential problem areas should be addressed prior to any transaction taking place – whether it is the simplest of domestic transactions or complicated international contracts.

For example, consider a simple transaction at a vegetable market – a customer negotiating the purchase of tomatoes from a vendor. Once a price and quantity have been agreed to there are implicit, if not explicit, rules that exist to facilitate even this basic transaction. The transaction is financed by the direct exchange of currency. This ensures that the seller gets paid. Unless the buyer and seller have developed a relationship of mutual trust over a long association, credit is seldom extended and payment by cheque is not acceptable. This is because the transactions costs associated with the seller verifying the credit worthiness of the buyer, or with chasing down the buyer if payment on the cheque is stopped, are simply too high. The buyer carries the tomatoes away from the stall removing any need on the sellers part to arrange transport.

Disputes are minimized because the buyer is allowed to visually inspect the tomatoes which will be purchased. *Caveat emptor* (buyer beware) applies to other aspects of the tomatoes' quality which the buyer cannot detect during the visual inspection. The quality of a tomato eventually consumed in the home of the consumer can be affected by the treatment it receives by the consumer after the exchange and over which the seller has no control. Hence, to prevent disputes, the implicit rule of *caveat emptor* normally applies to this type of transaction.

Transactions are, however, seldom so simple. Payment terms are negotiated based on letters of credit and 30 or 60 days for payment are pre-specified. Who pays for and arranges transport is subject to negotiation. Formal contracts are drawn up which attempt to carefully set out the exact conditions of the transaction and to outline an agreed course of action if problems arise. Contracts are an attempt to reduce the probability of disputes and the eventual costs associated with resolving them. If disputes do arise, they are ultimately solved by litigation in the courts. For international transactions, these potential problem areas become more complex and potentially more costly.

The increase in costs associated with international transactions arise for a number of reasons. Firstly, there is no international commercial law supported by a supernational legal system. As a result, if one party fails to live up to the terms and conditions of an international contract, the costs associated with solving the dispute rise and the risk of not achieving a satisfactory outcome increases. Secondly, as both the distances and the time involved between when the goods are shipped and when they are received in the buyer's premises tend to increase with international transactions, the potential for problems to arise while goods are in transit increases. Even if distances are short, time can be added due to the need to clear customs. Thirdly, two currencies will be involved in the transaction and this will complicate the negotiations surrounding payment. Fourthly, establishing the trustworthiness of the other party to a transaction is likely to be more costly when it has to be done at a distance and across cultures. While these costs and risks cannot be eliminated, specialized international institutions exist to help reduce both the costs and risks. In most cases, a range of services exist from which firms can choose. Costs vary and finding a mutually satisfactory mix of services is a subject for negotiation between exporter and importer.

Introduction to Part Five

An exporter is faced with the problem of ensuring that payment will actually be received for the product sold to the foreign firm. In the best of all worlds, exporters would be paid in their own currency deposited in their domestic bank by the importer prior to the shipment of the goods. There would be no risk for the exporter. This procedure, however, may not be acceptable to the importer because, once the exporter has received payment, the importer is vulnerable if the exporter chooses not to honour the contract and fails to ship the goods. The importer may attempt litigation in the courts of the exporting country but legal costs may be prohibitive and the courts may be biased in favour of their own country's firms. Faced with this prospect, the importer may simply refuse to conclude the deal. On the other hand, the exporter may not be willing to risk shipping its goods and trusting the buyer to pay once the goods have been received. The exporter would be faced with litigation costs and the possibility that the importer's national courts are biased. A number of alternative means of payment have been devised which reduce the ability of firms to act opportunistically. These will be discussed in detail in Chapter 14.

Most international transactions involve a time lag between when a deal is negotiated and when the goods are finally delivered. Problems can arise as a result of the need to convert payment from one currency to another. This is because exchange rates are not normally fixed. Even when they are fixed, the possibility of devaluation always exists. A change in exchange rates over the time lag between conclusion of the contract negotiations and receipt of the goods will mean that one party may not receive the amount which it expected. A change in the exchange rate can wipe out the profits expected in the international transaction. The perceived exchange rate risks may be high enough for one party to prevent a successful conclusion to negotiations. Again, private market mechanisms exist which can reduce these risks, but at a cost.

Specialized enterprises have developed to facilitate the movement of goods between countries. There are institutions which help to reduce the transactions costs faced by firms wishing to export using sea or air transport. Air freight forwarders act to consolidate the shipments of a number exporters so that bulk rates can be secured for their customers. Unique documents have been developed to standardize and facilitate the movement of sea freight. International insurance markets exist and the apportioning of liabilities among carriers, warehousers and the contracting clients is relatively standardized. Firms involved in exporting are faced with choices of transportation and insurance which must be weighed carefully when an export sale is being negotiated. It is often necessary to use customs brokers to facilitate the passage of goods across borders. The price negotiated in the contract can be used to apportion these costs between buyer and seller. For example, f.o.b. prices mean that the seller is responsible for all costs up to and including when the goods are loaded aboard the aircraft or ship that carries them abroad. This means that the costs of transport via the international carrier, insurance costs and the costs of delivery to the buyer's premises are paid by the buyer.

However, c.i.f. prices mean that the costs of international transport and insurance are paid for by the seller. Prices can also be quoted on the basis of 'ex works' where the importer takes responsibility for all aspects of the transaction after the product leaves the premises of the exporter. Prices may also be quoted 'as delivered' to the premises of the importer. Some firms may be able to negotiate better rates than others for transport and insurance. As a result, these aspects of the transaction need to be carefully negotiated.

As there is no system of international commercial law enforced by a supernational organization, national courts remain the last resort for legal recourse in the case of a contract dispute. The slowness, costs and the possibility of national bias associated with the use of courts has led to international arbitration being provided by the private sector as a cost reducing alternative. Arbitration by neutral parties can be chosen at any time by the mutual agreement of the disputing parties. International contracts often specify the use of arbitration if a dispute subsequently arises.

The costs of organizing international transactions tend to be higher than those associated with strictly domestic transactions. Firms, however, have the option of using a number of institutional arrangements which have developed in the private sector to reduce the costs faced by any firm wishing to undertake international transactions. The key is to choose the right mix of instruments to minimize these costs given the particular circumstances surrounding the transaction.

Financing international transactions 14

ARRANGING FOR PAYMENT

The financing of international transactions has three elements:

1. Arranging for payment.
2. Securing foreign exchange.
3. Reducing the risks associated with changes in the exchange rate.

When considering export transactions, one of the most important points of negotiation is ensuring that payment is received. The converse, of course, is to ensure that the goods paid for are actually received. When a business deal is negotiated with a firm located in a country which has a different business ethic, whose personnel are not well known, and where recourse to the court system is costly at best and biased at worst, an exporter is prudent if he worries whether it will be paid. The transaction is simply open to opportunistic behaviour on the part of the other party to the contract. Full insistence on pre-payment in advance, however, leaves the importer open to opportunistic behaviour. The exporter may simply fail to ship the goods once payment has been received. While this may appear to be a pessimistic view of business practices, the very existence of a number of elaborate mechanisms which attempt to overcome the problem of ensuring payment suggests that examples of firms choosing to behave opportunistically are sufficiently numerous to create a demand for these services.

The probability of non-payment is most acute when the business arrangement being negotiated is not likely to be repeated. If future mutually advantageous deals are probable, then neither side in the transaction has a incentive to act opportunistically by failing to pay (or failing to ship) the goods. Repeat business is the best insurance policy against opportunistic behaviour. It also allows time for the parties to become familiar with each other and to establish a relationship based on mutual trust. If such a continuing relationship can be built up over time, the costs of ensuring payment will be minimized.

Open account

The least cost method of organizing payment is an **open account** system. The exporter simply ships the goods and invoices the buyer with payment being due at a specified time after the goods are received. The importer pays with his own cheque and the only costs are the bank clearing charges. Of course, this is similar to most domestic transactions. The exporting firm must, however, be willing to pay any charges associated with technical problems related to payment and suffer the consequences for cash flow of any delays. Communicating with foreign banks and tracing down any problems with payment, even when the buyer is not behaving opportunistically, will increase costs. Open account, however, is probably a reasonable method to use with foreign customers with whom one has built up a successful ongoing business relationship.

If a firm uses an open account billing system and the buyer refuses to pay, the cost may be greater than in the case for a similar situation in the domestic market. This will be true even if litigation costs are no higher and the national courts in the buyer's country are not biased. For example, over the period that the goods are in transit, the foreign firm may become insolvent or simply change its mind and refuse to accept the goods. The exporter still owns the goods but is faced with the choice of either finding another foreign buyer or bringing the goods home. Finding another buyer in a foreign country may take considerable effort and expense (e.g. to fly out sales personnel). Making alternative arrangements may take considerable time and, as a result, storage costs will be incurred. If the goods are to be brought home, then the extra cost of international transport and insurance may have to be borne. In some cases, the import tariffs and customs duties associated with importing the goods back into the country will have to be paid. The final result may be that it is less costly to sell the goods off at a considerable discount in the original country of destination.

Outright refusal to pay may not be the preferred strategy for firms having to consider the prospects of future business relations. Buyers, however, may still have considerable latitude to act opportunistically by attempting to re-negotiate the agreed price. For example, the buyer may claim that the goods have not arrived in the condition specified in the contract and refuse to take delivery. They may then propose a price reduction. It may be very costly for the exporter to verify the condition of the goods (e.g. flying out company personnel on short notice may be prohibitively expensive). The exporter, faced with either finding another buyer or transporting the goods home, may find the original buyer's reduced price offer the least costly alternative (Kerr *et al.*, 1990). The buyer is speculating that the seller will be sufficiently unsure about the validity of its claim and that future deals will not be affected. The great majority of international arbitrations relate to disputes over the condition of delivered goods and the appropriate price discount. This suggests that verification problems are common.

Documentary collection

Banks specializing in international transactions provide a range of services which can be used to reduce the risk of non-payment. One method is to arrange for documentary collection. The bank acts as an intermediary between the seller and buyer. The buyer cannot gain control of the goods unless payment is made. This removes the opportunity of refusing to pay once the goods are received – increasing the sellers security. Once a deal is negotiated, the seller ships its goods and then takes the documents that will secure the release of the goods from either the shipping company or a warehousing firm in the buyer's country to its bank. The seller's bank then sends the documents to a bank in the buyer's country which it considers to be reliable. When the goods arrive, the buyer is notified. The buyer must make payment to the bank before it can receive the documents that will release the goods. The buyer takes the documents to where the goods are held, presents the documents and takes delivery. The bank in the buyer's country forwards payment to the seller's bank. The bank charges a percentage of the shipment's value for this service.

Risks still remain for the exporter. As there is normally a time lag between when the goods are shipped and when they are received, the buyer may decide that it no longer wishes to purchase the goods. Hence, the buyer may simply not attempt to claim the documents from the bank in its country. The result is that the seller has incurred all the cost of shipping its goods and, effectively, has no buyer. The seller's bank may be instructed to make a protest through a Notary Public that the bill has not been paid at maturity, but that is the extent of its obligation. Neither bank provides any guarantee of payment. The 'protest' can form the basis of litigation but the seller is still faced with the costs and risks of litigation in a foreign country. One way an exporter can reduce its potential losses is to negotiate the quoted price on a f.o.b. basis. This means that the importer pays for the cost of international transport and insurance and, hence, will be less likely to walk away from the shipment. At the time that the shipment must be paid for, however, the cost of transport and insurance represent a **sunk cost**. Based on its perception of the current market the buyer may still not want to accept the goods.

If the importer does not collect the documents, the exporter is faced with finding and conducting negotiations with a new buyer and paying storage or demurrage charges. The alternative is to pay for the goods to be transported back to the seller's country.

To provide a measure of standardization, and hence to reduce the costs of becoming informed about documentary collection procedures, the International Chamber of Commerce, a non-governmental organization supported by business, has developed uniform rules for collections. Its conventions are followed by most banks dealing in international transactions.

Documentary Letters of Credit

Documentary Letters of Credit represent the next level of security for ensuring payment in international transactions. This is because the buyer's bank, and possibly a bank in the seller's country, act as guarantors of payment. A list of pre-specified conditions, however, must be met. Documentary Letters of Credit have two aspects. Firstly, there is a Letter of Credit whereby the importer's bank guarantees payment if the exporter fulfils a set of pre-established criteria by a certain date. Secondly, there is a package of pre-specified documents which provide the evidence that the seller has fulfilled its contractual obligations.

Once a contract is agreed upon, including the list of documents which will act as the proof that the exporter has fulfilled its obligations, the importer contacts its bank to draw up a Letter of Credit which specifies the amount to be paid to the exporter. The importer's bank guarantees payment to the exporter. It is the bank's responsibility to secure payment from the importer. The Letter of Credit also sets out the documents that the exporter must provide the bank with before payment can be made.

The documents required to complete the transaction will vary depending on the nature of the goods. The exporter must provide proof that the goods have actually been shipped – bills of lading for sea transport, railway consignment notes, waybills for trucks, air waybills for air freight, etc. An invoice giving a complete description of the goods will be required. The accuracy of the description may have to be verified by independent experts. This provides the importer with assurance that the exporter is actually shipping what is required. This is very important because the bank only deals in documents and in no way guarantees the quality or quantity of the goods actually shipped. If the documents conform to the requirements specified in the Letter of Credit, then the bank will make payment. The bank has no interest in whether the goods shipped conform to the specifications agreed in the contract. Hence, it is important that the documents required in the Letter of Credit reflect the goods envisioned in the original contract. If the exporter is to arrange insurance for the shipment, then proof of insurance will be required. Documents which provide evidence of health inspection may be required for shipments of food and live animals. Independent chemical analyses may be required in the case of potentially dangerous goods.

The documents required can be complex. It is the responsibility of the bank to scrutinize the documents carefully before releasing payment. If there is a discrepancy in the documents which the bank does not detect, then the buyer can refuse to pay the bank. In one study of Documentary Letters of Credit, 50% of the documents failed to conform to the pre-established conditions on first presentation to the bank (Paliwoda, 1991). At best, having to amend the documentation to ensure compliance can delay payment. Rectifying discrepancies can be expensive, however, if the goods have already been shipped. In some cases, it may mean cancellation of the contract. The bank can attempt to contact the buyer to determine if the discrepancy is acceptable. Payment will only be made, however, once the bank is completely satisfied. The extra costs associated with these documentary discrepancies means that exporters must exercise considerable diligence to ensure that the documents are correct. Otherwise, what is supposed to be a low risk transaction will still be subject to a considerable degree of risk.

Even if the documents conform to the pre-established criteria, there are different types of Documentary Letters of Credit – each of which involves different degrees of risk. **Revocable credits** can be cancelled by either the exporter or importer at any time before the documents are presented. This means that the exporter is at risk if the goods have already been shipped or if the order has been produced to a buyer's unique specifications. In the former case, the exporter will still own its goods but they will be in a foreign country without a buyer. In the latter case, the exporter will be in possession of goods which may be of only limited use to other customers and, hence, can only be sold at a discount. Revocable credits should only be used when the seller is sure of the buyers need for the goods.

Irrevocable credits cannot be altered by either party unilaterally. The conditions can only be changed by the mutual agreement of both parties. In normal commercial conditions, irrevocable credits are sufficient to ensure that the seller will be paid. The importer's bank acts as a guarantor.

Irrevocable credits, however, may not provide sufficient security of payment if the exporter is concerned about the ability of the importer's bank to fulfil its role. This concern may arise due to problems with the bank's solvency or because of a high degree of political risk in the buyer's country. It may be possible to arrange for a bank in the exporter's home country, or a reputable bank in a third country, to guarantee payment. This is called an **irrevocable confirmed credit**. Obtaining this guarantee may not always be possible if the bank which the exporter asks to provide the guarantee perceives that the risk is too great. The exporter's bank, however, may be better able to assume the risk than an individual company and, hence, be willing to provide the service. It can spread the risk over a large number of international transactions in a number of countries. Further, the bank in the importer's country may be far more reluctant to default to a major international bank than it would be to default to an individual exporting firm. Defaulting to another bank could threaten its ability to engage in international transactions in the future. In some cases, the same considerations may influence the actions of government agencies allocating foreign exchange. They may be more reluctant to refuse foreign exchange which is to be paid to a foreign bank than if payments to an individual foreign company are involved.

While irrevocable confirmed credits ensure that the exporters get paid, they do not protect the importer who is dependent upon particular suppliers. While the buyer will not have to pay for goods that are not shipped, if the exporter simply fails to show up with the documents by the specified time – does not ship the goods – then the importer is faced with a breach of contract. It will be forced to search out alternative suppliers and to initiate legal proceedings for breach of contract in the seller's country.

The precautions which have to be taken to ensure against either an involuntary failure to pay or opportunistic behaviour by buyers may appear excessive. Approximately 20% of exports are facilitated through the use of Documentary Letters of Credit suggesting that businesses feel that the risks are real. Letters of credit may cost 0.25% of the value of the shipment but volume discounts are available in some cases.

To reduce the cost of acquiring information, the private sector has developed widely accepted rules for drawing up and using Documentary Letters of Credit. These rules are provided by the Uniform Customs and Practice for Documentary Credits of the International Chamber of Commerce.

Factoring and discounting

In some cases, exporters may not wish to wait for payments from importers, particularly when long delays are involved. Further, they may not be willing to attempt to collect foreign debt themselves. They may find it simpler to pay someone else to deal with these inconveniences and assume the risks involved. The large international banks have institutionalized these functions through subsidiaries known as factors.

For firms which simply suffer from cash flow problems, factors provide a discounting service for international transactions. The exporter turns its invoices over to the factor in return for an immediate payment which can be equal to 75% (or less) of the invoices' face value. When the invoices are due they must be re-purchased by the exporter at face value. The foreign buyer continues to pay the exporter directly. If the foreign buyer fails to pay the debt, securing payment is still the responsibility of the exporter. The buyer may not even know that its invoices have been discounted.

When the exporting firm has no interest in being involved in collecting bad debts or payments in arrears from foreign customers, they can use the service called **factoring**. In this case, the firm acting as the factor becomes responsible for collecting foreign debts. The exporter continues to invoice the foreign buyers but the buyer pays the factor directly.

The factor keeps a running ledger of the invoices, informs the buyer when it is in arrears and is ultimately responsible for any bad debts. A limit to the amount of invoice debt the factor will accept will be negotiated. This limit will depend on the degree of risk perceived by the factor. Factors are particularly useful for firms which have small export sales or are new in a market. Factors are experienced in determining the credit worthiness of firms in foreign countries. They have staff – or hire foreign firms – to collect accounts in arrears. If export sales volumes are small, the costs of carrying out these activities themselves may be prohibitively high for exporters.

The factor charges a commission for its services and discounts the value of the invoices based on its assessment of the risks involved. The exporter, however, receives immediate payment while the factor may be willing to accept invoices with term of payment of up to 180 days.

Transactions costs may also be reduced for the exporter because it only has to deal with one factor instead of a large number of foreign customers. As each country will have a particular degree of risk, its own institutional rules and a unique business culture, staff savings can be significant when the exports of the firm are spread over a large number of small markets.

Factoring, however, may create other problems for the exporter. The buyer may take offence at having its credit worthiness implicitly questioned when the seller chooses to use factoring. Further, a factor may be less knowledgeable regarding the special circumstances which may arise in a industry than an exporter who is directly involved. As a result, importers may feel that factors are less sensitive to their problems than an exporter. They may choose not to do business with the exporter at a future date. As a business relationship grows, the need for factoring declines. An exporter must weigh the risk of destroying the possibility of developing an ongoing business relationship against the risk of a relatively unknown importing firm failing to pay.

The decision to use the services of a factor as a means to overcome problems with cash flow should be considered carefully. Given the high costs associated with foreign market entry, exporting should not be approached as a short-term opportunity. A severe cash flow constraint might suggest that the time is not right to initiate a program of export sales. The discounts and fees charged by factors will lower the profitability of exporting in the short run. This may mean less resources for developing products better suited to foreign tastes and, hence, reduce profits in the long run. If the firm is unable to service a growing market because the upper limit on the value of invoices established by the factor is reached, then the firm may not be able to fully service the market. The exporter's reputation as a reliable supplier could suffer and future developments in export markets affected.

Forfaiting

Discounting and factoring are arrangements for problems which arise from short-term delays in payment. The delay in payment which is acceptable to factors would seldom exceed 180 days. Many export arrangements, however, are based on payment schemes set out in long-term contracts. This will often be the case when capital goods such as industrial machinery are being exported or when the construction period is very long as is the case with power plants, railways, hydro-electric facilities and factories. Foreign buyers are allowed to make payments over time. The buyer may, for example, need to sell some of the output produced with imported machinery to pay for the machinery. A problem only arises when the foreign buyer cannot enter international capital markets directly to obtain financing for the imports. Often, this constraint is the result of restrictions on accessing capital put in place by the buyer's government. Further, past actions of the importer's government may have led lending institutions to believe that commercial transactions with firms in that country are too risky. Special arrangements have been required for long-term contracts with command economies and developing countries. It should be emphasized that the risks or constraints discussed here arise from conditions outside of the control of the importing firm. Commercial criteria must first be used to assess the ability of the importer to fulfil its contractual obligations.

The exporting firm has two problems: it needs to reduce the risk of not being paid by the buyer and it needs to secure the means to finance the deal over the life of the contract. These two services are combined by firms which engage in **forfaiting**. The term arises from the French term, *à forfait*, which implies the forfeiting of rights. The forfaiter accepts a risk by giving up the right to ask the exporter for repayment of the loan used to finance an export contract. Most firms which offer forfaiting services are located in Switzerland, Austria, Germany or the UK.

The need for this type of service arose from changing commercial conditions. In the late 1950s the capital goods markets changed from a seller's market to a buyer's market. In addition, the process of de-colonization led to an increase in the number of capital importing markets where levels of political risk were high. Command economies also began to purchase western machinery and equipment. The strictly controlled capital and foreign exchange markets of command economies meant that exporters required access to long-term export financing if they were to be able to successfully negotiate a sale. In response to this demand, forfaiting evolved to provide a medium-term means for exporters to finance the credits required by importers. Typically, if the services of a forfaiter are required, financing will be needed for approximately 80% of the export sale. To ensure good faith on the part of the importer, immediate payment of 20% of the value of the contract is normally required.

The forfaiter acts as the guarantor of last resort against non-payment by the importer. The exporter receives financing for the arrangements in the contract and is freed from having to undertake collection activities if the importer defaults on his payments. The exporter receives immediate payment against the importer's promises to pay in the future. The forfaiter both discounts the value of the promissory notes and charges a commission for its services. Transactions financed through forfaiting are complex and involve at least five parties:

1. The exporter requiring financing.
2. The importer who promises to pay for the goods and services provided by the exporter.
3. The importer's bank which must provide a guarantee for the importer.
4. The forfaiter which acts as the guarantor of final recourse.
5. An investor, usually an international bank, which purchases the importer's promises to pay at a discount from the forfaiter.

A typical forfaiting arrangement is organized as follows. The importer and exporter agree to a schedule of deliveries and/or work over a number of years. Payments on a fixed schedule are agreed subject to a forfaiter being willing to finance the undertaking. The exporter obtains a commitment from the forfaiter for financing. The forfaiter offers the exporter a fixed discount rate on the future receipts and agrees to make payment to the exporter upon receiving the importer's promises of payment. The importer draws up a number of promissory notes against the delivery of the goods and services. The importer then arranges an **aval** with a bank acceptable to the forfaiter. This is the only guarantee that the forfaiter has against its loan to the exporter because it has forfeited its rights to seek repayment from the exporter if the importer fails to honour its promissory notes. This guarantee must not be conditional on the exporter fulfilling its part of the arrangement with the importer because the forfaiter has no right to seek repayment from the exporter. Hence, the importer's bank must assess the trustworthiness of not only the importer but also the exporter.

Once the aval has been arranged, the importer delivers the endorsed promissory notes to the exporter. The exporter endorses the promissory notes and delivers them to the forfaiter and receives the previously agree discounted payment. The forfaiter endorses the notes and sells them to investors on international money markets. The investor holding the promissory notes presents them to the importer at the appropriate point in time and receives payment. If payment is not forthcoming, the investor presents them to the importer's guaranteeing bank and demands payment under the terms of the aval. Only if both the importer and the importer's bank default will the investor present the notes to the forfaiter who has guaranteed them. The forfaiter pays the investor and then must attempt to obtain payment from the defaulters.

The forfaiter is fundamentally a country risk specialist who must assess the risk that the notes will be honoured by the importer's bank. Forfaiters also assemble packages of discounted promissory notes which will be of interest to investors. The offerings of forfaiters represent a high yield component of an investor's portfolio. Forfaiters tend to limit their commitments to offerings of promissory notes whose due date is in less than 7 years. Presumably, they find it difficult to assess risks with a sufficient degree of accuracy for longer periods into the future.

The discount rates applied by forfaiters are determined by the cost of money in the Euromarket for the period of financing. The additional fee which the forfaiter charges ranges from 0.1 to 0.125% per month (1.2 to 1.5% per year). The exact rate will be determined by the forfaiter's assessment of the degree of risk in the importing country.

This long and detailed discussion of forfaiting arrangements underlines the difficulties which are associated with assuring payment for some international transactions. Clearly, it is an extremely complex system that the parties to a transaction would seek to avoid. This suggests that when forfaiting is used, the perceived political risks must be significant.

To fully understand the services which forfaiters provide – and that exporters are willing to pay for – it is necessary to examine a transaction in detail. Before entering into a contract the exporter must make a commercial assessment of the likelihood that the importer will pay. If that assessment is not positive it is unlikely that the deal will be acceptable to the bank chosen by the importer to provide the guarantee. In other words, the bank must have a positive assessment of the importer's willingness and ability to pay prior to the contract being signed. The bank must also assess the likelihood that the exporter will fulfil its contractual obligations. The 'investor' must assess the reputation of the forfaiter before it will accept the discounted promissory notes on offer. Hence, the only risk which the forfaiter must assess and set fees against is the risk that the importer's bank will fail to honour the conditions of its aval. While it is true that banks do fail due to poor management, this does not happen sufficiently often to justify the fees charged by forfaiters. The real question is why an exporter would choose to pay for the services of a forfaiter if they could obtain the same unconditional guarantee for the promissory notes from the importer's bank. Over £2 billion of exports are financed by forfaiting each year suggesting that the problem of political risk requires closer examination.

Political risk

Political risk arises when normal international business practices may be adversely affected in the future by political events. It may involve a change in the relationship between a firm operating in a foreign country and that country's government. It may arise because the government of a foreign country can no longer guarantee the peace and security required for the smooth functioning of businesses. Political risk may also arise as the result of a deterioration in the political relations between the governments of two firms engaged in an international transaction.

Governments can adversely affect businesses, including banks, by imposing regulations which reduce profitability. Changes in legislation or poor economic management can adversely affect the operations of firms. Examples might be government legislation restricting access to foreign exchange or the inability to control inflation. Governments can affect ownership rights through expropriation.

If a nation's government is faced with insurrection or social unrest, firms may find it increasingly difficult to conduct business. Politically motivated strikes may prevent workers from arriving for work. The transport of inputs or outputs may be affected. Fuel, electricity and water supplies may be disrupted.

Governments may also lack the ability to enforce commercial law. This will mean that the cost of doing business will rise. Without strong enforcement of commercial law, there will be less constraints on opportunistic behaviour. If promises to pay cannot be enforced, transactions will have to be undertaken in cash. The use of cash payments is both cumbersome and time consuming. All of these are major problems in the former command economies. Doing business in cash also means that business people are easy targets for hold-ups. If robbery and theft cannot be controlled by the police force, then firms will have to spend additional resources to secure their premises and hire private security guards. For example, most firms in the Philippines employ large numbers of security personnel. When the government cannot guarantee the commercial environment, a fertile ground is created for organized crime to regulate the conduct of business. Of course, organized crime extracts a heavy price for this service. In Russia, for example, firms must pay protection money to organized crime if they wish to operate in peace.

Corruption is another source of political risk. If government officials do not fear prosecution for demanding bribes, the cost of doing business will rise as they are able to privately charge for the services they are paid by the government to provide. Firms dealing with corrupt officials become subject to their whims. While relatively formal rituals may evolve to facilitate the payment of bribes, firms may suddenly find their activities at risk if government personnel change and new rituals have to be established. Further, firms who have been actively engaged in bribery may find themselves under investigation if the government initiates an anti-corruption campaign. If the firm is involved in corruption in high places, a change of government may find the firm identified with the old regime and the subject of investigation by the new government.

When governments clash, long-term commercial arrangements may suddenly be at risk. Restrictions may be put on payments to firms or individuals in the country with which there is a dispute. The assets of the other nation's citizens may be frozen. Iraqi assets in Britain were frozen at the time of the Gulf War. Business travel may be restricted. Direct air flights may be suspended between the countries, adding to the cost of transportation. A number of countries, including the US, do not allow their airlines to provide services to Libya. Border inspections and customs clearance may become more difficult and time consuming. The movement of certain goods may require special licences or may be banned entirely. In some cases, the international community may impose sanctions on governments whose behaviour it considers unacceptable. Sanctions were placed on trade with South Africa until the fall of the apartheid regime. All of these events can make it more difficult for firms to live up to their previously agreed commitments. They may not be able to continue with existing mutually profitable business arrangements with firms in the other country.

Assessing political risk requires that firms expend resources to acquire information. Some easily available proxies for the economic performance of governments can be found in the ratings given to government bonds by firms such as Standard and Poor's. As the assessment of political risk is complex, however, a number of specialized private firms provide this service. Firms who are in the process of negotiating a major foreign contract may well wish to employ such a firm. The hiring of these firms on a short-term basis may be more effective than keeping political risk specialists on staff. The assessment of political risk, however, is to a considerable degree an art rather than a science and, as a result, the quality of the work produced may be difficult to assess. A firm has no recourse if the assessment is not accurate. When the services of a forfaiter are employed, for example, the forfaiter has a direct interest in the results of its assessments because of the guarantees it provides.

The range and complexity of private sector mechanisms which exist to ensure that payment is received when international transactions are entered into suggests that the risk of non-payment is high. In addition to private mechanisms, many governments provide guarantees of payment – export financing guarantees. In some cases they can be obtained at lower rates than those commercially available. In other cases they may be available for situations where the private sector is unwilling to accept the risk. Often government guarantees can be used to secure private sector financing. Securing government funds or guarantees, of course, is a skill in itself and firms may have to expend considerable resources to be successful. Further, governments tend to move at a pace which is frustrating for firms attempting to take advantage of an export opportunity.

ACQUIRING FOREIGN EXCHANGE

One of the major complications arising in international transactions is that at some point one of the parties to the transaction will have to convert the currency it uses in its own country into the currency of the country of the other firm. This has two aspects. The first is the costs and problems associated with converting or acquiring foreign currency. The second relates to the problems created when rates of exchange change over time. As many international transactions involve a time lag between when a deal is concluded and when payment is finally made, there is the possibility that changes in the exchange rate can reduce the profits expected from the transaction or even turn a profitable transaction into one where a loss is incurred. There are, however, institutional arrangements whereby firms can protect themselves against adverse movements in the exchange rate. Problems associated with changing exchange rates and the actions firms can take to protect themselves from these changes will be discussed in the next section. The problems and costs associated with the acquisition of foreign currency will be dealt with here.

No universally acceptable international currency has evolved even though the existence of such a currency would considerably simplify international commerce. The costs, both in terms of the fees charged for currency exchange and in the delays which may surround the acquisition of foreign currency should not be underestimated. For example, it is a popular exercise for the press in the EU, where currency markets are very advanced, to illustrate these costs by starting with some nominal amount, say £100 in a British bank. The currency then follows an orderly progression through the banking systems of the 12 member states with the conversion commissions and other bank charges deducted at each stage. Typically, very little remains of the £100 when the cycle is completed with the re-deposit of the residual amount in a British bank. The complete cycle of transactions may also take more than 6 weeks. This example certainly overstates the unit cost of converting currencies because there is usually a lump sum charge per transaction made by a bank as well as a percentage commission. Even these lump sum charges, however, may become important constraints to some types of international businesses such as mail order houses due to the large cost each consumer faces when they must arrange international payment.

The movement to an internationally accepted currency has been resisted by national governments because the loss of currency sovereignty means that they would have much less control over their national economies. Macro-economic policies, particularly the ability to establish independent interest rates through the use of monetary policy, requires a national currency.

In the past, gold may have come close to serving as an independent international currency. International contracts were delineated in gold and, while national currencies existed, they were freely convertible to gold. While the exchange rate between the local currency and gold could change over time, the costs of exchange were minimized. This **gold standard** system of exchange worked reasonably well in an era when national governments were much less involved in macro-economic management of the economy. The restrictions which the gold standard places on governments' freedom of action makes the system no longer acceptable. Of course, gold is costly to transport and its purity must be verified. Gold is also far too cumbersome to be used to finance the volume of international transactions which currently exist.

At times, other currencies such as the US dollar have gained considerable international acceptance. Using a single currency as an international standard allows the country which issues the currency considerable freedom in its economic policy. Other countries may be adversely affected. Even in sub-groupings of states such as the EU, where most internal trade barriers have been removed and the transactions costs associated with currency exchange are high, the movement to monetary union and a single currency has been hotly debated and stoutly resisted by some countries.

Convertible currencies

The simplest way for a firm to eliminate the costs associated with currency conversion is to impose all of the costs on the other party to the international transaction. An exporting firm, for example, could insist that all payments be received in its national currency. All of the costs of currency conversion would be paid by the importer. Of course, whether the importer will agree to assume those costs depends upon the relative bargaining position of the two parties during negotiations. If the exporter's competitors are offering to accept payment in the importer's currency, then it may not be possible to require payment in the seller's national currency.

In the long run, the costs of exchanging currencies will be reflected in the prices which firms are willing to pay or must charge. Even if it is possible to impose the costs of currency conversion on the other party to the transaction, it may not be desirable to do so. Banks or other financial institutions in different countries may charge different rates to convert currency. Further, firms dealing in large quantities of foreign currency will be eligible to receive preferred rates. By accepting the task of currency conversion and, hence, reducing transactions costs, the firm with the ability to secure a preferred rate will be able to make the entire deal look more attractive.

Controlled access to foreign exchange

While there are direct costs associated with exchanging currencies in economies where currencies are freely convertible, there may be far larger indirect costs imposed on international transactions when currencies are not freely convertible. Governments may wish to control access to foreign currency for a number of reasons. They may wish to control the international purchases of individuals for ideological reasons or to prevent the transfer of assets out of the country. In most cases, however, control over the acquisition of foreign currency is used to ration shortages of foreign currencies. If a government is following a macro-economic policy which fixes its exchange rate at a level where the demand for imports exceeds the value of exports which foreigners are willing to purchase, then some form of foreign exchange rationing will be required. This means that the domestic currency is overvalued relative to the particular foreign currency. If market forces were allowed to operate, the cost of purchasing foreign currency should rise. The government may not wish to allow the price of foreign currency to rise because it will increase the price of imports, including some whose price the government wishes to keep low for political reasons. In a number of African countries, the government keeps down the price of foreign currencies so that food can be imported at low cost to feed the people in large coastal cities.

If a government deliberately overvalues its currency, there is excess demand for foreign currency at the official exchange rate. Governments must develop mechanisms to apportion the limited quantities of foreign exchange among those who wish to acquire it. This usually means that the government designates some imports as having a higher priority than others. For example, capital equipment, essential inputs for industrial production and food staples may be designated high priority items. Luxury consumer goods and tourist trips abroad will be given lower priorities. Only when all the demands for foreign exchange for higher priority imports have been satisfied will foreign exchange be allocated for lower priority items.

Even if the products which constitute an import transaction are in the high priority category, the agency charged with rationing foreign exchange will have to be satisfied that the products fall into the priority category. At the very least, extra paperwork will be involved and there will be delays until bureaucratic approval is received. If the goods involved in the deal have been designated as lower priority items, then the entire transaction may be considerably delayed until the country's foreign exchange position improves sufficiently for an allocation to become available. For some goods, this position may never be reached and the deal cannot be completed. Failure to complete a transaction can be particularly costly when the exporting firm is producing a product to meet an importer's unique requirements. There may be no alternative market for the product.

Governments may not be willing to consider allocating foreign currency to the importer until the goods are actually received. If an allocation of currency is not subsequently made, then the exporter is faced with the choice of bringing its product back home or abandoning it. Even if currency is eventually made available, the exporting firm may suffer from cash flow problems as a result of the long delays. The risks associated with non-convertible currencies need to be anticipated by firms wishing to engage in international transactions.

If the official exchange rate is set at a rate where the domestic currency is overvalued relative to a foreign currency, there will be excess demand for the foreign currency. Black markets will arise. As the foreign currency is in short supply, the black market conversion rate will be at a rate where it takes more units of domestic currency to acquire the same quantity of the foreign currency than at the official rate. Conversely, this means that more domestic currency can be acquired for a unit of foreign currency on the black market. In effect, this makes goods priced in local currency more attractive. Importers will wish to purchase more goods than at the official exchange rate. Firms may be tempted to use the black market to acquire imports.

Of course, using the black market is illegal and the importing firm must weigh the risks of being caught and assess the likely penalties. These decisions become particularly difficult when competitors have decided to use the black market to acquire imports. The competitor will be able to offer the same imported goods at a lower price than an importer who acquired them using the official exchange rate.

As there can be a considerable incentive for importers to use the black market, governments are likely to put in place stringent regulations relating to the acquisition of domestic currency. These restrictions will require proof of the rate of exchange used to finance the transaction before the goods can be released for export. As a result, additional time will have to be spent arranging proof that currency was exchanged at the official rate.

Governments which do not wish their citizens to acquire foreign exchange may set up elaborate mechanisms to inhibit the functioning of black markets. The government of China, for example, for years operated a system of dual currencies – one which was convertible and one which was not. This meant that all business people visiting China had to purchase convertible Chinese currency at the official rate. Every transaction to purchase local Chinese commodities became a challenge because individual Chinese would refuse to give change in convertible currency, even if they had it (Kwaczek and Kerr, 1986). Officially they were not allowed access to the convertible Chinese currency. The only alternative was to seek out official tourist stores which dealt in convertible Chinese currency, a time consuming activity. The net result was that western business people were likely to spend more in China than they otherwise would have. The cost of doing business in China was increased. Adding layers of complexity to currency exchange will inevitably add to the cost of doing business internationally.

CHANGES IN EXCHANGE RATES

In the past, most countries followed fixed **exchange rate** policies. Currently, however, many countries follow flexible or 'floating' exchange rate regimes. The exchange value of the currency is determined, at least within certain limits, by the forces of supply and demand in international money markets. This change has made international transactions more complex for firms.

Under a fixed exchange rate policy, the rate at which a nation's currency could be exchanged for each other currency was set by the government. If demand by foreigners for the nation's currency exceeded the supply provided by domestic firms seeking to purchase foreign currencies – implying that the relative price of the domestic currency should rise – then the government or its central bank would sell additional domestic currency into the international money markets. Foreign currency was received in exchange. This foreign currency formed the county's foreign exchange reserves. If the supply of domestic currency in international markets exceeded the demand for the currency at the fixed price – implying that relative price of the domestic currency should fall – then the government would intervene in the market by using its foreign exchange reserves to purchase domestic currency. In this way the fixed rate was maintained.

Fixed exchange rates

Fixed exchange rate regimes meant that, except in exceptional circumstances, firms did not have to be concerned about changes in the exchange rate between the point in time when a deal was agreed and when payment was received. The exceptional circumstances, however, could have devastating consequences. The system worked well as long as the fixed rate reflected the underlying economic forces in the two economies and exports equalled imports – including flows of monetary capital – over the long run. If the demand for imports consistently exceeded the exports which could be sold to foreigners, then the amount of domestic currency being supplied into the international market to finance imports would exceed the demand for the currency by foreigners to purchase exports. As a result, the government would be consistently running down its foreign reserves to defend its currency. Foreign reserves, however, are not inexhaustible. Once they have been exhausted, the government can no longer defend the rate at which the exchange of currencies was fixed. When this occurred, the government was forced to devalue the currency, fix the rate at a new level.

Devaluations tended to be quite large changes in the exchange rate. As a result, one party to an international transaction – agreed to prior to the devaluation but where payment did not take place until after the devaluation – was certain to lose. Hence, while fixed exchange rates in most instances simplified international transactions for businesses, when a devaluation appeared likely, international transactions became extremely risky. As a result, mutually profitable business deals were often put on hold for long periods when a government appeared to be having difficulties with its foreign exchange reserves.

Devaluations were common in the 1930s. After World War II the US and the UK took the lead in designing new international monetary institutions – known as the **Bretton Woods system**. The International Monetary Fund (IMF) was its central organization. The Bretton Woods system was a fixed (pegged) exchange rate regime. While devaluations were still possible, they could not be used as part of strategic macro-economic policy. The IMF managed a pool of gold and currencies which could be allocated to countries faced with devaluation. The system of pegged exchange rates could not be sustained and in 1973 the exchange rates of the major industrial nations began floating.

Fixed exchange rates restrict the ability of governments to pursue independent macro-economic policies. Some governments still attempt to follow fixed exchange rate regimes by pegging the value of their currency to the currency of a major country, e.g. dollars, pounds or deutschemarks. In most developed economies, however, the exchange rate is allowed to float. Central banks may, at times, actively intervene in the exchange markets by buying and selling foreign reserves. They intervene to prevent wide swings in currency values or to support the currency at levels which the government feels represent psychological thresholds for business confidence.

Flexible exchange rates

Variable exchange rates complicate international commercial activity. Changes in the exchange rate must be anticipated for each international transaction. Given the delays involved in organizing the international movements of goods, almost every transaction will be subject to a degree of exchange rate risk. The movement by governments to flexible exchange rates with the collapse of the Bretton Woods system led to the development of a number of institutions which allow firms to manage this risk.

The exchange rate may, of course, move to the advantage of the firm which is arranging payments. There will be a period between the placement of an order and when payment is due. A buyer in an international transaction can choose to use the **spot** (or current day's) **rate** to acquire the required foreign currency at any time. However, if the firm is risk averse, a number of alternatives to this speculative behaviour exist.

Currency Accounts

Banks often offer **Currency Accounts** as one of their services. This allows the firm to open a bank account in foreign funds removing the risks and costs of exchanging currency for every transaction. Currency Accounts are particularly useful when a firm is both selling and buying in a foreign market – so that there are both inflows and outflows of foreign currency. The firm can choose to exchange currency only when taking profits – which can often be delayed until the exchange rate is favourable. Of course, if the account moves into a deficit position then funds may have to be transferred to it when rates are unfavourable. Currency Accounts however, are not particularly useful for firms involved in one way trades, e.g. exporting but not importing, or when foreign transactions are undertaken on an intermittent basis.

Forward Exchange Contracts

Banks also offer **Forward Exchange Contracts**. These can be used most productively at the point in time when firms are negotiating the price at which an international transaction will take place. A Forward Exchange Contract is a promise by the bank to purchase or sell foreign exchange at a specified rate on a certain date – the future date when payment on the contract must be made. The advantage of Forward Exchange Contracts is that the firm knows the future exchange rate it will face. This exchange rate can be used in determining what price to set. The bank assumes the risk that their quoted forward rate is not the actual exchange rate at the time when payment comes due.

Fixed date contracts are only useful when the date when funds must be exchanged is known perfectly. It may not be possible, however, to know the exact day when a customer's payment will arrive. A **limited option** contract allows currency to be exchanged at any point within a 30 day period. The 30 day period might commence in 3 months time.

Unrestricted **option** contracts are also available. They allow currency to be exchanged on any day over the life of the Forward Exchange Contract. Of course, the exchange rates offered in limited option and option contracts are adjusted to reflect the risk which the bank is assuming by providing this degree of flexibility.

Borrowing foreign currency

Firms may also have the option of borrowing foreign currency. An importer may borrow foreign funds from its own bank on the day that negotiation of the contract is concluded. The current exchange rate is, of course, available to the firm. The borrowed foreign currency can immediately be exchanged for the firm's local currency – meaning the known 'spot' rate becomes the effective exchange rate for the transaction. The domestic currency could be invested or applied against debts owing in the domestic currency. As foreign currency payments arrive over time from the customer, they can be used to repay the foreign currency loan. The interest rate on the foreign currency loan will reflect the rate of interest applicable in foreign country whose currency is being borrowed. This is because this is the rate at which the bank will have to borrow the currency offered in the loan. Of course, large banks are able to borrow foreign currency at rates lower than individual firms, hence the reason that they are able to offer the service at advantageous rates.

Hedging currency on the futures market

The exchange rates at which banks can offer a Foreign Exchange Contract will be established in the **futures markets** for foreign exchange. Futures markets for some agricultural commodities have existed for over 100 years. They represent formal markets where individuals can exercise their opinions about prices in the future. As the future cannot be seen clearly, differences in opinions regarding future prices are natural. When opinions are sufficiently strongly held regarding future prices, individuals may be willing to speculate financially based on their opinion. Speculators have no interest in actually selling or acquiring the commodities on whose price they are speculating. They are only interested in capitalizing on their skill at predicting prices. The formalization of speculation in futures markets provides a service for those who have an interest in reducing the risk associated with storing commodities for future sale or acquiring commodities at some time in the future. This activity is known as **hedging**. Basically, speculators assume the risks for those who wish to hedge on the futures market. Of course, if their speculations are correct, they will receive any windfall gains.

Under a flexible exchange rate system, a foreign currency is simply another commodity whose price is uncertain in the future. Futures markets in foreign exchange are relatively new financial instruments which have developed as a result of the movement from fixed to flexible exchange rates (Powers and Vogel, 1981). Assume a firm is about to enter into a foreign contract where payment will be made at some date, e.g. 6 months in the future. It can through a broker, buy or sell a futures contract to purchase foreign currency. Contracts are for standardized amounts of currency. At the date of maturity, the futures contract is closed out and no foreign exchange is actually taken delivery of. The spot market is used to acquire the foreign exchange needed to pay for the goods exported. Losses on the spot market should be offset by gains in the futures market or visa versa. The net result is to fix the rate of exchange for the original transaction involving goods. A detailed explanation of the working of a futures contract can be found in Gillis *et al.* (1990).

A firm may wish to use the futures market rather than a bank to manage its exchange rate risk. The ability to buy and sell futures contracts increases the firm's flexibility in dealing with exchange rate risks and also removes the bank as an intermediary – of course saving the bank's charges. Hedging currencies, however, may only be advantageous for major users of foreign exchange due to the large size of individual futures contracts (Gillis *et al.*, 1992).

Problems associated with payment are endemic in international transactions. Even when a foreign firm's willingness and ability to pay on time is not in question, the risks associated with variable exchange rates will remain. A large number of institutions have evolved in the private sector which allow firms wishing to engage in international commercial activities to reduce the transactions costs and risks associated with arranging for payment. If the institutions did not reduce transactions costs they would not survive. Identifying when to use a service provided by an individual institution is the challenge for firms engaging in international commerce. The mechanics of some of these institutional arrangements are extremely complex and evaluating the worth of the various services available is no easy task. Most contingencies can be addressed through the use of one or more of the existing institutional arrangements. It is still up to the individual company to determine which events have a sufficient probability of occurrence to warrant the use of a particular service.

REFERENCES

Gillis, K. G., Yoshida, S., Hobbs, J. E. and Kerr, W. A. (1990) A futures market for Japanese beef imports: is it the next logical step? *Kitami Daigaku Ronshu*, **24**(3), 33-67.

Gillis, K. G., Jameson, K. and Kerr, W. A. (1992) Transnational hedging – an added complexity for feedlot management in Canada. *Journal of International Farm Management*, **1**(3), 81-91.

Kerr, W. A., Hobbs, J. E. and Gillis, K. G. (1990) Reducing the risk of exporting to Japan: The development of market information, in *Selling Beef to Japan*, (eds D. K. Elton, W. A. Kerr, K. K. Klein and E. T. Penner), Canada West Foundation, Calgary, pp. 171-91.

Kwaczek, A. S. and Kerr, W. A. (1986) A note on the current Chinese experience with Gresham's Law. *Economic Notes*, **15**(1), 134-48.

Paliwoda, S. J. (1991) *International Marketing*, Butterworth-Heinemann, Oxford.

Powers, M. and Vogel, D. (1981) *Inside Financial Futures Markets*, John Wiley and Sons, New York.

Moving products between countries   15

THE MOVEMENT OF GOODS AND INTERNATIONAL TRANSPORTATION

As with the financing of international trade, a large number of specialized institutions have developed to facilitate the international movement of goods. Their effect is to reduce the transaction costs attached with physically transporting goods between countries.

Transporting goods between countries can take place using four mediums – ships, aircraft, rail and road vehicles. The bulk of internationally traded goods is carried by ships, although one should not overlook the use of road and rail transportation which often accounts for a high proportion of the trade carried between countries on the same continent. The carriage of goods by air, although small in volume terms (1–2%) is, however, large in terms of value (20%). Two modes of transport (shipping and air transport) will be discussed in this chapter as they account for the movement of the major portion of the value of internationally traded goods.

A TAXONOMY OF SEABORNE TRADE AND CARGOES

Cargoes can be of several types depending upon the type of shipping service used to carry them. The two most important categories are **bulk cargoes** and **general cargoes**. Bulk cargoes tend to be raw materials or semi-processed commodities.

Bulk cargoes can, in turn, be broken down into liquid cargoes such as petroleum, gas and chemicals and dry cargoes such as grain, iron ore, coal, bauxite and phosphate rock. Both these types of bulk cargoes are carried in specialized ships, for example, tankers in the case of liquid cargoes. They tend not to be packaged or protected physically in any special way except for the protection provided by the hull of the ship. Loading and unloading can be carried out by specialized equipment, but by and large, the operations are simple and routine.

General cargoes are made up of goods such as consumer products and machinery. The size of general cargoes is usually smaller than bulk cargoes and they often require specialized packaging and handling. Recently, with the expansion of trade in certain manufactured goods such as cars, specialist ships have been built for their transport. As a result they can almost be treated as bulk commodities.

The modern day bulk carrier has taken over the role of the latter day tramp freighter, it sails between ports picking up and dropping off cargoes and hardly ever enters its home port and may never visit its nation of registry.

Ships and shipping services

To transport goods by ship between countries, exporters/importers usually use the services of maritime brokers to acquire the appropriate vessels to carry their cargoes. The majority of cargoes are carried by independent shipping companies since very few exporters or importers own their own vessels. One major exception is the large transnational oil companies who own very large tanker fleets to transport petroleum and its derivative products. Some of the oil companies requirements are, however, also provided by independent shipping firms.

For the transportation of dry bulk cargoes, commodity dealers and others wishing to ship these commodities can approach ship owners directly. More commonly, however, these two parties are brought together by **shipbrokers** via the Baltic Exchange in London (Cochran, 1994). As with any market, the Baltic Exchange provides convenient and effective cost reducing place for sellers and buyers to exchange information. Brokers provide a service which matches buyers' requirements with the vessels available.

The Baltic, like many of the other City of London institutions, traces its origins back to a coffee house. When it was established in 1744, the bulk of the trade its customers dealt in was with the Baltic states, hence its name. Today's Baltic Exchange has 600 member companies, employing 2000 brokers who are entitled to trade on its 'floor'. It currently handles approximately two thirds of all the world's open market bulk cargo movements. Deals struck on the 'floor' stipulate the cargo to be carried, its size, the terms of carriage and the rate which is expressed in US dollars. The rules and regulations governing membership of the exchange, its ability to resolve disputes between members and its use of standardized contracts reduces the risks associated with international carriage.

The Baltic also plays a major role in tanker charters for liquid bulk transportation. Specialized brokers and agents, working mainly in London but also in New York and other minor regional centres, also arrange shipping on behalf of the shippers and ship owners. As with dry bulk carriers it is unlikely that tankers ever see their home port or nation of registry.

Bulk carriers are very similar, if not identical, and their characteristics and the reputation of their owners are well known to all. The rates at which ships are hired are reported daily in the trade papers such as *Lloyds List* and the *Journal of Commerce*. This availability of information at little cost suggests that the market for dry bulk and liquid carriers approximates that of the economists' model of perfect competition (Metaxas, 1978). Standardization, low cost information and the large number of brokers means that both ship owners and potential shippers do not have to spend time and resources identifying customers/ship owners and determining their reputations. Transparency pricing reduces negotation costs.

In contrast, the system under which general cargoes are transported is made up of a number of well organized international cartels (Ademuni-Odeke, 1988). General cargoes are carried by ships that have a fixed route and a timetable that applies to both arrivals and departures. These timetables are adhered to irrespective of whether the vessels are fully loaded or not. This is the so-called **liner trade**, since a company's vessels ply a particular route or line. The liner trade is often arranged around **conferences** which are, essentially, a cartel formed by the companies involved in certain routes. The conference sets rates of carriage, conditions for transportation, routing and timetabling. By controlling the membership of the cartel and maintaining other barriers to entry, i.e. restricting specialized port facilities to the members of the cartel, the conference is often able to restrict competition. The justification, for restrictive competition is that in return shippers face lower transportation risks. To have their goods transported exporters and importers can approach the liner companies directly or again use brokers.

The majority of liner conferences were formed in the latter part of the 19th century and the early part of the 20th. The transformation of European colonies into independent states and the rise of economic nationalism led many countries to question the composition of the conferences since the shipping companies of developed market economies dominated their membership. As a result, and to improve their development prospects, many less developed countries began to seek access to these conferences on behalf of their shipping companies. In many ways this was a logical move, ships are not very sophisticated pieces of capital equipment – the technology is not very complex and the human skills required can be obtained without too great a financial outlay. In other words, a developing country with a modicum of capital and human resources can fairly easily acquire a comparative advantage in shipping services.

Through UNCTAD, developing countries began to put pressure on the conferences for access under a specific code of conduct (Ademuni-Odeke, 1988). This code of conduct proposes that trade between two countries should be split between the ships of the nations involved on a 40%–40% basis, leaving the remaining 20% to be covered by ships of 'third' nations. This code has met with a great deal of opposition principally from the US which views it as anti-competitive. The EU has similar reservations although it concedes that its member states can sign the code as long as specific pro-competitive clauses are included. The EU has made it clear that the 40% limit must include equal access to all of the EU's shipping fleets and not just that of the signatory.

More recently the EU has been examining the workings of two major conference agreements to ascertain whether their price fixing and capacity controls are anti-competitive. The European Commission is monitoring the Trans Atlantic Agreement and the Europe Asia Trades Agreement which were signed in 1993 to stem the large losses incurred by ship owners on these routes. These agreements currently account for just over 70% of the container trade between Europe, the US and the Far East. European users of these routes argue that the practices of these conferences has raised the costs of carriage which has adversely affected the competitiveness of their goods (Walters, 1994).

The relatively small size of consignments of manufactured goods and the specialist packaging often required for their transportation makes them ideal for transport in containers. The advantage of **containerized carriage** is that the consignment can be loaded off the ship onto a lorry or railcar and transported to the factory, warehouse or directly to the retail outlet once having cleared customs. By carrying goods in containers, ship owners are able to use large vessels that give economies of scale. These modern-day liners contrast not only in size but also in structure to those seen up until the late 1950s and early 1960s. Small consignments were carried on a number of decks within their hulls – the so-called 'tween' deckers. Some of these older ships are still used on routes which have not been containerized although these routes are becoming fewer and fewer. For this trade, liner companies may revert to hiring ships on the open market – often via the Baltic Exchange.

The chartering of ships

The hiring of ships is referred to as **chartering**. There are several types of chartering, varying not only on the length of the period for which a vessel is hired but also on the nature of the shipment involved.

The simplest form of charter is the **single voyage charter** where a ship is hired to carry a particular amount of cargo between ports and either a lump sum is paid or a rate established per ton carried. A **trip charter** is similar to a single voyage charter but involves payment on a per day (or per diem) basis. Ship owners often prefer this type of charter since they are paid a rate even if delays occur.

Longer-term arrangements also exist which involve the hiring of a vessel or vessels for specified periods of time, i.e. 3 months, 1 year, 5 years, etc. These arrangements can be carried out on the basis of **consecutive voyages** which is like the single voyage charter except that the vessel is hired for a number of specified voyages carried out one after another. The **time charter** involves the ship being made available for a specific period of time and allows the charterer to employ the vessel between any ports required. Sometimes a company may want to hire a vessel, use its own crew and operate it as it wishes. This form of hiring is known as **bareboat chartering** and has been used by transnational oil companies as a way of increasing the size and flexibility of their fleets.

Owners of large fleets sometimes strike deals with the owners/purchasers of bulk commodities to transport a fixed amount of cargo between ports. These so-called **contracts of affreightment** allow owners to maximize the utilization of their fleets as individual vessels are not specified. The ship owners are, however, often required to specify the size of each shipment and the time of delivery.

It can be seen from the variety of contracts of carriage available that the international shipping industry provides considerable flexibility for those needing to export. This flexibility minimizes the difficulties involved in transporting goods over great distances. For cargo owners wishing to have regular deliveries, time charters, contracts of affreightment and bareboat charters are particularly useful not only in guaranteeing regularity of delivery but also in allowing transportation costs to be known in advance. This is important when prices are being negotiated in an export contract.

Single voyage and trip charters are more useful to exporters that need either to supplement their own capacity or where the product to be transported is highly seasonal or affected by other factors such as market fluctuations and political factors. This flexibility allows firms to take advantage of short-term export opportunities without making a major investment or long-term commitment in ships.

From the ship owner's point of view, the longer term charters provide revenue stability. Single voyage and trip charters can, on the other hand, be very lucrative especially when market conditions lead to a shortage of ships.

Conditions of carriage and service

As was indicated above, the prices of carriage or freight rates are determined largely by the open market. These rates, however, are quoted on a particular basis, dependent on the amount of service to be provided. The most common forms of price quotation are:

1. Free on board (f.o.b.).
2. Free along side (f.a.s.).
3. Cost, insurance and freight (c.i.f.).

Free on board, as discussed in Chapter 8, means that the exporter/seller of the good pays for the loading of the vessel and guarantees that the goods were placed on board the vessel damage free. The purchaser/importer pays for the insurance and the unloading of the vessel. Free along side implies that the seller places the cargo alongside the vessel in good condition. After that, the goods are the responsibility of the buyer who must incur loading costs and other costs such as insurance involved in the safe importation of the goods to their final destination. Cost insurance and freight indicates that the price of the good includes the cost of transportation, the insurance premium and the cost of the goods. In other words, the seller meets all the charges that are necessary to ensure the carriage of the goods to their destination in good condition. Those negotiating to ship cargo should carefully assess shiploading, insurance, etc., and compare them to the pricing options available. When considering arranging these services privately firms should be careful not to underestimate the potential monitoring costs.

The insuring of cargoes

An interesting feature of ocean transportation is that the carrier is not responsible for any loss or damage to the cargo unless negligence can be proved. As a result shippers, exporters and importers need to acquire insurance for their goods. This is usually taken out with underwriters who specialize in this work. Marine underwriting is a very complex area and tends to be carried out by the larger insurance companies and specialized institutions such as Lloyds of London. Again, to ease the procedure standardized contracts are used to cover one consignment or a series of consignments. Transaction costs for firms are, as a result, reduced.

AIR FREIGHT AND TRANSPORTATION

As has already been mentioned, air freight accounts for only a very small proportion of the international movement of goods, approximately 1–2% of trade by volume. In value terms, however, about one fifth of international trading is accounted for by air freight. It is one of the most rapidly growing forms of transport. The reasons for this are fairly straight forward. The current inability of aircraft to lift great weights and their high running costs means that they are inappropriate mediums when it comes to transporting low value bulky items. Aircraft are occasionally used in emergencies to transport heavy items but in general they are not used for the transportation of such goods. In contrast, aircraft are an ideal mode of transport when it comes to high value low density products such as diamonds, cut flowers and newspapers. Most importantly, of course, air freight is used when the speed of delivery is important.

The growth in air cargo

The growth in air transport can be accounted for by two principal factors: the ability of modern aircraft to carry heavier loads of up to 30 tons in the case of jumbo jets and the increase in demand for high value low density products. Other factors that are also of importance include:

1. The reduced transit time of air transport when compared to sea.
2. The location of airports near to important markets or centres – which may not be the case with sea ports.
3. The ease of cargo transfer between aircraft.

All these factors reduce the costs of shipment. Direct transportation costs however, may not be the only item that may give air freight an advantage over other forms of carriage. For example, lower transit times can translate themselves into lower inventory and stock requirements. The ease of shipment and lower journey times can lead to lower insurance costs. Finally, in the case where products are perishable or need to be shipped to a market quickly to take advantage of high prices, air transport may be the only mode of transport.

The supply of air services

Aircraft are provided either on a scheduled or chartered basis and therefore are akin to the services provided by ship owners; however, the regulation of air transport by countries has shaped the industry's structure and as a result it differs considerably from sea transport.

Nation states have taken a very active role in the regulation and promotion of their national airlines and, hence, a whole series of complex bilateral agreements exists between countries. These agreements control the number of flights between nations, the airports where foreign access is permitted and whether foreign airlines are allowed to pick up and carry passengers and cargo within a country's domestic market. These agreements do not have sea-going counterparts. It has usually been the practice to allow ships of any nation access to ports except when hostilities exist between nations or where cargoes are deemed to constitute a danger to the country.

Most of the major airlines offer cargo services and there are also some specialized cargo-only carriers. The bulk of air freight is offered on a scheduled basis so that shippers know exactly the times of departure and arrival. This enables a reduction in the uncertainties associated with transport. Where volumes do not warrant specialized cargo-carrying aircraft, consignments are transported in the holds of regular passenger aircraft.

The chartering of aircraft is usually confined to cases where the cargo requires specialist handling facilities or where access is required to areas which do not have regular scheduled flights. As with sea transport, the chartering of aircraft is carried out via brokers who bring together cargo interest and aircraft owners. Again, some of these arrangements are facilitated on the Baltic Exchange.

REFERENCES

Ademuni-Odeke (1988) *Shipping in International Relations*, Avbury, Aldershot.
Cochran, I. (1994) *The Baltic Exchange*, Lloyds List Publications, London.
Mextaxas, B. N. (1971) *The Economics of Tramp Shipping*, Athlone Press, London.
Walters, J. (1994) EU shipowners sail into ill wind. *The Observer Business News*, **19** (June).

16 The settlement of international commercial disputes

WHY DISPUTES ARISE

All but the simplest of international transactions will involve the use of a contract. Almost all international movements of commodities will take time to organize and involve the delivery of goods or services to a specified place in another country. Of course, many international transactions will be complex and include:

1. Specifications for quality and other performance criteria.
2. Dates for delivery and payment.
3. Arrangements for transportation, insurance and payment of customs duties.
4. Penalties for non-performance of the contract's provisions.
5. Appropriate remedies in cases when the contract provisions cannot be fulfilled due to no fault of the parties to the transaction.

It is not possible, however, to account for all future contingencies when a contract is being drawn up. In legal terms, this means the contract is not complete. As a result, there will be circumstances when a contract provides no guidance as to the appropriate remedy. Lack of completeness in contracts can also provide the opportunity for one party to act opportunistically.

Even when a contract appears to cover a set of circumstances, firms may disagree in their interpretation of events. While commercial disputes are often settled by private discussions between the two parties, in some cases no agreement can be reached privately. The dispute must then be settled by a disinterested third party. In the case of disputes between firms in one country, two options are generally available – litigation through the courts or commercial arbitration. Arbitration is arranged through the private sector while litigation takes place under the auspices of the nation's judicial system and, therefore, is backed by the state. This means that the state can use its powers to enforce the settlements imposed by the courts. In the case of arbitration, the decision to abide by the decision is largely voluntary.

There will be times when those who lose an arbitration will not comply with the decision. In some cases, national courts will act to enforce the decisions made by arbitrators. If national courts will not enforce the decisions of arbitrators, the party seeking redress will be forced into using the courts to judge the original complaint. Given that recourse to the courts is the ultimate step, why do firms – particularly firms involved in international commercial activity – tend to choose arbitration to settle their disputes rather than the courts? The answer is complex and forms the basis of this chapter.

DIFFERENCES IN NATIONAL LEGAL SYSTEMS

The major reason arbitration is the preferred method of settling international commercial disputes is that there is no supernational legal system to which governments are willing to delegate the powers of their courts. As a result, national courts remain the final adjudicators of commercial disputes. Institutions such as the EU's European Court have begun to take on the role of a supernational court for firms operating within the EU but such institutions remain the exception. For the most part, countries guard the sovereignty of their courts very closely.

Commercial law and court procedures vary considerably among countries. Even when the legal systems in two countries are based on the same set of legal principles, differences will arise over time because all legal systems are continually evolving. The absence of a supernational legal system means that firms wishing to enter into international transactions are faced with choosing which country's legal system to use if a dispute arises.

The fundamental problem is that a legal decision brought down by the courts in one country cannot be enforced in another country. Assume that the firms were agreed that the courts in the exporter's country were to be used to settle disputes. If the importing firm refused to pay and a verdict was brought down against it in the courts, the judgement could not be enforced in the country of the importer. Hence, the exporter would have no assurance that it would be paid when it entered into a contract. On the other hand, if the importer's court system were agreed to, then if in the importer's opinion the exporter failed to fulfil the terms of the contract, a judgement in the courts of the importer's country could not be used to force the exporter to comply. The importer would have no means of ensuring the exporter's performance when the contract was signed.

It might be possible to draw up two contracts for each transaction – one for each country. Differences in national legal systems, however, are significant enough to make it virtually impossible to construct parallel contracts which will convey the same intent and be interpreted in the same way. Subtle differences in the meanings of words in two languages can lead to alternative interpretations. Even if the same language is used, the legal interpretation of words can differ between countries. Attempting to construct two contracts would lead to considerably increased legal costs and would not lead to a satisfactory convergence between the two contracts. As a result, this practice is uncommon.

Even if firms are not concerned about the willingness of the other party to the contract to abide by a ruling made by another country's national court, firms may be concerned about national bias in the courts. In many countries, the courts are not an independent arm of government but rather, are considered as an integral part of the government's policy-making machinery. As a result, they may actively promote the interests of their nation's firms to the detriment of foreign firms. Even when courts are independent of government, individual judges may not act in an unbiased fashion towards foreign firms. Further, courts and judges may not be free from corruption and, hence, may be induced to act in the interests of their own nationals. It may even be the case that a firm may not trust its own courts, feeling that they may be 'in the pocket' of foreign firms. As a result, a firm may wish to seek an alternative to the legal system in its own country.

Negotiations over which national court system should be used to settle contract disputes are likely to be protracted. This may raise the transactions costs of reaching a contractual agreement to unacceptable levels. International arbitration is a transaction cost reducing method of settling disputes when contracts involve parties in two or more countries.

International arbitration relies on the willingness of parties to a dispute to voluntarily submit to both the process and decisions of an arbitrator. If either party refuses to submit to arbitration, then national courts remain the means by which disputes must be adjudicated. Agreement to proceed to arbitration can be delayed until a dispute actually arises. Often, however, the parties agree in the contract to proceed to arbitration if a dispute arises. The actual forum within which the arbitration will take place can also be stipulated in the contract. Even if arbitration is voluntarily agreed to in the contract, firms may choose to act opportunistically and refuse to abide by the agreement if a dispute arises. Arbitration is not backed by the power of the state as is the case with rulings from national courts. Firms may even allow the agreed arbitration to proceed and, if the decision reached by the arbitrator is not to their liking, the firm can refuse to abide by the ruling. Some national courts do operate to enforce arbitration rulings but, if nothing else, this will involve considerable legal costs. Arbitration will always be open to opportunistic behaviour by one of the parties.

Examples of opportunistic behaviour by firms who have voluntarily agreed to use arbitration for the settlement of disputes is not, however, common. If it were it is unlikely that international arbitration would enjoy the popularity that it does. Most firms perceive it to be in their best interest to have an efficient and unbiased means to settle disputes. As disputes will arise from time to time, firms need a means whereby they can be settled. Refusing to live up to a commitment to submit to arbitration can harm prospects for future business dealings between the two firms. Even if the firm does not contemplate future business dealings with the party with which it is in dispute, failure to live up to its arbitration commitments can lead to a loss of reputation. Contracts will be more difficult to negotiate with other firms in the future.

INTERNATIONAL ARBITRATION VERSUS NATIONAL COURTS

International arbitration provides a solution to the problems associated with differences in legal systems. Arbitration procedures tend to be flexible, thereby allowing the concerns of both parties to be taken into account when the structure of a particular arbitration is agreed. Further, elaborate and transparent procedures exist to allay any concerns relating to bias.

The use of international arbitration has other advantages in the resolution of disputes. Litigation through national courts may not be particularly suited to the needs of international commerce. Litigation tends to be a very slow process. Firms may suffer from problems with cash flow or disruptions to production while they await a decision from the courts. Business records, accounts and technical standards are likely to vary among countries. The particular standardized formats used by businesses may, in part, be the result of regulations of national courts regarding the preparation of evidence. Having records transformed to comply with the rules of evidence in another country may add considerably to the time required for litigation. Arbitration proceedings can be organized to allow for more flexible rules of evidence.

The period of time allowed for the completion of an arbitration can be specified in a contract. In the case of perishable commodities, the two sides can agree to abide by the decision of a single independent inspector charged with making a decision on the spot. It is often possible to have an arbitration decision reached for a relatively complex case in 6 weeks – a case that might normally be 3 years or more in litigation.

Litigation can also be very expensive. Lawyer's fees can be sufficiently high to deter at least some firms from pursuing their cases. This can bias proceedings if one party to a transaction is large and well financed. Hence, the threat of litigation can be used strategically against a smaller firm. Arbitration proceedings can often be conducted without lawyers. Even if there are legal issues which require the services of lawyers, as arbitration procedures tend to involve much less time than litigation, lawyers' fees are reduced.

As courts are public institutions, their proceedings tend to be transparent. All citizens may have access to court rooms, not just the interested parties. In many disputes, discussions of the technical details of products or processes are involved. Firms may not wish their trade secrets to be discussed in open court for fear of the information becoming available to their competitors. Arbitration proceedings can be conducted in private, thus safeguarding the confidentiality of information.

Most judges tend to be lawyers by training. As a result, they may lack the technical sophistication to judge a commercial dispute which involves complex engineering, scientific or managerial concepts. Even if expert witnesses are used in the courts, judges may not be able to understand their arguments or assess the quality of their information. Further, litigation tends to be adversarial with the lawyers from each side presenting their best case to a court which is largely passive. It is up to the lawyers to manage their case in such a way that the judge reaches the desired decision. Arbitrators, on the other hand, are selected on a case by case basis and can be chosen for their technical expertise. Arbitration procedures may also allow arbitrators to take a proactive role – questioning witnesses, seeking clarification and calling in experts of their own. As a result, an arbitration decision is much less dependent on the relative skill of the lawyers preparing the case.

In some countries, courts have little flexibility when awarding claims. As litigation is an adversarial system, arguments are heard and the court may decide on an all or nothing basis. The claimant either wins or loses its case. The inability to fulfil the conditions of a contract, however, may not be the responsibility of only one party. Arbitrators are able to make decisions on the basis of reasonable business practices and can apportion the responsibility accordingly.

In international arbitration, the concerns of firms relating to national bias are handled through a number of mechanisms. The care and attention taken to prevent bias in international commercial arbitration suggests that it is an important concern of businesses. While international arbitration can be carried out by individual arbitrators, it is common practice for panels of arbitrators to be used – often of three or five members. If, for example, a three member panel is used, each party will nominate one arbitrator with the third, who will act as the chairman of the arbitration panel, being jointly chosen by the two parties or some disinterested third party. A normal procedure would be for the two parties to attempt to find a third arbitrator which is acceptable to both. If a suitable third arbitrator cannot be agreed upon, then a disinterested third party will make the choice. Often, the two parties will use the services of an international arbitration centre which maintains lists of potential arbitrators. It is also common for individual parties to be able to reject at least one or more of the independent body's choices for the chairman of the arbitration panel. The arbitration rules chosen by the parties may state that the chairman cannot be a citizen of the home country of either of the contending parties. Allowing the firms to nominate their own member(s) of the panel provides assurances for the nominating party that their arguments will receive a fair hearing in the proceedings.

It is also common for the procedures for selection of arbitrators by the disputing parties to include time limits. If the time limit is exceeded, the independent body under which the arbitration is taking place will select the arbitrators. This prevents firms from acting opportunistically to delay or thwart proceedings by failing to appoint arbitrators.

National bias is also prevented by allowing for a choice of venues for the arbitration – presumable a mutually acceptable neutral country. Selection of the venue is often decided as part of the negotiations leading up to the signing of the contract.

Arbitration can also allow the parties to choose the legal system whose principles will govern the arbitration and by which the decision will be interpreted. This may be the legal system of either claimant or a third legal system which is acceptable to both parties. It is not uncommon that a dispute between companies whose home offices are in the US and Japan to be heard by an arbitration panel in Sweden with a Brazilian chairman and the proceedings interpreted according to Swiss commercial law.

The problem of national bias and inappropriate (or non-existent) commercial law was particularly important for transactions with state firms or state trading agencies in command economies. In the communist system, courts were considered direct instruments of state economic and social policy. Further, the command economy required no domestic system of commercial law because all firms were agents of the state and, if a dispute arose, it was resolved by bureaucratic decisions. This system put western firms at risk to both arbitrary decisions and national bias. The risks were often too high for contracts to be entered into. The result was that trade which command economies would have found beneficial was stifled. International arbitration became the norm for commercial relationships between firms from market economies and enterprises in command economies.

The decisions of arbitration panels are usually made public and arbitrators must provide the reasons for their decisions. This allows firms to assess both the technical ability and fairness of individual arbitrators. This improves the ability to make informed choices when choosing arbitrators. In national legal systems, judges tend to be assigned by the state. The parties to the dispute have no input into who will try their case. Arbitrators who do not provide decisions which are both technically competent and unbiased will not be selected and, over time, dropped from the list of available arbitrators.

While these procedures appear to be complex, they can be seen primarily as transactions cost reducing compared to firms being unable to agree on which national court will be used for litigation. This reduction in costs allows a mutually beneficial international transaction to proceed.

Critics of arbitration suggest that it provides less protection for individual rights than national courts. The primary means of protecting individual rights in the courts is the use of **due process**. The flexibility of arbitration procedures, whereby the rules are selected for convenience, fails to provide the same degree of protection as is the case with formal litigation. Firms voluntarily selecting to use international arbitration over the use of litigation are giving up the additional protection provided by national courts for the lower transactions costs associated with arbitration.

Firms choosing to use arbitration are not, however, totally protected from the interference and possibly bias of national courts. National courts may choose to overturn or augment the decisions of arbitration decisions if:

1. They are seen to contravene in a fundamental way the intent of domestic legislation or the principles of justice that the courts apply.
2. Third parties might be adversely affected by the arbitration decision.
3. The arbitration decision was not in the national interest.

Arbitration can take many forms and there are other forms of dispute resolution which are near to arbitration. Expertise, for example, can be used as a form of arbitration. The power of experts may, however be more limited. The parties to a dispute can agree to appoint an expert to judge the quality of goods with regard to whether they fulfil the specifications set out in the contract. His/her opinion may not, however, be binding. If the opinion is given as evidence to an arbitrator then the expert is not serving an arbitration function. If it is agreed that the expert's opinion will be binding on the parties without further interpretation or if the expert is also empowered to adjust the price of goods to reflect their true quality, then the expert is also acting as an arbitrator. A distinction is sometimes made between this type of arbitration, where only technical aspects of quality are being decided and when arbitrators provide legal interpretations. National courts seldom choose to interfere when an arbitration deals solely with technical issues of quality. Courts are more inclined to intervene when matters of law are concerned, if for no other reason than to prevent the erosion of the state monopoly on justice.

Once arbitration is voluntarily agreed to, it is binding on the parties to the dispute. Conciliation, on the other hand, is not binding on the parties to the dispute until a mutually acceptable solution is found. Arbitrators may be asked to decide cases in a manner which is concerned with equity rather than strictly according to legal principles. Hence, the decision may be similar to that which would be reached by conciliation. By agreeing to arbitration, however, firms agree to be bound by the decision even if they would not voluntarily accept it.

While arbitration may be used as a replacement for national courts for cases which could have been brought before the courts, arbitration may also be used to decide on problems which could not be brought to the courts. Arbitrators can fill in gaps in contracts or alter their conditions to reflect changing circumstances. In some legal jurisdictions, contract law does not allow the courts to intervene to complete contracts or to alter their terms.

If a contract is not complete, then a mutually beneficial commercial arrangement may be threatened by the inability of the parties to agree on a mutually acceptable solution. While a solution may have been mutually agreed upon during the negotiations leading up to the signing of a contract, at some later date the circumstances may have changed. At that point in time, firms may have made unequal resource commitments. For example, a food processor may have signed a long-term contract with an importer to provide a specialized line of confectionery products which would not be marketable in the processor's domestic market. To fulfil its contract, the processor must make a considerable investment in specialized equipment. The prices specified in the contract will make this investment profitable. After the investment is made the importer's government may pass new health regulations which will require the processor to make additional investments so that their confections can be exported. As the legislation was not anticipated when the contract was signed, the agreed prices do not reflect the additional costs. As the processor has already made a considerable investment in specialized equipment, it may wish to re-negotiate the prices. The importer, who has not made any resource commitment may feel no urgency to re-negotiate. Negotiations will not take place on an equal basis. The contract did not anticipate the problem and is incomplete. Arbitration will provide a solution to the unforeseen problem, eliminating the possibility of a contract threatening impasse.

Arbitration may be used to alter the conditions of a contract in cases when adhering to the original conditions would be to the detriment of both parties. Courts may not be allowed to alter contracts – only interpret the existing contract. For example, a price may be agreed to in a contract but the exporter's costs may increase dramatically as a result of some unforeseen circumstance. If the exporter keeps to the contract price it will go broke. The importer, however, may not be able to organize an alternative source of supply on short notice and for the exporter to cease production would be detrimental. The courts could only force the seller to honour the price specified in the terms of the contract. An arbitrator can be used to find a solution which is reasonable given the changed circumstances.

Conciliation may be used prior to arbitration. In other words, conciliation may be attempted as a first stage in the arbitration process. If the effort at conciliation fails, the dispute can be resolved through arbitration. The arbitration panel may be better informed of the problems faced by parties to a dispute as a result of the search for a mutually acceptable resolution of the problem through conciliation. This information can make it easier for the arbitrator to produce a reasonable decision.

Conciliation and arbitration may serve as useful alternatives when litigation is not an accepted part of business practice. In Japan, while litigation procedures exist, they are avoided due to the loss of face associated with even an accusation that a contract has not been strictly honoured. Japanese firms are practised at finding mutually acceptable solutions. Western businesses put a great deal of effort into designing complete contracts. Using litigation to settle disputes is part of their business culture. If a western firm finds itself in disagreement with a Japanese firm, it may attempt litigation in the Japanese courts. The Japanese firm's executives would lose face. Future business with the Japanese firm will be precluded and other Japanese firms are unlikely to be willing to deal with the western firm. On the other hand, western firms may not have the skills required to arrive at a mutually acceptable arrangement with the Japanese firm. Conciliation or arbitration can provide a solution, particularly if it takes place at a mutually agreeable neutral venue outside Japan and the procedures are conducted with discretion. No loss of face will be involved and a subsequent loss of reputation will be avoided by the western firm. Clearly, the transactions costs are far less than in the case of litigation.

As arbitration, unlike litigation, can be conducted confidentially, technical secrets can be kept from competitors, Arbitration also allows firms to keep information secret from customers, the general public and the tax system. A firm may wish to prevent consumers from finding out about defects in its products. Companies may not wish to reveal financial difficulties to creditors. A firm may wish to avoid a loss of reputation which would reduce the value of its franchises to customers in foreign countries. Even if a suite in the courts is won, damage to a firm's reputation may arise from adverse publicity surrounding the case. The merits of the particular case may have nothing to do with the loss of reputation. Hence, firms will find arbitration preferable to the public scrutiny which an action in the courts allows.

The widespread use of arbitration in international transactions may simply be a reflection of the costs imposed by national courts because they are no longer a legal system suitable for business purposes. In particular, national courts – with their domestic mandate – may simply not be oriented to the efficient handling of disputes arising in international contracts. Businesses may be seeking to establish an efficient system of commercial law through the development of the institutions of international arbitration. Establishing an efficient system for litigation may no longer be possible on the national level due to the monopoly over the creation and interpretation of law given jurists by legislators. As with any monopoly, jurists may have an incentive to formulate laws and legal procedures which reduce the effort they must expend (**X-inefficiency**) and/or which enable them to extract monopoly rents. The monopoly price represents an increase in transactions costs for firms.

[Simply put, X-inefficiency arises when there is a lack of competitive pressure to force the personnel of firms to act efficiently. The most obvious examples are excessive expenditures on executives' comfort – ostentatious offices, corporate jets, etc. It may also be manifest in organizational slack whereby procedures are put in place to reduce the effort required of executives. An interesting discussion of X-inefficiency in the context of the transactions costs associated with monitoring contracts can be found in Lang (1980). One obvious example of this type of inefficiency in the legal system is the delays that can be obtained by lawyers to help them with scheduling their court appearances. The net effect is to allow them to increase the number of clients they have and, hence, increase their income. Of course, the delays impose considerable costs on businesses. The time limits imposed on international arbitration proceedings, where no monopoly of jurists exist, is a clear example of the design of procedures by business for business.]

The absence of a jurists' monopoly in international law has allowed an efficient system for arbitration to develop. Given that there is an almost unlimited choice in the arbitration procedures and that there is a high degree of competition between the institutions which formally offer arbitration services, international arbitration is a low cost method of dispute settlement.

Further, both the formal legal language used and the non-transparent procedures used in the courts requires that lawyers be employed for even the simplest and most straightforward of disputes. Business people often have to spend considerable time and effort informing lawyers of technical complexities because they are not allowed to ask questions in court themselves. Arbitration removes these inefficiencies and the costs associated with them.

Even when the courts or the legislation underlying them do not have a national bias, the principles which form the basis of countries' legal systems differ. These differences can lead to a considerable degree of risk for firms wishing to enter into an international transaction. Legal scholars and national courts have not been able to reach agreement on matters relating to conflicts between nations' laws. While in some cases the parties to an international transaction may be able to choose which national law will apply to the contract, in many cases the question of which court will have jurisdiction cannot be determined when the contract is being drawn up. As the rulings of the courts will not be the same in different countries, members of the legal profession will not be able to give an unqualified answer to businesses regarding a contract's interpretation. It may not be possible to answer how damages will be assessed in the case of non-performance of contract obligations. The circumstances when revisions to contracts may be expected differ from legal system to legal system. In one national jurisdiction certain types of clause may be allowed but they may not be allowed in another jurisdiction. The best a lawyer can do is to inform the firm of the difference and the likely consequences. Lawyers are unlikely to be able to devise a contract which provides an equal degree of risk reduction in both jurisdictions. As a result, the prices firms eventually agree to in a contract will be less attractive (mutually beneficial) than if the level of risk could be harmonized. In some cases, no mutually acceptable price can be agreed and the transaction will be called off.

Arbitration allows the parties to choose a single set of rules. This decreases costs and, hence, increase the probability that a mutually acceptable contract price can be arrived at.

THE INSTITUTIONS OF INTERNATIONAL COMMERCIAL ARBITRATION

There has been a gradual evolution of international commercial arbitration. The process has become more formal. Although arbitration existed even in Roman times, it is in the 20th century that it has flourished. In part, the growth in the use of international arbitration is the result of the massive increase in the volume of international trade which has occurred in this century. The increase in the demand for international arbitration services has led to the development of permanent institutions. The increased use of arbitration may also reflect the decline of colonialism in the latter half of the 20th century. Colonialism acted to reduce the problems arising from differences in international laws in two ways. Firstly, it meant that one justice system was likely to apply to all commercial arrangements among the political units which made up a colonial empire. Secondly, direct trade between colonies of different nations was often discouraged. Trade between colonies and the colonial power was promoted instead. As a result, trade between different legal jurisdictions was reduced. The demise of colonial empires has meant that trade links have expanded between nations with different legal systems. Legal systems have also proliferated as the systems of justice in newly created states evolve independently.

The formalization of arbitration has been manifest in two ways. In the past, arbitration tended to be used on an *ad hoc* basis to resolve a dispute which had already arisen. It is common current practice, however, for parties negotiating a contract to make specific provision for international arbitration. In other words, arbitration is selected by firms in anticipation of disputes. This suggests that the general cost-effectiveness of international arbitration is accepted by firms conducting international business. Previously they would consider the merits of arbitration on a case by case basis.

Secondly, arbitration has been formalized through the development of generally accepted rules for procedures. These rules have been devised by international organizations or at permanent centres which offer facilities for arbitration. Rules for the procedures to govern international arbitration may be specified by firms without any reference to a formal centre where the arbitration will take place. In most cases, an international arbitration centre will allow firms wishing to avail themselves of its services to choose any set of arbitration rules they prefers. Firms can also choose to use a set of arbitration rules developed by an arbitration centre without using the services of the centre. The international organizations which have devised arbitration rules may also offer the services of a centre. The centre, however, is likely to allow a different set of rules to be used if it is the wish of the parties. This underlies the flexibility which characterizes the international arbitration system and contrasts with the rigid rules which are applied in the litigation systems of national courts. The formalization developing in international arbitration reduces business costs by providing procedural models for arbitration and specialized facilities. In other words, firms do not have to incur the costs of developing their own rules and finding a location with the mix of services which will maximize the efficiency of an arbitration.

While exact statistics on the pre-selection of international arbitration do not exist – because they are private contract information – the practice of including arbitration clauses is widespread and is promoted by many trade organizations. Arbitration is very common when the quality of the goods traded is easy to verify. It is less common when goods are complex – automobiles, apparel, electronics. This is probably because the complexity of the goods increases the costs of verifying quality, which in turn increases the cost of arbitrators' investigations. As a result, firms will have an incentive to work harder at arriving at a negotiated decision amongst themselves. The absence of the use of arbitration in an industry does not, however, imply that national courts are used as an alternative.

Many of the cases brought to arbitration centres are settled before the arbitrator reaches a decision. As arbitration is approached from a conciliatory rather than an adversarial perspective, the atmosphere at arbitration proceedings is much more likely to lead to a private settlement than when litigation is chosen.

Unless the domestic courts in a firm's country are willing to enforce awards, a firm entering into arbitration cannot be compelled to comply with the arbitrators decision. David (1984) suggests that failures to comply with the rulings of international arbitrators are rare. Failure to abide by awards leads to loss of reputation and subsequent difficulties when contracts with other firms must be negotiated in the future. This increases a firm's transactions costs in the long run.

A choice of arbitration institutions

Arbitration is often arranged under the auspices of industry organizations concerned with particular commodities. More broadly based disputes can often be referred to Chambers of Commerce. In Britain, the Chartered Institute of Arbitrators was established in 1915. In the US the American Arbitration Association was founded in 1926. The International Centre For Settlement of Investment Disputes between States and Nationals operates under the auspices of the World Bank. The Chamber of Commerce of Zurich is prominent in international disputes as are the Netherlands Arbitration Institute, the Stockholm Chamber of Commerce and the London Court of Arbitration. These four institutions have well publicized rules for arbitration procedures which firms can use if they choose. The Inter American Commercial Arbitration Commission was chartered in 1933. Many major trading cities have centres which provide arbitration facilities.

Each arbitration centre has its own rules regarding the selection of who is eligible to be on the list of arbitrators. Some centres require arbitrators to pass examinations or to possess an independent technical certification. Often, however, no formal qualifications are required and persons are added to the lists based on their reputations. In some cases, arbitrators can refuse to serve while in other cases they agree to provide their services on demand when they agree to be added to the list. Persons remain on a list for a fixed period or they remain on indefinitely depending upon the rules of the particular centre. Even if an arbitrator who is in demand finishes a term, many centres allow the parties to select arbitrators who are not on their list.

While arbitration proceedings are private, it is in the interest of firms engaging in international commerce to be able to identify high quality arbitrators. As a result, a great deal of information is made available. A large number of academic journals and other publications are dedicated to the reporting and study of arbitration awards. Firms can study this information when they need to select an arbitrator. Parties to disputes will not be able to reach an agreement to appoint arbitrators who appear to be biased and will challenge arbitrators that they do not consider fit. If the list of arbitrators maintained by a centre has a large number of potential arbitrators whom parties consider unsuitable, the parties are free to choose an alternative centre for future contracts. As a result, arbitrators have an incentive to keep the quality of their arbitrations high.

The International Chamber of Commerce

The most prominent organization involved in offering international arbitration services is the International Chamber of Commerce (ICC). Created in 1919, the ICC's only legal status is as an association registered under French law. It is, however, a federation of national organizations from more than 50 countries. These national organizations have the sponsorship of industry organizations and associations in their countries. The ICC has produced a widely accepted code for international arbitration and maintains a Court of Arbitration. The Court of Arbitration is appointed by the Council of the ICC. The United Nations has produced arbitration codes for those who do not wish to have their arbitrations subject to any commercial organization. The operation of the ICC, however, probably deserves closer examination because it sets the standard with which other international arbitration organizations must compete.

The ICC's Court of Arbitration is located at the organization's headquarters in Paris. The Court of Arbitration does not itself settle disputes. The Court only confirms and selects arbitrators according to its 'Rules of Conciliation and Arbitration'. In the case of arbitration, the preferred procedural choice is a single arbitrator mutually agreed to by the participants. The Court simply confirms the appointment. If the use of a single arbitrator is agreed to but the parties cannot agree on a arbitrator, the Court will make the appointment. The two parties have only 30 days to arrive at a mutually acceptable arbitrator.

If an arbitration tribunal is requested by the parties, then each party may nominate one arbitrator to be confirmed by the Court. The third arbitrator is appointed by the Court and chairs the tribunal. If one party fails to nominate an arbitrator the Court will appoint one. If the parties cannot agree on the number of arbitrators, the Court will appoint a sole arbitrator. If a decision to appoint a single arbitrator is challenged by one of the parties, the Court will judge whether the case is sufficiently complex to warrant a tribunal. The Court's decision is final. If a tribunal is approved, the parties have 15 days to nominate their arbitrators.

For the arbitrators it appoints, the Court relies for nominees on lists of potential arbitrators maintained by the National Committees which constitute the ICC. The rules state that sole arbitrators or chairs of tribunals cannot be citizens of the countries of the firms which are involved in the dispute. A firm is allowed to challenge the appointment of an arbitrator but the Court judges the merit of the objection and its decision is final.

Clearly, these rules provide firms with considerable flexibility while providing protection against national bias. The rules are also constructed to prevent opportunistic delaying tactics through a failure to respond to a call for nomination of arbitrators. It is in the interest of the National Committees to maintain lists of capable unbiased arbitrators as firms can choose to use the services of a different arbitration court if they are not satisfied.

Selection of individuals for the lists of nominees available for appointment as arbitrators varies among arbitration institutions. Competition has meant that, as a rule, they will have available individuals from countries other than the country which is home to the institution. Individuals from a large number of countries are normally included so that suspicion of national bias is removed. The right to challenge or refuse arbitrators is fairly universal but the rules are constructed to prevent these rights being used opportunistically for the purpose of delaying the proceedings.

According to ICC rules, if recourse to arbitration by the ICC is explicitly written into a contract, then either party can ask for arbitration upon supplying evidence from the contract. If there is no mention of arbitration in the contract, or if no particular arbitration body is specified in the contract, then either party can ask the ICC for arbitration. The other party will then be informed but if they do not agree that the arbitration should go ahead under the auspices of the ICC, the ICC will refuse to hear the case. Again the emphasis is on flexibility.

The rules allow firms to chose arbitration only when a problem actually arises. They allow firms to choose the appropriate arbitration body once the nature of the dispute is known. If the dispute relates to a question of product quality, for example, an arbitration system established by the industry organization concerned with the product can be used. Such specialized organizations are likely to have product experts on their list of potential arbitrators. They will be more efficient at arbitrating this type of dispute than more general ICC arbitrators.

Of course, if either the use of arbitration or the choice of arbitration institution to be used for the arbitration are not pre-specified, a firm may be open to the refusal of the other party to agree to arbitration. They may also object to a particular venue. These trade-offs will have to be considered at the time the original contract is being negotiated. The greater the degree of mutual interest in continuing the business relationship, the more likely that the arbitration procedure will be kept flexible.

Any party to a contract can request arbitration from the ICC. If arbitration by the ICC has been pre-specified in the contract between to two parties, then the defendant named in the case is informed of the claimant's request for arbitration and is provided with all documentation supplied by the claimant. The defendant must reply within 30 days and submit the basis of its case. It must also make any counter claims at that time. The original claimant then has 30 days to reply to the counter claims. Again, there is an emphasis on rigid timetables to prevent the tactical use of delay.

If arbitration by the ICC was pre-specified in the contract between the two parties and one party refuses to submit to arbitration, then the arbitration will still take place. This protects the claimant from the defendant refusing to live up to the prior commitment to arbitrate. In this case, the Court of Arbitration appoints an arbitrator in place of the one which the defendant would normally nominate.

If one of the parties objects to the arbitration, the Court of Arbitration decides on the validity of the objection. The Court's ruling is binding. Even if the party does not agree with the Court's ruling, the arbitration will proceed. This may appear as a wasted effort if one side refuses to live up to its arbitration commitment. However, this strategy cannot be allowed to thwart the arbitration process. In any case, a firm's refusal to co-operate with the arbitration procedure itself may not mean that it will not abide by the arbitration ruling. More important, however, is that having the arbitration take place and a ruling given increases the damage to the defendant's reputation by forcing them into a position of having to formally refuse to abide by the decision. As the Court of Arbitration cannot actually enforce its rulings – unless the defendant's national courts have agreed to enforce the ruling – compliance relies primarily on there being the potential to damage the reputation of the company. If a firm refuses to abide by a ruling, then other firms are less likely to enter into contracts with the offender because they will not feel that they are protected by the agreement to arbitrate. If the defendant were simply able to thwart the arbitration process by refusing to agree to arbitration, there would be no direct evidence of the defendant's wrongdoing. This would make the task of diminishing the firm's reputation more difficult. Without a judgement, the defendant could simply claim that it was not guilty and, hence, was refusing to participate in the arbitration because it saw no need for the proceedings. While the firm may be seen by some as automatically guilty by its refusal to submit to arbitration, others will still have doubts. It is also important that the claimant's case be heard to ensure that its reputation is not diminished by the defendant's public protestation of innocence. By increasing the transparency of the entire arbitration proceedings, their effectiveness is increased. This reduces the risks associated with international transactions.

The parties to the dispute may specify the country where the arbitration should take place. If they cannot agree, the Court of Arbitration will decide the country of arbitration. This provision relates primarily to the problem of preventing national bias. This is because under ICC regulations, the parties to the dispute have three options regarding the rules governing the conduct of arbitration hearings. Firstly, the parties can choose the procedural rules for arbitrations set out by the ICC. The parties can also choose any other rules for the conduct of arbitration proceedings that they can agree on. The ICC has no particular interest in promoting the rules of arbitration it has developed. If the parties have not specified any set of rules for the arbitration, then the legal rules of the country where the arbitration will be held will apply. This allows the parties to choose a legal system with which they are both comfortable. It also ensures that there will always be a set of procedural rules available for any arbitration.

The arbitrator is given wide latitude in the procedural rules established by the ICC. The arbitrator is specifically empowered to be proactive – unlike some judicial proceedings where the judge simply applies rules of order and passively evaluates the case on the basis of the presentations of advocates. The emphasis is on the arbitrator being able to obtain, as quickly as possible, any information that will aid him/her in reaching a decision.

The arbitrator may call witnesses. As a result, only those considered relevant can be called. The arbitrator can appoint technical experts to provide information on product quality, on the quality of work undertaken as part of a contract and on the diligence of the parties in arranging for shipping, etc. The arbitrator can call upon legal experts to provide for the interpretations of points of law. The means by which witnesses and experts inform the arbitrator are not constrained by rules of evidence, cross-examination, etc.

Each party is allowed to submit its case in writing and provide all the documentation it feels is appropriate. The arbitrator is charged with attempting to decide the case based on the materials presented by the parties. This gives an incentive for firms to provide complete information to the arbitrator. Otherwise, the arbitrator may make the decision based on the information provided by only one side. Relying on written submissions to provide the basis of a settlement reflects an attempt to keep costs to the parties low. Expensive visits to neutral countries where the arbitration is taking place are avoided. This is an attempt to provide equal access to the arbitration process for all firms. Firms are often dissuaded from pursuing litigation in the courts simply because the costs of a court action are prohibitive. Of course, large firms, or those in a stronger financial position, can use the threat of a court action as a bargaining tactic. Arbitration seeks to minimize these types of tactical advantages. Either party to an arbitration, however, does have the right to request a hearing. Only the party who requests the hearing must attend. As the arbitrator controls the hearing process, its tactical use by one party is minimized.

If the arbitrator is unable to decide the case on basis of the documents provided, a hearing may be scheduled. If one party fails to attend the summons of the arbitrator, the arbitration hearing will still proceed. This prevents a failure to attend from being used to strategic advantage.

Hearings are held in private. Hence, unlike formal legal proceedings, the confidentiality of information is protected. Confidentiality is particularly important internationally where patent protection may be poor. This is clearly a procedure preferred by business which is not available in national courts with their reliance on public scrutiny of proceedings and concerns relating to the public trust.

The parties can appear before the arbitrator themselves. This is stated explicitly in the ICC rules to emphasize that the proceedings are not based upon representation by legal council. The intent is that business people should not be intimidated by the process and that the less formal nature of proceedings will allow the arbitrator to obtain the information directly from those involved. A party is also allowed to be represented by local agents whom they designate, thereby reducing travel costs.

The ICC rules regarding arbitration procedures states the parties 'may also be assisted by council or solicitors' (United Nations, 1973, p. 83). The intent is clear, parties should represent themselves. Some firms, however, may be uncomfortable with the idea of making direct representations. Representation by council is encouraged in other rules of arbitration and represents an element of competition for the ICC.

Under the rules of the ICC, arbitration proceedings are expected to be concluded and a verdict reached within 60 days of the arbitrator having been appointed. Again, the stress is on keeping the time involved to a minimum. The arbitrator, however, is allowed to ask the Court of Arbitration for an extension of this period in complex cases. It is the arbitrator and not the parties that must seek the extension.

When a tribunal rather than a single arbitrator is being used, the award is based on the decision of a majority vote. If there is no majority, only then does the chairman make the award. This means that the chairman, appointed by the Court of Arbitration, cannot overrule in the case when the two arbitrators selected by the parties themselves agree on an award. This is in keeping with the notion that businesses themselves should know best and that the Court, through the arbitrator it appoints, should only make the award when all other avenues have been explored. Of course, if the arbitrators selected by the parties fail to agree, then the independent arbitrator makes the decision.

When an award is made by the arbitrator, it is submitted to the Court of Arbitration which can alter the form of the award and, if it feels necessary, point out aspects of the case to the arbitrator's attention. The former simply ensures that awards will conform to legal or other conventions. The substance of the award, however, cannot be changed. This allows greater freedom to use individuals as arbitrators who have important technical knowledge but only limited knowledge of arbitration procedures and the associated legal requirements. Reaching an informed decision in an arbitration is more important than the formal protection of rights. This flexibility is an overt attempt to prevent a group of individuals gaining a monopoly over arbitration institutions similar to that enjoyed by lawyers in the judicial system.

An arbitration award is final. When submitting to arbitration by the ICC, the parties wave all rights to appeal. This prevents an appeal process from being used strategically as a way of increasing costs for a party which is financially weaker. It also prevents the use of appeals as a delaying tactic. Other arbitration systems do allow for limited forms of appeal. The national courts in some nations, however, provide for the direct appeal of arbitration awards.

The Court of Arbitration attempts to ensure that, where possible, an award is enforced without comment by national courts. Many national court systems, however, refuse to surrender that prerogative, believing that to do so would undermine their monopoly on justice. The parties to the dispute also agree to 'carry out the award without delay' (United Nations, 1973, p. 83).

The arbitrator also assesses the costs arising from the arbitration procedure and apportions who should pay the costs. There is even a provision that allows the ICC to require that, prior to the actual arbitration proceedings, one or both of the parties deposit an amount sufficient to cover the cost of the arbitration with the ICC. Clearly the ICC itself is concerned with ensuring that it will get paid.

This in depth examination of the ICC rules is provided to illustrate the types of costs than may arise in international commercial transactions. Obtaining an arbitration award appears to be fairly straightforward. The arbitrator considers the arguments and evidence provided by the parties to the dispute, invites in experts, considers their advice, arrives at a decision which apportions the blame and then makes an award. All of the additional complexity built into the procedures is either to prevent national bias being present in the decisions or to prevent the arbitration procedure itself from being used to strategic advantage by either party. While the ICC rules are simple, as well as being simply stated, they are carefully constructed to minimize opportunism. Hence, the ICC arbitration rules provide considerable insights into the types of opportunism which may be practised in international commerce.

ENFORCEMENT OF ARBITRATION AWARDS BY NATIONAL COURTS

Those who offer international arbitration services are, however, cognizant of the risks associated with having to rely on voluntary compliance for restitution. As a result, there are ongoing attempts to have national courts recognize and enforce the awards of international arbitrations. Arbitration centres have made provisions for their arbitrations to be decided according to the principles, but not the procedures, of individual country's laws. This can remove the potential for a conflict in legal principles. Conflicts over legal principles make it much more difficult for national courts to uphold arbitration awards.

While national governments have often been willing to enforce arbitration awards made by international arbitrators, they have been less willing to recognize the awards in the absence of the right to review the awards. If national courts wish to scrutinize the awards of international arbitrators, to some extent the purpose of choosing arbitration is defeated. The case will still end up in the courts. Further, review by national courts reintroduces the possibility of national bias into the proceedings.

On the other hand, the position of national courts is understandable. If they do not review the cases they are expected to enforce, they may be enforcing awards made on criteria that violate the principles of the law they are expected to uphold. This problem has meant that the relationship between international arbitration and national courts varies considerably among countries. The relationship tends to evolve slowly with international arbitration institutions asking for more enforcement and less review while national courts tend to give ground only grudgingly.

The Convention on the Recognition and Enforcement of Foreign Arbitral Awards (United Nations, 1959) came into force on June 7, 1959. Over 60 countries have signed the Convention. For the most part, the signatories will apply the rules of the Convention to arbitrations undertaken in any state which has signed the Convention. When signing the convention a country agrees to:

> ... recognize arbitral awards as binding and enforce them ... There shall not be imposed substantially more onerous conditions of higher fees or charges on the recognition or enforcement of arbitral awards ... than are imposed on the recognition or enforcement of domestic arbitral awards.

The Convention provides a number of conditions under which the state need not enforce an arbitration award. Most of these relate to cases where a court believes that the arbitration was carried out under a flawed procedure. Governments, however, can also refuse to recognize or enforce and international arbitration award if:

(a) The subject matter of the difference is not capable of settlement by arbitration under the law of that country; or
(b) The recognition or enforcement of the award would be contrary to the public policy of that country. (United Nations, 1959)

Clearly, considerable latitude is available for intervention by the national courts. As a result, most arbitration awards are not submitted to the national courts for enforcement. Voluntary compliance with the terms of an award remains the rule rather than the exception.

Within the EU, the European Court has been established to act as a means to adjudicate disputes. Commercial disputes arising when contracting parties span two or more countries who are members of the EU are included. The procedures of the Court are, however, cumbersome. Generally, direct appeal to the court is not possible. A dispute must first be pursued through all levels of appeal in the domestic courts of a member state. Only then may the appeal be taken to the European Court. The court can only decide if the decision violates laws of the EU. The European Court relies on the national courts for enforcement. The entire process is very time consuming. Clearly, this is a legalist approach to dispute settlement and not particularly suited to the requirements of international commerce.

As with the other private institutions which evolved to facilitate international trade, international arbitration exhibits a great deal of flexibility in its forms and institutions. This allows firms undertaking international transactions to search out the particular arbitration system which bests suits their requirements. As a result, the transactions costs associated with the settlement of disputes will be kept low.

REFERENCES

David, R. (1984) *Arbitration in International Trade*, Kluwer Law and Taxation Publishers, London.

Lang, M. G. (1980) Marketing alternatives and resource allocation: case studies in collective bargaining. *American Journal of Agricultural Economics*, **62**(4), 760–5.

United Nations (1959) Convention on the recognition and enforcement of foreign arbitral awards. *Treaty Series*, Vol. 330, p. 38, No. 4739.

United Nations (1973) Rules of conciliation and arbitration of the International Chamber of Commerce, in *Register of Texts of Conventions and Other Instruments Concerning International Trade Law, Vol. II*, United Nations, New York, pp. 77–85.

Summary of Part Five

Any initial attempt to study the private sector institutions which have evolved to facilitate international commercial transactions is likely to quickly overwhelm the most inquisitive of minds. The sheer number, diversity and complexity of the institutions and how they interact with each other represents a closed and Byzantine world which few outsiders comprehend. Even those on the inside seldom have an understanding of the wider system within which their particular institution operates. No discussion of this system can ever be complete. In this section, an attempt has been made to lay out the major constraints faced by those who wish to engage in international transactions. A number of the major institutions which have evolved in the private sector to reduce the costs these constraints impose on firms are examined. A few have been examined in depth to show the reader that details can be important. Small differences in the services provided by the institutions can considerably affect the viability of an international business deal. As these services are provided in the private sector, they are provided at a cost. Given the complexity of the system, firms wishing to use the services available face a large number of choices which must be evaluated on the basis of the costs and expected benefits. As many of the benefits relate to the reduction of risk, evaluations will be particularly difficult.

Three major problems have been examined:

1. The problems associated with ensuring payment – including problems associated with exchanging currencies.
2. The problems associated with physically moving a good between firms in two countries – including insurance.
3. The settlement of disputes in the absence of a supernational commercial legal system.

While these problems have been examined in turn, in reality they represent parts of a complete system that will govern any international transaction. The method of transport affects payment assurance through the nature of the documents required for collection. The bank guaranteeing a forfaiter may require that the parties to the transaction agree to insert a clause in the contract specifying arbitration of disputes concerning an exporter's performance. An insurance claim against damage in transport may be evidence required for an arbitration.

Acting in combination, these institutions may reduce the risks associated with international transactions to a greater degree than the sum of their individual contributions. The institutions often operate in layers with the organization ultimately assuming the final portion of the risk being totally removed from the original transaction – having no interest in the goods or services actually transacted. The complexity of the system may lead firms contemplating entering international transactions to wonder how transactions are completed at all. Yet without these institutions, it is unlikely that many international transactions would take place. The risks would simply be prohibitive.

This suggests that the economic implications of these institutions are simple. They reduce the transaction costs associated with international commerce. Transactions costs in economists models have been likened to friction in the models of physicists. The private institutions of international commerce simply act as lubricants to reduce friction. It is, however, difficult to measure their contribution to efficiency. It is interesting to note that governments have found them to be so efficient at reducing the costs of international transactions that they have found it necessary to invent and interpose their own brand of friction or transactions costs into the international trading system. These government imposed transactions costs take a number of forms. In the face of low transportation charges, governments impose tariffs. In the face of private institutions which efficiently transfer funds between countries, governments impose currency restrictions. Restrictions are imposed on arbitration awards by national courts. Government red tape counteracts efficient exchange of the documents which facilitate the transfer of products between firms in two countries. If the private system were less efficient at reducing transactions costs, one suspects that there would be far less interference in international commerce by government. The efficiency imparted by the international commercial institutions allows the effects of changing comparative advantage to be transferred among countries very quickly – often far faster than governments are willing to tolerate. Protectionist policies have been the result.

The long struggle at the GATT and in other international forums has been undertaken in a period when the technology available to international commercial institutions has been relatively static. New technology is now becoming available to these institutions. The revolution in electronic communications technology makes it possible for the transfer of information and funds virtually instantaneously. This shortens the time required for verification, for arbitration and even the physical transfer of goods. Governments already complain that they cannot control international movements of funds. Their ability to manage the economy is handicapped by instantaneous flights of capital. As information transfers become instantaneous, managers all over the world can react to the same signals at the same time. How governments respond to this increase in efficiency and, hence a reduction in their ability to control events, will affect the future functioning of international commercial institutions.

Firms wishing to enter into international transactions will also benefit from the electronic communications revolution. It will allow them to dispense with some international institutions while they will become more reliant on others. If instantaneous visual transmissions between firms are inexpensive, disputes over quality will be reduced because the exporter will be able to verify his product's arrival condition through high resolution television pictures. Electronic sensors in individual containers allow the exact time of damage to be determined – greatly simplifying insurance claims. Banks can be directly accessed electronically, meaning the time it takes to arrange financing will be reduced. With better information, banks will be able to put together more favourable financing packages. The commercial world will become more integrated, reducing cultural and procedural difficulties. International transactions will become more common and they will lose some of their distinctive character. The need for specialized institutions will remain, however, as long as nations retain a considerable degree of economic sovereignty.

The ability to act opportunistically will also be reduced with improved information flows. Opportunities to act opportunistically arise because the costs of monitoring activities is too high or because of the time required to complete transactions. Both monitoring costs and time will be reduced because of the revolution in electronic information technology.

It is interesting to note that many economists who have had an interest in studying the international system have felt that the transactions cost associated with international commerce could be safely assumed away. They did this to be able to concentrate on the 'friction' imposed on the international system by government – tariffs, subsidies, import quotas, etc. This suggests that the transactions costs are probably low, attesting to the efficiency of the institutions. Why economists did not devote more time and effort to the study of opportunistic activities by firms is less clear. After all, it would appear that most of the institutions of international commerce exist primarily to reduce the costs of opportunistic behaviour. There is little better proof than the very existence of the institutions to suggest that firms do act in an opportunist manner if an opportunity presents itself. If the international commercial system is to be better understood, far more research will be required on the ways firms actually behave.

PART 6

Future trends in international trade and commerce

Introduction to Part Six

Both the number and value of international commercial transactions are increasing at an increasing rate. International business, in all its manifestations, is the world's major growth industry. International trade in goods and services is growing at a more rapid rate than the domestic economies of all developed countries. While all areas of the world are exhibiting increases in international activity, it is the trade between developed countries which is expanding the fastest. This suggests that their economies are becoming more closely integrated. Developing countries, with a few obvious exceptions, remain relatively isolated and outside the main stream of international commerce.

Closer integration of national economies may be viewed by some with distaste. It is difficult, however, to ignore the growth – and development – potential arising from international commerce. Negotiations to liberalize trade follow a tortuous course as politicians struggle to satisfy those with vested interests in preserving a degree of economic isolation. Rumblings about the neo-colonial nature of the institutions of international commerce are still heard in some quarters. In spite of these difficulties, barriers to trade and commerce continue to decline. New GATT agreements are reached. The EU accepts new members. The US and Canada are willing to accept Mexico – with its dramatically different economy – as a full trading partner. The former command economies are clamouring to join the EU. Countries in the western hemisphere are requesting that the NAFTA be broadened to accept new members. Developing countries are unilaterally reducing the trade barriers put in place over decades in the name of development strategies based on import substitution. These changes suggest increased opportunities for international business.

The major challenge for individual businesses is to determine how best to take advantage of the opportunities available to them. The answer to this complex question lies first and foremost in the people they employ. No matter to what degree new technologies reduce the cost of organizing international transactions and restrictions placed on international commerce by government are removed, doing business internationally will be more complicated than doing business at home. The continued integration of the world economy will mean two things. More individuals in any firm will be directly involved in international business and a broader range of employees will be in direct contact with people having different business practices and cultures. Receptionists will have to deal directly with foreign businessmen, both on the phone and in person. As first impressions are extremely important, receptionists will need to be more sensitive to nuances of both spoken and body language. The electronics revolution will make it far more likely that production problems will be sorted out between foremen on the production line in two countries rather than through cumbersome communication through a number of layers of management. Both foremen must be better informed about the production technologies in use and the psychological profile of the person being dealt with. The receptionist and the foreman need a better standard of education as well as additional training provided by the company.

Managers and executives will be far more likely to be directly involved in international business arrangements. It will be increasingly difficult to isolate export departments or international divisions from the rest of the firm. Instantaneous electronic communication will break down divisional barriers within firms. To be competitive, the export division will require that there be three-way direct communication between themselves, their production, engineering or finance divisions and the foreign firm with which they are negotiating.

International contacts are also likely to broaden to include more countries. Managers will have to deal with a much wider range of business cultures than in the past. This leads to questions regarding the type of education which will be appropriate for the executive of the future. The focus of most MBA programs and undergraduate business degrees has been on providing managers with skills which will enable them to contribute to improving the internal performance of the firm. Their education has emphasized better planning, control and staff motivation. Great strides have been made through the widespread use of the principles of internal management. While internal management will always be important, as the international component of a firm's business increases, more of the gains in efficiency will come from reducing the costs associated with organizing international transactions. These cost savings will come primarily from reducing the friction created by the failure to correctly communicate across cultures.

As the electronic communications revolution reduces the technical difficulties associated with organizing international transactions, the costs associated with individuals failing to communicate will become more prominent. The rise of transnational corporations can be seen as a means by which the gains available from better internal management could be extended into international business. For the most part, transnationals simply transferred domestic management systems to co-ordinating activities in other countries. By imposing a uniform managerial structure, problems with cross-cultural communications are reduced. In essence, however, the cross-cultural interface was simply displaced further along the production and distribution chain. Of course, transnational corporations can seldom remove all cross-cultural contacts and have had to adapt their local organizations accordingly. One characteristic of transnational corporations is that their internal management systems will often differ to a considerable degree from those of the domestic firms in the countries within which they operate. Of course, the greater the degree of cultural difference, the more stark the contrast. While additional gains in efficiency are probably available from further extensions of better internal management practices transnationally, those gains will be limited. At some point the firm must interact with foreign business people or consumers. Cross-cultural differences will remain and reducing their associated costs will become increasingly important.

Reducing the costs associated with the failure to communicate across cultures will require a different type of manager. A good manager will still need to be cognizant of the parameters which affect internal efficiency. As better internal management practices become matters of routine, the manager's role as an innovator and promoter of such practices will be reduced. This suggests a re-orientation of managerial education toward the skills which will help reduce cross-cultural communication problems. A greater emphasis on language skills, cultural difference in business practices, tolerance of foreign practices and, if possible, some direct foreign experience are suggested. A more liberal arts approach to executive education is suggested, but with a focus. A signpost may be provided by the curricula of the increasingly popular international MBA programs. While some basic management skills are included in most curricula, the emphasis is on building cross-cultural understanding and tolerance. Finding a means to capitalize on the opportunities made available by those skills provides the programs' focus. The best of these programs encourage an international student body and job placements in foreign countries. It is interesting that many of these programs have arisen outside state funded education systems. Hence, they may be another manifestation of the private sector establishing institutions catering for the needs of international business in the absence of supernational publicly funded institutions.

Ensuring a successful future in international commerce will require a different orientation for many firms. Expanded opportunities will be available both to firms wishing to directly engage in international commerce and those specializing in providing the services which facilitate trade. The economic question remains the same – how do institutions, both public and private, affect the efficiency of international transactions?

Facing the future 17

DISEQUILIBRIUM AND CHANGE

Change is the word which best describes the economics of international business. While the world economy is probably never close to equilibrium, the economic factors currently driving its evolution are more powerful forces for change than have been seen in the last half of the 20th century. Change will create opportunities for some firms engaged in international commerce. Opportunities will be reduced for others. The expansion of trade relations will never lead to all businesses being 'winners'.

The changes currently underway should lead to a net increase in trade and other international activities. International commerce will continue to be a growth industry. While expanding trade is often 'sold' on the basis of increasing export opportunities, over the long run every expansion of exports must be accompanied by an expansion in imports or investment abroad. The gains to society from increased trade do not arise from increases in exports. They arise from the movement of resources – raw materials, people and capital – from inefficient uses to efficient uses. Unfortunately, the movement of these resources does not take place instantaneously or costlessly. The expansion of trade will impose economic losses on those who own the resources employed in declining industries. Shareholders in these industries will suffer a loss in the value of their capital. Labour will become unemployed. These problems are unavoidable in an economy that trades. Of course, the owners and employees of businesses which are internationally competitive will prosper. Changing fortunes are the inevitable result of disequilibrium.

RESOURCE MOBILITY

Governments will always be faced with pressure from businesses and labour groups whose wealth and livelihood are threatened. This pressure can be dealt with in a number of ways. Governments can give in to the pressure of protectionists and intervene in the functioning of international markets in ways which slow down the rate that resources leave an inefficient industry. Of course, this means that part of the nation's resources are inefficiently employed. Trade restrictions and other measures can prevent the exit of resources from an industry made uncompetitive by imports. These policies are often put in place 'temporarily' in the name of restructuring – to allow the industry to become internationally competitive again. The evidence suggests that attempts at restructuring are seldom successful. Even if they are successful, the costs will often far exceed the benefits to society.

Governments can also choose to ignore pleas for protection, take no action and allow industries to decline. Those who find themselves unemployed will be force to rely on the support mechanisms of the nation's social welfare system. Of course, most governments will follow some mixture of policies as they weigh the importance of various interest groups and the welfare of the society as a whole. The role of politicians is to make the difficult trade offs which give to some and take from others. Almost all changes in policy, including changes in trade policy, are choices concerning who will be the winners and who will be the losers.

Neither protectionism nor *laissez-faire* – non-interventionist – approaches to trade policy attack the root of the problem. The problem with the changes which arise from disequilibrium in the international economy is that resources do not move quickly and costlessly from declining to expanding industries. In some cases, where specialized capital is involved, there is little that can be done to increase its mobility. Due to the increasing rate of technological change, however, a considerable proportion of fixed capital is obsolete in less than a decade. In the case of labour, however, it should be possible to develop policies which improve mobility, both between industries and, if necessary, geographically.

Keeping labour employed in declining industries by the use of protectionist measures or having them languish on various forms of social assistance for long periods is not efficient. Alternatives need to be found to assist those who lose as a result of changing international competitiveness. While most governments have policy initiatives that attempt to reduce labour's immobility, the majority of policy effort is normally directed at either protectionism or the social welfare system. Policies aimed at improving resource mobility have, in most cases, had only limited success. A greater investment in children's education will probably reap high rewards in the long run. However, far more thought and research into policies which will increase resource mobility will be required before effective policies are likely to arise. Economists who develop trade theory have added little to this debate. Most of the models which are used to examine trade problems make the assumption that resources move instantaneously and costlessly between sectors.

The fundamental question of resource mobility will become more important as the rate of change in the world economy accelerates. The major contributor to international disequilibrium is the increasing rate of technological progress. The individuals who can take advantage of these technological changes are those who can adapt quickly to acquire new skills which have a high degree of technical sophistication. In short, individuals need to have intellectual mobility. The more people a society has who are intellectually mobile, the greater the likelihood that it will prosper in the increasingly global economy. Nations which fail to create an intellectually mobile labour force will see their unemployment lines increase. The pressure for protectionism will rise. Businesses need to lobby governments to make the investments in human capital required to enable them to take advantage of international opportunities. More importantly, firms will also have to provide additional training for their employees. Further, for those firms doing business internationally, there may need to be a reversal of the recent management strategy whereby employees have been shed in favour of contracting out. The skills which are useful in reducing the costs associated with poor cross-cultural communications are likely to be specific to individuals. Success in reducing these costs will depend, to a considerable degree, on the establishment of ongoing relationships with foreign individuals. As a result, while the people who repair a firm's computers may be relatively interchangeable and, hence, the service can be purchased on contract, those who have developed working relationships with foreign businesses will not be interchangeable. It is probably not surprising that those firms which specialized in international transactions in the past had reputations as lifelong employers. The special relations with comprador families nurtured by the Hong Kong trading houses lasted over many generations. Japanese trading houses provided the model for Japanese lifetime employment policies. Conducting international business successfully in the future will mean approaching it from a long-term point of view.

INCREASING DIVERSITY

Beyond the revolution in electronic communications technology, there are a number of major trends which are likely to foster the expansion of international commerce. The first is that as incomes rise, consumers tend to wish to diversify the range of products they consume. Part of their craving for diversity will be supplied by foreign products. The variety of consumer products which are available nationally, but not yet internationally, is still enormous. Firms will find lucrative niche markets satisfying consumers' craving for the exotic.

While rising incomes allow consumers to better fulfil their quest for diversity, the internationalization of communications provides them with information about foreign lands and cultures. Increasingly, consumers have direct and indirect access to foreign programming transmitted by satellites. They watch television commercials for foreign products. They are made aware of new products and fads faster and in a much more visual way than in the past.

Consumers are also increasingly well travelled, meaning they experience foreign products first hand. This tends to break down resistance to foreign products and leads consumers to seek them out when they return home. Trade is increasingly based on quality and product characteristics rather than on comparative advantage in relatively homogeneous industrial inputs. Predicting changes in trade flows becomes much more difficult.

Consumption of services is growing faster than the consumption of goods. While some services are tied to localized on-site delivery – restaurant food, car repairs, hairdressing – many are not. With access to modern communications technology, book editing can be undertaken anywhere in the world. Architectural drawings can be done on a computer as easily in Russia as they can in Washington. Programs to control robotic production can be written in Vancouver, tested in Aberdeen and used in Tokyo. The distinction between products and services is becoming blurred. Is writing a new computer program an aspect of production or a service? Is debugging that program still production?

Services based on human rather than physical capital – consulting, market research, management advice and even accounting – are increasingly mobile. As the world becomes increasingly technical, the technology itself must be serviced. Trade in services will continue to increase. Trade in services is likely to require less transport and insurance than trade in goods. Problems associated with ensuring payment and the settlement of disputes will remain. As the quality of service is, in general, much more difficult to verify than the quality of goods, disputes are likely to increase.

Sourcing of components on an international basis is also likely to expand. Further integration of the global economy will result. Improvements to both the speed and reliability of transportation have released manufacturing firms from reliance on local suppliers. Components can be bundled together into final products which are tailored to the preferences of local consumers. Some companies have become specialists at searching out the components which are available internationally and then bringing them together for assembly. Assembling components is a relatively simple procedure in many cases. This increases the weighting given to the international procurement divisions of firms relative to their domestic manufacturing divisions. For those firms that are involved in international sourcing of components, reducing the costs associated with poor cross-cultural communications is imperative.

Few firms are, as yet, truly international. Companies remain identified with particular countries – even if their ownership may be truly international and their formal headquarters in a different country than that with which they are identified. While their international business has increased, they retain their national character. This national character is expressed primarily in management organization and ethic. The management of few companies would be considered truly multinational.

DEVELOPING COUNTRIES AND FORMER COMMAND ECONOMIES

Firms in most developing countries have been less affected by the forces of change which are leading to increased international economic integration. Certainly, some components are sourced in developing countries. Exotic products are exported to satisfy the craving for diversity by consumers in rich countries. The fact remains, however, that a much smaller proportion of firms in developing countries engage in international commerce. Firms from developing countries are much less likely to instigate an international transaction than those in the developed countries. Trade between developed and developing countries is initiated by firms in developed countries seeking products or markets. Trade among developing countries remains small. A large proportion of this trade is organized and facilitated by firms headquartered in developed countries. Part of the reason is technological. Many firms in the developing world have not been able to finance the acquisition of modern electronic communications technology. Often they do not have staff well enough trained to utilize this technology effectively and their governments have not provided the infrastructure required to support its use.

More importantly, however, many firms in developing countries do not have the resources to actively seek out international markets. The costs of market entry are too high to be financed out of current profits. Banks in developing countries will not provide financing for ventures with such slow payoffs and high risks. In many cases, business practices are so different that firms find it impossible to overcome problems with cross-cultural communications. Business practices are, in part, governed by the commercial environment fostered by the government. Where contract enforcement is weak and other aspects of commercial law underdeveloped, business is conducted on a cash basis and remains based on family ties or long-standing personal relationships. Vertical co-ordination based on these business practices is very expensive in terms of managerial time and effort.

Firms in western countries, where commercial law is well developed and enforced, have to a considerable degree substituted contracts for commercial relationships based on personal trust. While it is possible to build relations based on personal trust when the number of other businesses being dealt with is small, it becomes impractical as the number of business contacts increase. The costs of building trust based on personal relationships increases greatly when that trust must be built with a business person in a foreign country. Travel costs alone can be prohibitive. In any case, firms in developed countries are likely to find the costs of building such relationships prohibitively expensive. They will prefer to deal with firms in other developed countries who use contracts to organize the transfer of goods and services.

If developing countries are to benefit from the opportunities that will arise from the growth of international trade, their firms must become proactive participants in international commerce. Developed countries will continue to impose barriers on the imports of some products from developing countries. The market power which some transnational firms possess will continue to limit the ability of developing countries to capture all of the benefits available from trade. The major challenge for developing countries is, however, to reform their systems of commercial law. Without a secure commercial environment, the transactions costs associated with organizing international commerce will remain prohibitively high for all but a small minority of their firms.

The absence of an effective system of commercial law would also appear to be a major stumbling block for the former command economies. Western firms have found that doing business in these countries is extremely risky, primarily because it is impossible to protect themselves from the opportunism of the firms with which they are dealing. They must also contend with the opportunism of other firms and government officials. In some cases, the vacuum created by an absence of enforceable commercial law is being filled by organized crime. The result has been that after considerable initial enthusiasm, western firms have become much more cautious in their dealings with the former command economies. The firms which continue to be interested in extending their activities to include the former command economies have found that they must fall back on the expensive process of building long-term personal relationships. Until these problems are overcome, the former command economies will, to a considerable degree, remain excluded from the benefits arising from the growth in international trade.

The main growth area for international commercial activity is likely to be among the developed countries. The rapidly growing economies of the Asia–Pacific rim are well on their way to becoming integrated into the international economy. While commercial relations with China remain difficult, if the Chinese economy continues to open its doors to trade and foreign capital it will continue to be a major area for growth. India is also showing signs of removing some of the barriers to trade and investment which have been an integral part of its long-term strategy of development based on self-sufficiency. The voluntary opening of two of the largest economies in the world will, however, add to the disequilibrium in the international system. It will take time for new market channels to be opened and for commercial opportunities to be identified and acted upon.

Issues for the international trading system

18

LIBERALIZATION VERSUS PROTECTIONISM

Whilst changing technology and the broadening of consumer tastes will provide the commercial opportunities internationally, governments will continue to influence both the opportunities which firms will be allowed to act upon and the manner in which they can be undertaken. The source of this influence will continue to be through the trade accords they negotiate with other countries and the regulations they unilaterally impose.

Trade liberalization is on the ascendancy as an official political ideology in most developed countries. Whilst formal protectionism raises its head once in a while in developed countries, it is clearly no longer a major political force. Protectionism has lost favour as a legitimate intellectual alternative to trade liberalization. It has, instead, become associated directly with individual vested interest. This does not mean that politicians can always ignore the concerns of these vested interests. Hence, protectionism is currently applied on a piecemeal basis as a political response to particular concerns. The increasing reliance on contingency protection measures by the US, for example, allows requests for protection to be dealt with on a case by case basis. By making it easy for those seeking protection to file suits, the process is de-politicized to a considerable extent. The interim trade restrictions in US contingency protection procedures provide a means by which intense pressure on politicians for protection can be dissipated. Individual vested interests are, however, finding it more difficult to have their concerns identified with the national interest. Even the Japanese rice import policy may be losing its credibility as one of the major guardians of the country's culture and morality. In general, however, agriculture in developed countries is an exception and remains closely associated with nations' welfare.

The reasons why protectionism has lost its political legitimacy are complex. Part of the reason is the evidence itself. The success of the EU, Japan's export based economy and the relatively open economies of Asia's 'four tigers' stand in sharp contrast to the stagnating economies following import substitution policies. Even Britain's Labour Party now openly embraces the EU.

Protectionism is also identified with direct government management of the economy. The conservatism of the Reagan and Thatcher years initiated a movement away from big government and the welfare state that, to a greater or lesser degree, has affected economic policy in all developed countries. Trade liberalization was simply the international manifestation of the move toward deregulation and market forces. The demise of communism, with its emphasis on self-reliance, as an intellectual alternative to market oriented policies is an additional contributing factor to the decline in the popularity of protectionism. The general reduction in the influence of labour unions, with their traditions of protectionism, has freed politicians from the need to listen as closely to their complaints.

Consumers, have for the most part, ignored pleas to buy American or buy British and instead purchased Toyotas, Sonys and Toshibas without a shred of conscience. The choices of consumers have not gone unnoticed by politicians. In particular, politicians realized that voters could not be denied access to the latest foreign consumer gadgetry. The improvement in domestically produced products brought about by sharp foreign competition was also not lost on politicians.

The *status quo* is not an acceptable alternative to liberalization. There was little support for leaving well enough alone when the Uruguay Round was being proposed. Expansion and closer co-operation are the bywords of the EU. The CUSTA was extended to include Mexico in the NAFTA. There are discussions regarding further expansions. Formal trade alliances have been proposed for the Pacific rim. The former command economies are applying for entry into the EU. In general, there is a momentum for change.

There are two major intellectual thrusts to the process of trade liberalism. One of the thrusts of trade policy is multilateralism. The other sees an expanded role for regional trade organizations. They are not necessarily contradictory. When transformed by political energy into government policy, however, the end result can be the creation of institutions which move trade policy in opposite directions. Multilateralism is firmly rooted in the liberalization tradition. The enthusiasm for regional trade organizations is much more pragmatic and reflects the art of the possible. Multilateralism is sometimes perceived as a spent force while great potential is seen in regional arrangements.

The political appeal of multilateralism, however, should not be underestimated. The vast amounts of political energy put into the Uruguay Round attests to its resilience. No major trading country seriously considered abandoning the GATT. In part, this is because the alternative – a total reliance on regional organizations – carries with it the unpleasant spectre of competition between trade blocs and protectionist beggar thy neighbour trade restrictions between blocks. Politicians fear that trade wars between blocks could be sufficiently destructive to wipe out many of the economic gains which have been made since World War II.

Trade blocs and multilateralism need not be incompatible. They share the common aim of trade liberalization. The WTO explicitly allows for regional trade organizations. The major problem with regional trade organizations is that making them work effectively can require a tremendous amount of political energy. Political energy tends to become focused on the problems of the organization. Further, there will be a need for political compromise among the countries in a regional trade organization. In some cases, accommodating competing national interests in a regional organization can be most easily accomplished by imposing costs on countries outside the regional grouping.

The EU provides excellent examples of the tendency to impose costs on non-members for the sake of internal harmony. The political energy required to keep the EU from self-destruction is enormous. The export subsidies of the CAP are simply a means by which reforming the system of agricultural subsidies could be avoided. By exporting the surpluses at subsidized prices, costs are imposed on other agricultural exporters who have subsequently lost their markets. For a long time the inability to negotiate meaningful reforms to the CAP eventually threatened the entire Uruguay Round. The failure of the member states of the EU to agree on how to rationalize the automobile industry has led to increased restrictions on Japanese imports and car makers.

One of the major proposals of the EU at the Uruguay Round was a relaxation of the principle of non-discrimination. This would have allowed selective imposition of trade restrictions on individual countries without the fear of multilateral retaliation. Being allowed to restrict the imports of selected countries would have reduced the cost of internal EU negotiations relating to access to sensitive markets within Europe.

The CUSTA contained elements which allowed increased restrictions on car makers in other countries. These provisions eased the passage of the Agreement through the legislatures of both countries. The difficulties which regional trade blocs face in achieving internal compromise are likely to increase as they expand the number of states they include. As a result, the trade concerns of non-members are more likely to be ignored. The final stages of the Uruguay Round negotiations became a search for compromise between the EU and the US. Other countries could only wait on the sidelines and hope the compromises reached did not significantly damage their interests.

Of course, the amount of political energy which was required to make even small amounts of progress at the multilateral GATT negotiations led to the interest in regional groupings in the first place. Much faster progress towards trade liberalization could be made when only a few countries were involved. Frustration with the slowness at the GATT negotiations provided part of the impetus for the negotiations between the US and Canada. Additional countries wish to join the EU rather than waiting for multilateral negotiations. The Uruguay Round of GATT talks, with over 100 nations participating, took 7 years to complete. If the issues were not so fundamentally important, it is unlikely that any agreement would have been reached.

The major problem with multilateralism is that the number of participants involved makes the negotiating process nearly intractable. It is not clear how multilateral institutions might be reformed to increase efficiency. Any change which increases efficiency will require that states relinquish some of their sovereignty over trade matters. Most countries show little inclination to do this. As a result, regional trade organizations retain their appeal.

The extension of the existing GATT organization into areas of international commerce not concerned with trade in goods was a major accomplishment of the Uruguay Round. Since the inception of the GATT, the progress made in reducing tariffs has been considerable. Progress has been so great that only limited gains are likely to arise from the remaining tariff reductions, at least among the developed countries. Trade in services, international protection of intellectual property and government procurement now represent areas of international commerce where the removal of barriers provides the greatest potential for gains from trade. Liberalization in these areas, however, is likely to be difficult. These are also areas where the examples from regional trade organizations can provide a guide. This is because they have been able to make greater progress due to the smaller number of countries involved.

TRADE IN SERVICES

Liberalization in the areas of services is likely to be difficult because the restrictions on trade in services are not often explicit border restrictions. They are, rather, integral parts of a country's domestic regulations. In some cases, it is be possible to arrange for delivery of the service from the home country of the foreign service company – proof reading manuscripts or computer data entry. Few restrictions, however, limit this type of trade. Franchised services – where the service is provided by citizens of the country importing the service – are also not heavily restricted. Problems may arise if the company selling the franchise is not able to send its employees to the importing country to provide training or to monitor the quality of the service. These problems are unlikely to greatly inhibit the franchising of services.

Far greater problems are likely to arise in the trade in services from the need to send employees to the importing country on a temporary basis. Problems with certification of professionals may also be important. The movement of people between countries has not traditionally been a trade matter but rather an immigration matter. Restrictions on immigration are, essentially, restrictions on the movement of one factor of production – labour. The forces of comparative advantage suggest that either goods or labour should move to markets where they receive increased returns. Immigration policy is, hence, bound up in employment policy. Countries impose immigration barriers in the name of keeping unemployment down, of keeping wages up and of maintaining the fiscal integrity of their social welfare systems. Regardless of the validity of these arguments, nations will jealously guard their rights to control imports of labour.

Traditionally, the movement of labour between countries tended to be a permanent movement. The labour component of the trade in services is far more likely to be transitory. If the provision of the service requires a full time labour commitment, then training a local employee would often be more cost effective. The labour component of an imported service is unlikely to be based on a significant labour cost advantage. If the wages associated with the provision of imported services were significantly higher in the importing country, the exporter's employees could always better themselves by finding a means of emigrating, either legally or illegally. The exporter of the service would have high labour turnover costs.

While immigration policy is primarily concerned with long-term employment, it can be used effectively as a short-term trade barrier. The most obvious example of this is when an international contract involves the bundling together of both goods and services. As the technology embodied in goods has increased in complexity, both the requirements for servicing and the sophistication of that servicing have increased. Hence, when goods are sold, the contract often includes within it a long-term service component. Without a service agreement, the individual buyer would be forced into employing trained staff to repair the equipment purchased. It is often more efficient for sellers to provide the service because the cost can be spread over a large number of sales.

When tied combinations of goods and services are marketed internationally, government restrictions on the international movement of service people can adversely affect sales. While tariffs and other restrictions on the movement of the goods portion of the transaction may have been eliminated as a result of international trade negotiations, the movement of the personnel required to service the goods may still be restricted. Exporting firms must then be willing to establish service subsidiaries in export markets. This may mean costly duplication and compliance with regulations regarding local participation in subsidiaries, labour laws, social security, etc. The price of the entire package may be increased considerably and, hence, total sales reduced. These problems are likely to be particularly acute in the market entry stage when the volume of sales cannot justify a full time service organization. Sending service personnel from the exporting country on a short-term basis may be the only cost effective alternative. If this is not allowed, export markets will have to be foregone. Hence, finding mechanisms to reduce barriers to trade in services will become increasingly important as the technical complexity of exports continues to increase. The CUSTA included special provisions for the short run movement of personnel involved in servicing industrial goods.

Removing barriers to the trade in professional services is a complex topic. Doctors, lawyers, accountants, engineers, etc., often have, as part of their mandate as professionals, the requirement to act as quality guarantors for those who use their services. Given the complexity of verifying quality, self-regulation by government sanctioned professional organizations has been generally adopted. In most cases, professional organizations have the right of certification.

Certification procedures in different countries have evolved independently and, hence, vary considerably. The process of certification is often tied to and influences the education prospective professionals receive at university. Individuals who have been certified in one jurisdiction may be forced to incur considerable **switching costs** if they wish to obtain certification in another country. Given that they have a state sanctioned monopoly over certification, and, hence, entry into the profession, professional organizations have the opportunity to undertake rent seeking activities. As the verification of quality can be exceedingly complex in professional services, it is difficult to determine when the standards for certification are necessary to guarantee quality for consumers and when they are being used as barriers to entry for the purposes of rent seeking. In any case, as quality cannot be guaranteed absolutely, professional organizations will always be able to make the claim that their regulations reduce risks for consumers.

Imports of professional services is likely to be perceived as a threat by a professional organization which is using its certification powers for purposes of rent seeking. Certification may not be based on an examination, but rather on long-term processes involving education, supervised experience and socialization. Evaluation of the contribution of these aspects of certification for those trained in a different country can be very difficult. Formal certification examinations often only serve the purpose of a final check on professional competency – they can be used to fail candidates but full certification relies heavily on the individual having passed all the previous steps in the process. Hence, it is probably not possible to design a single examination which can substitute for these long-term professionalization processes. Professional organizations sometimes attempt to devise special exams for foreign applicants. As these will inevitably be more demanding that those devised for domestic students – in an attempt to substitute for the professionalization process – they are open to charges of discrimination.

The problem of trade in professional services can be approached in a number of ways. Professional organizations in different countries can be asked to harmonize their regulations. This will mean protracted negotiations. Harmonization may also require the co-operation of educational institutions. The harmonization of the government regulations which affect the services will also be necessary. Overcoming determined opposition from professional organizations may be very difficult. It may be easy for professionals to enlist public support for their political battles. The trust they have built up can be used to unsettle consumers. References can easily be made to 'inferior' foreign standards when verification of standards is beyond the competence of individual consumers. Harmonization can be a long and difficult process.

One alternative is for the government to extend **national treatment** to individuals who have been cerified by foreign professional organizations.

National treatment means that individuals who hold foreign certification will have the same rights to practice their profession as those with domestic certification. This approach can succeed as long as quality differences are actually small and if foreign professional organizations are effective guarantors of quality.

The CUSTA and the EU have included elements of both harmonization and national treatment in their provisions for trade in services. The EU's provisions for the free movement of professionals needs to be closely observed. Problems have already arisen regarding the inability of professional organizations in other counties to verify the qualifications of dentists certified in Italy. A second alternative – establishing a supernational body to devise a common certification program – has not generally been attempted due to the difficulty of structuring an examination which can evaluate the long professionalization process.

Liberalizing trade in professional services can be likened to the problems associated with removing non-tariff barriers. Many non-tariff barriers arise from differences in domestic regulations put in place to protect the public interest. That the regulations also have an ability to restrict trade is an externality that can be used by vested interests to their advantage. As in the case of non-tariff barriers, there are political costs to removing the economic instruments useful to professionals vested interests.

A new **General Agreement in Trade in Services (GATS)** was reached as part of the Uruguay Round. The GATS is a parallel agreement to the GATT and will be administered under the auspices of the WTO. All members of the WTO will be members of the GATS. Any disputes arising in trade in services will settled by the WTO. A broad range of services is covered including investment, temporary movement of personnel and cross-border operations. The services provided by government such as the police and education are not included.

A commitment to improve the transparency of regulations concerning services has been made by GATS members. Countries have agreed to open the services market to varying degrees. Once a commitment has been made a country must, in principle, extend the concession to all other GATS members. There is a provision for exceptions, allowing discriminatory treatment to creep into the agreement. The exceptions are expected to be removed within 10 years. Future negotiations are expected to reduce or remove restrictions on access such as limitations on the number of foreign providers of services, on the total value of services, on the number of transactions undertaken by foreign firms and on the number of employees foreign providers of services are allowed to hire. Over time, negotiations will take place regarding reductions to restrictions on the cross-border movement of people providing services, the harmonization of professional, technical and licensing standards and the control of trade distorting subsidies in service industries. While commitments have been made to liberalize trade in financial services, maritime transport, telecommunications and international air flights, these services are treated as special categories.

The GATS, as yet, remains largely an agreement of intent. Its success will depend upon the concessions countries will grant in future negotiations. One strong clause in the agreement is that, while previously granted concessions may be withdrawn or modified after 3 years, compensation must be paid. If the parties cannot agree on compensation it will be awarded by arbitration.

PROTECTION OF INTELLECTUAL PROPERTY

The internationalization of protection for **intellectual property** is not fundamentally a trade issue. It was included in the Uruguay round negotiations by developed countries so that it could be directly tied to concessions in the trade in goods and services. The issue does, however, have a trade aspect. Products which use intellectual property as an input are often exported back to the country where the intellectual property originated. If the intellectual property has been used without full compensation being paid, it means that the low cost imported product competes directly with the product of the firm which incurred the costs of developing the technology. As a result, incentives for companies who develop technology are adversely affected.

While intellectual piracy is not a new phenomenon, it has increased in importance due to the revolution in electronic technology. The proportion of a good's cost accounted for by physical materials has fallen considerably. Computer chips are inexpensive to manufacture. The major component of their value is supplied by the intellectual effort incorporated in the chip's design. The flexibility that these chips give to product design means that industrial production is much less standardized than in the past. Further, the rate at which intellectual property is becoming obsolete is increasing. The fixed costs of developing intellectual property, as a consequence, have to be recouped from fewer and fewer sales. Given its increased importance, the incentives for using intellectual property without compensation have risen.

As the unauthorized use of intellectual property increases, however, the lower the returns to investing in such activities become. The rate of technological change is reduced. Politicians in developed countries are concerned with sluggish growth in their economies. Protection of intellectual property has become an international issue in the same way that patent protection was once a public issue within national economies.

Resistance to increased international protection for intellectual property has come, for the most part, from developing countries. There are three reasons for this. Firstly, as most intellectual property is developed in rich countries, they are able to maintain or increase their higher standard of living – an equity issue. Secondly, as patents are only a very crude instrument for providing returns on investment, they also allow firms to extract monopoly profits. Thirdly, governments in some developing countries may not be able to effectively police the use of intellectual property.

As the proportion of the value of goods made up by intellectual property rises, a nation's economic prosperity increasingly depends on its ability to generate new technology. Most new intellectual property is developed in advanced economies. Part of the reason for this is that major corporations locate their research and development activities in their home countries. The much larger expenditures which developed countries can afford to make on education and publicly funded research is also important. In the view of some developing countries governments, closing the development gap may simply not be possible without transfers of either human capital or the technology itself. As foreign assistance in these areas remains at levels far below what is required to close the gap, some governments in developing countries see the uncompensated use of intellectual property as the only means available to acquire the technology required for them to close the gap. While some governments openly espouse this view, others simply choose to ignore the unauthorized use of intellectual property.

Even if governments in developing countries accept the argument that those who invest in the development of new technology are entitled to a return on their investment, they find the mechanism used by developed countries to provide that return unacceptable. Developed countries want patent protection extended internationally. Further, they want developing countries to vigorously enforce patent protection. Patents endow the developer of new technology with the property rights to the use of the technology for a specified period. This allows the holder of the rights to act as a monopolist. Exercising monopoly power provides the basis for the return on the investment made in new technology. This means, however, that the returns actually received are not directly tied to the size of the initial investment. As a result, the rates of return on investment for developing new technology may exceed that required for a competitive return on investment.

The issue of a competitive rate of return for investments in research and development is complex because it involves risk and risk spreading. The firms investing in research and development argue that rates of return on a successful development must cover losses on other unsuccessful research ventures. Governments in developing countries, however, object to paying the monopoly rents that contribute to returns on investment which exceed competitive returns. This argument is particularly prevalent in the case of pharmaceuticals and agricultural inputs such as seed. Governments in low income countries argue that their citizens are too poor to pay high prices for essential drugs and farmers too poor to pay for high priced inputs. As long as they are not involved in the development of new technology, they have little to lose from allowing their citizens access to low cost domestically produced generic products. This is why developed countries have wanted discussions on intellectual property to be tied to other trade issues where they can exert some leverage.

Some developing countries may also feel that they are unable to expend the resources necessary to enforce intellectual property rights.

Further, they may not have the capacity for effective enforcement. If they agreed to improved international protection for intellectual property, they may not be able to live up to their commitments. This would put them in violation of their international commitments and leave them open to withdrawal of trade concessions.

These are the fundamental issues which must be dealt with regarding the protection of intellectual property. For businesses that develop new technology, the lack of international protection increases the risks associated with those investments. Lowering the risk may take many forms, including direct transnational operations or vertical integration to better ensure control of the new technology.

The Trade-Related Aspects of Intellectual Property Rights (TRIPS) were a major concern of developed countries at the Uruguay Round. The negotiations concluded with a wide ranging Agreement on Trade-Related Aspects of Intellectual Property Rights, Including Trade in Counterfeit Goods. The central theme of the agreement is that countries agree to enforce the property rights of other countries' firms and citizens. This commitment extends to patents, trademarks, films, sound recordings, computer software, integrated computer circuits, trade secrets, test data and the misuse of geographic indicators, e.g. labelling bottles of wine produced in Canada as originating in France. While the conventions covering different types of intellectual property vary, that the intellectual property of foreigners should receive the same protection as that given to the country's own nationals is the general principle applied. Further, the protection extended to one country's nationals must be extended to all other countries – the principle of non-discrimination.

With respect to patents, developing countries which do not have comprehensive patent protection must enact legislation to cover those areas of technology not currently covered. They have 10 years to complete the task. In terms of other aspects of the agreement, the least developed countries have 11 years to bring their legislation and practices into conformity with the agreement. Other developing countries and former command economies must conform within 5 years while developed countries agreed to conform within 1 year. Hence, the agreement would appear to provide a considerable degree of protection for intellectual property rights. Enforcement will, however, be of paramount importance.

The agreement obliges member governments to provide procedures and remedies in their domestic laws to ensure that intellectual property rights can be effectively enforced. The procedures put in place must allow for judicial review. Excessive time delays and costs are not to be allowed. There is no requirement, however, that extra resources need to be dedicated to the enforcement of intellectual property rights or that enforcement should receive any priority. Countries with weak or ineffective judicial systems are still likely to have poor intellectual property rights protection.

The remedies which countries have agreed to put in place include injunctions, damages and the right of judicial authorities to order disposal or destruction of infringing goods. Countries are expected to provide criminal procedures and penalties for the most blatant abuses of trademark counterfeiting and copyright piracy. Clearly, in the negotiations an attempt was made by developed countries to have the problem of enforcement addressed. Enforcement, however, is ultimately dependent upon bureaucrats or the courts acting vigorously to identify and pursue infringements. Judging the effectiveness of the agreement will have to wait until these latter aspects of enforcement can be assessed. Under the Uruguay round agreement, a Council for Trade-Related Aspects of Intellectual Property Rights has been established within the WTO. Disputes are settled within WTO procedures.

GOVERNMENT PROCUREMENT

Liberalization of government procurement procedures is another area where the potential for gains from trade are significant. Government involvement in national economies continues to increase despite efforts in many countries to reverse the trend. Governments typically purchase in excess of one quarter of the goods and services sold in any year. For the most part, government procurement contracts have been reserved for domestic producers. If foreign firms are allowed to bid on government contracts, it is often on conditions that discriminate in favour of domestic firms.

In some cases, foreign bidders are excluded for legitimate reasons of national security. In most cases, the restrictions are the result of politicians giving in to pressure from lobbyists. Politicians have a role as the champions of the nation's products. They are often put in a difficult position when the government they represent is purchasing foreign goods and services. This inconsistency is not lost on opposition politicians and voters. Given that the goods and services purchased are often complex, explaining foreign purchases on the basis of strict commercial criteria to the satisfaction of voters is often difficult.

The result is that the goods and services purchased by government often enjoy near autarky levels of protection. Hence, the potential for gains from trade are probably significant. Opening up government procurement contracts to foreign bidders is likely to be difficult. Those politicians who perceive trade liberalization as an engine for global economic growth will, however, promote liberalization – if for no other reason than the expected size of the potential gains.

The opening of procurement contracts to foreign bidders is likely to lead to lively debate within political parties themselves. As suggested above, it will leave politicians open to criticism that they are abrogating their responsibility to champion domestic products. There are numerous examples of apparently trivial violations of their roles as champions of national products such as driving a foreign made car or vacationing in foreign countries which have become major political issues. Fear of the effects of this form of criticism on a much larger scale may lead to considerable opposition to liberalization of procurement contracts.

Further, the awarding of procurement contracts may be one of the ways political parties reward their supporters. Allowing foreign bidders will reduce the party's power base and, subsequently, resources. Resistance can be expected within the party if this is the case.

It will prove difficult to devise a mechanism for awarding contracts which will withstand international scrutiny. Governments have been at pains to devise bidding systems which allow criteria other than lowest price to be considered in domestic sealed bid auctions. In many cases, the perception of the ability of the firm to complete the project or to deliver on the quality specifications is as important to the decision to award the contract as the price. The problems created by the **winner's curse** phenomenon makes reliance on bid price as the only criteria problematic at best (Cullen and Kerr, 1989). Making the allocation of government procurement contracts a sufficiently transparent process to overcome bidders suspicions of bias has proved virtually impossible for purely domestic contracts. It will likely prove even more difficult when contracts are opened for international bidding and suspicions of national bias are endemic. New international institutions will probably be required to monitor government procurement procedures if liberalization takes place.

The CUSTA made specific provisions for the opening of government procurement contracts to firms in the other country. This was done on the basis of reciprocity whereby each country agreed to open all contracts that exceeded pre-specified minimum values. Small contracts are still reserved for domestic firms. Both Canada and the US are federations with multiple levels of government with constitutionally guaranteed powers. Both the Canadian provinces and the individual US states as well as local governments in both countries have considerable economic independence. This includes control over their own procurement processes. Attempting to have the Agreement's procurement provisions extended to lower levels of government would have led to a constitutional challenge in both countries. As it was a mutual problem, the procurement provisions were restricted to contracts of the national governments. This type of arrangement would not be suitable for countries with a more unitary government system because it would mean that all contracts in the country with a unitary government structure would be open while a portion of a federation's contracts remained closed to international bidders. Wider acceptance of the liberalization of procurement contracts is likely to be subject to difficult negotiations.

While negotiations on government procurement were not formally part of the Uruguay Round, 12 countries – including the EU signing as one – signed an Agreement on Government Procurement in December 1993. The agreement will, however, be part of the WTO. Most developed countries including the US and Japan are party to the agreement, as well as Hong Kong and South Korea. Other countries are encouraged to join.

The basis of the agreement is the opening up of contracts over a certain size to bids from the other countries signing the agreement. The size of the contracts open to foreign bids will change with the level of government involved. For national governments, the threshold is

US$176 000. It rises to approximately US$270 000 for states, provinces, departments and prefectures while for utilities it is US$540 000. For construction contracts it is US$675 000.

This system of thresholds leaves politicians considerable flexibility if they wish to exclude foreign bidders. Almost any contract can be re-bundled into smaller units and separately tendered. In other words, if a contract is sufficiently large that foreign bids must be allowed under the terms of the agreement, it could simply be split into two (or more) smaller contracts and foreign bidders excluded.

The principles underlying the agreement on government procurement are transparency and **national treatment**. The signatories have agreed to widely disseminate information on contracts including technical specifications, time limits, required documentation and submission procedures. Institutional arrangements are to be put in place for unsatisfied bidders to be able to challenge procurement decisions. Foreign suppliers and foreign goods and services must be given no less favourable treatment than domestic suppliers.

The agreement comes into force at the beginning of 1996. Its wider success will, of course, depend on the number of additional countries which join over time.

TRADE BLOCS

Liberalization of services and government procurement, as well as agreements over increased protection of intellectual property, will be much easier within regional groupings of countries than it will be in the multilateral forums of the WTO. As a result, regional groupings are likely to become increasingly influential and important regulators of international commerce. The danger is that these regional groupings may take on the characteristics of competing trade blocs. This will mean that, while trade barriers are coming down within the blocs, trade barriers between the blocs may remain in place. There is already considerable trade tension between the major focal points around which trade blocs will have to coalesce. The US and the EU are at loggerheads over agriculture. The US and Japan are in conflict over access to Japanese procurement contracts and the Japanese distribution system. Japan and the EU battle over imports of Japanese cars and electronics.

The prospects for further expansion of the EU and the embryo of an American-led bloc in the western hemisphere has not been lost on other countries. If blocs are developing, countries must fear not belonging to a bloc. The worst case scenario for a small country is having to go it alone in a world where trading blocs are building trade barriers around themselves. If trade blocs become the focus of political activity, the protection offered small countries by multilateral institutions will wane. The fate of Australia and New Zealand when Britain entered the EU is a lesson lost on few small countries. The safe course is to become a member of a bloc.

Countries such as Sweden, Austria and Finland perceived great benefits from being members of the EU, they also feared being left on the fringes of international commerce. The number of countries wishing to negotiate some form of expanded NAFTA, in part, reflects these fears. As regional groupings expand, negotiations for the acceptance of new members will become more difficult and the terms of accession less favourable. Hence, it is better to attempt to join a group as early as possible. The scramble to join potential trade blocs will, of course, increase the economic power of the bloc. This will increase its ability to act independently. As blocs become larger they will also become more unwieldy. Additional political energy will have to be expended to progress internally. This will increase the likelihood that the trade concerns of other blocs and non-members will be ignored.

The potential for a third bloc on the Asia–Pacific rim also exists. As yet, there is little evidence that it is in the process of forming. The natural focal point is Japan but other Asian nations appear to fear Japanese hegemony. Memories of Japan's last attempt at the formation of an economic bloc, its wartime **Greater East Asia Co-Prosperity Sphere** may still be too sharp. Further, while growing rapidly, the markets of other Asia–Pacific rim countries are not yet large enough to replace the US and Europe as Japan's major markets. Events in China could change the balance. China is a natural counterbalance to Japanese hegemony and its market potential is huge. If the EU and the western hemisphere begin to act more as contending trade blocs, Asian countries may well find the will to follow suit.

If true trade blocs arise, some developing countries will find themselves drawn into one of the bloc's sphere of influence but without full membership. Others will be increasingly isolated. In both cases, their bargaining power over trade issues is likely to be decreased. Trade will not be their engine of growth.

While the increased speed at which trade barriers can be reduced when a small group of states co-operate is appealing – there is also great danger. While some disputes between blocs are to be expected and not likely to disrupt trade flows significantly, the spectre of full blown trade wars between blocs is also possible. Trade between Japan, the US and the major countries of the EU exceeds that with their regional trading partners. This trade is also increasing rapidly. A full scale trade war would be devastating to all the major economies. As a result, political effort will be required to prevent a further deterioration in relations. At present, the only forum available is the WTO. The future is likely to see a seesaw between the forces of regionalism and the forces of multilateralism. If trading blocs begin to seriously conflict, multilateralism will ascend. Frustration with the slow progress possible through multilateralism will see renewed regional efforts.

BUSINESS INPUT INTO TRADE ISSUES

It will be important for businesses to watch closely the evolution of the international trading environment. Changes in trade regulations will provide opportunities. Falling barriers will open new markets. Change will also mean new threats from foreign competition. Increasing barriers will lead to opportunities to produce substitutes for foreign products. It will also mean that some markets will become closed. The opportunities provided by the reduction in barriers provided by regional groupings of states are likely to be easier to identify and act upon. The threats presented by competitors from within a bloc are also likely to be more vigorous. Information will be the key.

Regardless of the actions of governments, technological change will be the most important factor influencing future international commercial activities. Governments are only likely to be able to act after the fact in reaction to commercial realities. Given the current political acceptance of the trade led growth thesis, firms which identify new opportunities that are constrained by trade barriers are likely to get a better hearing from government than those wishing to close off a competitive threat from foreigners.

Foreign non-tariff barriers may not be in place to protect any identifiable vested interest but may rather have been put in place to regulate a situation which no longer reflects the commercial reality. The restriction only remains in place due to the inertia of government. Firms who find their opportunities constrained by such foreign regulations cannot be complacent. They will have to press their government strongly to negotiate with the foreign government for the removal of the obsolete trade restriction. If the pace of technological change continues to accelerate, more redundant regulations which act as non-tariff barriers are likely to become evident. Firms seeking out international opportunities will be the first to identify these constraints. They will need to form much more of a partnership with government than in the past, when the major thrust of trade negotiations was the reduction of general purpose trade restrictions – tariffs, import quotas, etc. Non-tariff barriers in the form of domestic regulations will be very diverse and less easily identifiable by governments. Industry must be prepared to take a more active leadership role. Further, the smaller scale negotiations of regional groupings of states will make it easier to identify particular areas of business concerns than is the case with multilateral negotiations.

While one of the major assumptions of this discussion of the future has been that the influence of protectionists is on the wane, this does not mean that they have been vanquished. It does appear, however, that protectionists no longer have the ability to become identified with broad-based national interest. The poor showing of Canadian political parties which fought elections primarily over whether to sign and subsequently to 'tear-up' the CUSTA, the difficult time had by most political parties opposed to their countries joining the EU, the weak opposition in the US against NAFTA, all attest to the protectionists fading influence. Those interested in protectionism, however, may also find themselves with new allies.

Environmental groups, frustrated with the rate of progress in cleaning up the environment in developing countries, have been attempting to tie environmental issues to trade issues. This would enable more leverage to be applied to governments in developing countries. The environmental groups have found willing allies among protectionists who see lower environmental standards as unfair trade advantages. While this line of reasoning is little more than the old cheap labour argument dressed up in a different guise, it has gained a degree of popularity. Certainly, the environmental record in developing countries is generally very poor and needs to be addressed. Tying it to trade issues will not, however, be likely to lead to a significant improvement. It should be noted that, along with poor enforcement of labour standards – the cheap labour argument – Mexico's less stringent environmental legislation was the major stumbling bloc to US approval of the NAFTA. The convergence of interest between the protectionist instincts of businesses facing vigorous foreign competition and the environmental movement may wield considerable influence in the right circumstances.

Other special interests, such as animal welfare groups and those concerned with endangered species may also wish to have their issues increasingly tied to trade sanctions. This increases their ability to influence events in other countries. The effectiveness of trade actions in influencing events in other countries was powerfully demonstrated when the European Community banned imports of seal products to protest at the method used in Canada's seal hunt (Jhappan, 1994). While trade sanctions have been used to try to influence the behaviour of nations regarding aggression and human rights, the broadening of the spectrum of issues where trade sanctions can be applied may considerably influence future trade patterns and international commerce.

Firms engaging in international commerce may have to be far more cognizant of the origins of the products they trade than in the past. While it may be relatively easy to identify when an endangered species is being used as an industrial input, it may be far more difficult to determine whether an imported input has been produced under environmentally acceptable conditions. Firms engaging in international commerce who fail to take account of such factors may risk considerable loss of reputation through adverse publicity.

As the world economy continues to become more integrated, fewer and fewer firms will remain isolated from international commerce. Businesses are, however, able to influence considerably the economic environment in which they operate.

REFERENCES

Cullen, S. E. and Kerr, W. A. (1989) International competitiveness and resource rents – insights from the Canada–US softwood lumber dispute. *World Competition Law and Economics Review*, **12**(3), 25–39.

Jhappan, R. (1992) Animal rights versus aboriginal rights: Canada's aboriginal peoples and the European Community, in *The European Community, Canada and 1992*, (ed. G. M. MacMillan), The University of Calgary, Calgary.

Summary
Part Six

The pace at which change is taking place in international commerce is increasing. Part of the reason for this is the rapid rate of technological change in a key component to the costs of doing business internationally – electronic communications. By increasing both the quantity and quality of information available to firms, as well as reducing the time it takes to transfer information, the ability to identify new potential markets is improving. More effective monitoring of transactions is also possible.

The rate of change is also increasing because governments in most countries have identified the liberalization of international trade as being important to improving the performance of their economies. A considerable momentum exists for the removal of trade barriers both multilaterally and within regional trade alliances. While those with vested interests in the status quo are still able to exert considerable pressure for protection, their efforts are less often identified with the broad national interest.

Both regional trade groups and multilateral negotiations continue to make progress in removing trade barriers. The progress in regional trade associations has been more rapid and helps to explain their current popularity. The EU and the NAFTA both have countries lined up wishing to join. Their example is being followed in other areas of the world. From Australia and New Zealand to South America to Africa, new regional trade groupings are being formed and old ones resurrected. Whilst 'Free Trade Areas' have existed in many parts of the developing world for a considerable period, they were largely ineffective in the era when policies of import substitution and an expanding role for government in the economy were the popular ideologies. The new regional trade groupings are the result of initiatives from governments which are attempting to deregulate their own economies, including their trade policies. They may succeed where their predecessors did not. Their success will, however, be limited without better access to markets in at least one of the major developed economies.

Even though progress seems painfully slow at the WTO, multinational negotiations remain a major focus for trade policy. There is still more agreement amongst countries about trade issues than there is disagreement. While the disagreements surrounding agriculture and cultural industries receive the publicity, and may at times appear to threaten the entire multilateral system, agreement in a large number of other potentially difficult areas was achieved fairly easily in the Uruguay Round.

Governments also perceive that for future large gains to trade to arise, liberalization will have to be applied in other areas – in particular trade in services and government procurement. Liberalization in these areas is being pursued both multilaterally and in regional trade organizations. The liberalization of services will be difficult because it will often involve the temporary movement of people. The liberalization of government procurement contracts will be difficult because of its direct influence on internal politics. Considerable progress in these areas has been made by both the EU and in the NAFTA. Their experience may prove valuable when attempts are made to extend liberalization in these areas to other countries. Reaping the full benefits of trade liberalization will also require government investment in reducing the costs of re-deploying resources, particularly labour displaced as a result of liberalization.

The interaction between firms engaged in international commerce and trade policy makers is likely to increase in the future. With many of the formal barriers to trade removed, trade opportunities may be increasingly affected by non-tariff barriers. The formal barriers such as tariffs and import quotas were imposed by governments for the expressed purpose of restricting trade. They were visible targets for liberalization. Non-tariff barriers are less transparent and individually affect only a limited number of international commercial opportunities. Firms, in the process of investigating commercial opportunities, will encounter these restrictions. Often these restrictions will not have been imposed with the intent of impeding trade. Companies will have to work more closely with governments than in the past to help identify the constraints on their opportunities and to suggest solutions.

The economics of international business can be approached from two levels – trade between countries and international transactions between firms. Economists have traditionally focused on the former. Considerable insights are provided by trade theory models and from the understanding they provide regarding the effects of the trade policies used by governments. The challenge is to use those insights effectively to commercial advantage. It is also important for business people to understand the flaws in some commonly held theories. Only then can reasonable business responses to trade policy issues be formulated.

The study of the economic forces underlying international commercial transactions is less well developed. The current institutional arrangements available to facilitate international transactions can be explained as attempts by firms to reduce the costs associated with those transactions. The evidence suggests that the international institutions which have evolved to facilitate international commerce are efficient. It would appear, however, that many of these institutions have as their primary *raison d'être*, reducing the risk of opportunist behaviour by parties to an international transaction. This suggests that economists need to spend more time studying how firms actually behave. Only then will better insights be gained into the interaction between trade policy and the other economic forces affecting the volume and organization of international transactions.

Exercise 1

While it is common to provide questions and exercises throughout a book, we have not done so. We believe that international trade and commerce needs to be approached as a system. Underlying economic forces, trade policies and international institutions, both public and private, together affect the choices firms make. We have decided to set only one exercise.

In light of what you have learned in this book rewrite the executive's tale that began the volume.

Hopefully, you will have a better ending than Tony.

Glossary of terms

Absolute advantage The ability to produce a good or service more cheaply than one's rivals.

Accounting profit The residual after deduction of all money costs, ie, sales revenue minus wages, salaries, rent, fuel, raw materials, etc.

Ad valorem **tariff** A tariff which is expressed as a proportion of the price.

Appellate body A body that adjudicates on trade disputes between countries.

Asset specificity An investment which once made has no or very limited alternative use, e.g. purchase of specialized plant or machinery.

Autarky A situation when a country is not participating in international trade.

Aval A contract of exchange. A form of guarantee given by a bank or other party to enhance the value of a negotiable instrument.

Balance of trade The difference between the value of visible exports and the value of visible imports. Thus a country may be in surplus or deficit on its visible transactions with one or all countries.

Baltic Exchange Freight chartering exchange in the City of London.

Bareboat charter A time charter under which the ship owner hires out only the ship letting the charterer employ the master and crew, provide fuel and stores and bear all the cost and responsibility of operating the ship.

Barter An agreement where goods and services may be exchanged for another specified set of goods or services. No currency is offered in exchange.

Beggar thy neighbour — Retaliatory trade policies designed to counteract other countries' trade restrictions. They usually lead to further retaliatory action which results in the reduction of trade volumes and benefits no one.

Bilateral agreement — Agreement between two nations.

Black market — An illicit trade in goods.

Bretton Woods system — An agreement reached in 1944 among finance ministers of 45 western nations to establish a system of fixed exchange rates.

Bulk cargo — Cargo consisting entirely of one kind of loose substance that does not need any packing, such as coal or wheat.

Bulk carrier — A ship intended for carrying cargoes of loose materials, such as coal ore or grain, which are not packed in containers.

Buy-back agreements — In order to obtain an order to supply plant, such as a factory, a firm agrees to buy a specified amount of the output of the plant when commissioned.

Cambridge School — A school of economic thought established by economists at the University of Cambridge, Great Britain.

Camproadors — Either employees of a trading house or their exclusive agents, employed to foster personal business relationships and trust between traders so reducing the cultural clash between businessmen and encouraging trade.

Capital — Assets which can be used in the production and distribution of goods and services, i.e. capital equipment. Also the money value of real assets.

Carrier of origin requirements — A requirement that imports be carried on ships/aircraft registered/owned by the country of destination or that exports be carried on the ships/aircraft owned/registered by the country of origin.

Cartel	A cartel is an association of independent entities that attempts to determine output/sales/prices so that members secure monopoly profits.
Charter	A charter is a contract by which an owner agrees to hire a ship or aircraft to a person or organization known as the charterer. The document relating to the conditions of the contract is the charter-party.
c.i.f.	Cost, insurance and freight. In foreign trade contracts the seller's price includes all charges and risks up to the point where the ship carrying the goods arrives at the port of destination. From that point the buyer accepts all costs and risks of unloading, lighterage and wharfing unless these have been included in the freight or collected by the ship owners when the freight was paid.
Classical economics	A tradition of economic thought initiated by Adam Smith and developed by others.
Closed economy	An economic system with little or no external trade.
Command economy	An economic system where resources are allocated by a state planning authority.
Commodity	A commodity is any useful but scare article or substance but especially basic foodstuffs or raw materials which need to undergo processing before they are ready for the end consumer.
Commodity broker	A broker who acts as agent for buyers and sellers in one of the commodity markets, receiving a brokerage fee for his services. In certain trades, brokers may buy and sell for themselves thus being dealers.
Common Agricultural Policy (CAP)	An integrated system of subsidies and rebates applied to the agricultural sector in the European Union.
Common Market	A group of countries who agree to remove all barriers to trade among members, to establish a common trade policy with respect to non-members and to allow full mobility of factors of production.

Community indifference curve	A locus of combinations of goods between which the community is, in some sense, defined as being indifferent.
Comparative advantage	A situation where one country is more efficient than another in the production of two or more products but is relatively more efficient in the production of one of those products.
Competitive advantage	A country's ability to produce a good or service more cheaply than other countries due to favourable factor conditions, successful related and supporting industries, appropriate firm strategies, structures and rivalry conditions as well as favourable demand conditions.
Concentration	A policy that involves concentrating on a small number of markets.
Conferences	An association of shipping companies formed for the purpose of setting rates, routes and timetables.
Confirmed credit	A letter of credit for which a bank has made itself responsible for honouring.
Conglomerate	A business organization generally consisting of a holding company and a group of subsidiary companies engaged in dissimilar activities.
Consecutive voyage charter	A contract between the shipowner and charterer covering a specified number of trips.
Constant returns to scale	The condition whereby an increase in the factors used in production by a given percentage leads to an increase in output by the same percentage. A doubling of inputs leads to a doubling of output.
Consumers surplus	The difference between the market price and what a consumer would be willing to pay for a good.
Container ship	A large fast ship specifically planned and built to carry containers.
Containerized carriage	Goods which are transported in a large metal case of standard shape and size. Their standardization greatly helps in

	transporting them quickly and cheaply (dimensions: 2.4 m × 2.4 m × 6.1 m or 12.2 m).
Contract of affreightment	An agreement between a shipowner and a shipper or owner of the cargo to transport a specified quantity between ports over a specific period.
Cost of search	The cost incurred by a firm in attempting to identify new markets for its products.
Countertrade	A form of barter in International trade where the buyer requires the seller to accept goods in lieu of currency.
Countervailing duties	An import duty imposed on a commodity to offset a reduction of its price as a result of an export subsidy in the country of origin.
Countervailing power	The balancing of the market power of one economic group by another. Advanced by J.K. Galbraith who suggested that the power of large manufacturers was balanced by that of large retail groups, and the power of large employers was balanced by trade unions.
Currency Account	An account opened in a foreign currency which may allow a firm to avoid the cost and risks of exchanging currencies for each foreign business transaction.
Customs union	A union among trading countries in which members dismantle trade barriers in goods and services and establish a common trade policy with respect to non-members.
Decoupled subsidy	A level of subsidy paid to an organization/firm regardless of its level of output.
Depression	A situation when output in the economy is below potential capacity for a prolonged period of time to damage another country's economy.
Due process	The formal working of a fair legal action. The regular and orderly course of the law through the courts.
Dumping	Selling goods overseas at a price lower than the exporter's home market or at a

	price lower than the cost of production or both.
Economic profit	The surplus remaining after the full opportunity cost of the factors of production have been met.
Economic Union (EU)	A union among trading countries that would have the characteristics of a common market plus harmonized monetary policies, taxation and Government spending policies, and would use a common currency.
Economies of scale	Lower costs per unit made possible by operating on a large scale.
Entrepôt	A centre at which goods arrive for subsequent transhipment.
Equivalence	A recognition that standards imposed on goods in one country can be 'equivalent' to those imposed in another country.
Exchange rate	The price or rate at which one currency is exchanged for another currency.
Export led growth	A term used to describe a situation where the bulk of the growth in national income and output is attributable to the growth in export earnings.
Externalities	Costs not fully accounted for in the price or by the market system.
Factor intensity	The ratio of capital input to labour input used in the production of a good.
Factoring	A means by which traders can receive immediate payment at a discount for goods sold from an intermediary known as a factor. The factor eventually receives payment from the purchaser.
False border trade	Trade in goods across border frontiers encouraged by an imbalance of sales taxes and excise duties in different countries. For example, trade in alcoholic beverages between Britain (expensive higher duty) and France (lower duty and cheaper).
f.a.s.	Free alongside ship/steamer price quotation. The seller's price where the goods are

	placed alongside the ship ready to be taken on board. The buyer must pay for the loading of the goods **but** if the ship cannot enter the port or tie up to the shore, the seller must arrange and pay for lighters.
Fixed capital	Capital such as plant, machinery and buildings.
Fixed costs	Costs which do not vary with output.
Flexible exchange rate	The exchange rate is determined by the market and governments do not intervene to establish its value.
f.o.b.	Free on board price quotation. In foreign-trade contracts the seller's price includes all charges and risks up to the point where the seller delivers the goods on board the ship named by the buyer at the named post of shipment. From that point, all risk and charges have to be borne by the buyer.
Forfaiter	A specialist private firm which assesses the risk of foreign trade transactions.
Forfaiting	A means of collecting payment similar to factoring.
Foreign Direct Investment (FDI)	The establishment or expansion of a firm's operations in a foreign country.
Forward Exchange Contract	A contractual form used by the money markets to fix an exchange rate for the future delivery of one currency for another.
Forward rates	Contracts that provide for two parties to exchange currencies on a future date at an agreed exchange rate.
Franchising	A form of licensing that allows a distributor or retailer exclusive rights to sell a good or service in a specific area.
Free trade area	An association of countries who between them abolish import tariffs and quotas, export subsidies and other Government measures designed to influence trade. Each country, however, maintains its own international trade measures *vis-à-vis* countries outside the association.
Full employment	A situation in which everyone in the

	labour force who is willing to work at the market rate has a job.
Futures market	Where buyers and sellers of commodities or financial assets contract to exchange items at a specified price at a specified future date.
General Agreement in Trade in Services (GATS)	The name given to the set of rules that will apply to trade in services. Negotiated in the Uruguay round its aim is to liberalize trade in services.
General Agreement on Tariffs and Trade (GATT)	The inter-governmental body that oversees multilateral trade agreements.
General cargo	Cargo consisting of various kinds of goods not of any particular kind, nor full cargoes of a single commodity.
Gold standard	A standard setting the relative price of international currencies in terms of gold.
Greater East Asia Co-Prosperity Sphere	Formed by Japan in World War II in an attempt to force formal economic integration of Asian economies.
Greenfield investment	An investment which creates an entirely new subsidiary/company.
Harmonization	An agreement between nations to conform to a common set of regulations.
Hedge	To counterbalance a present sale or purchase with a sale or purchase for future delivery as a way of minimizing loss due to price fluctuation. To make counterbalancing sales or purchases in the international market as protection against adverse movements in the exchange rate.
Hegemony	Leadership – especially by one state.
Homogeneous products	Goods and services which are considered to be perfect substitutes.
Horizontal integration (lateral integration)	The merger of two or more firms in the same business activity.
Import quota	The quantitative limit placed on the importation of a specific commodity.
Import substitution	A policy adopted by many developing countries that involves the systematic

	encouragement of domestic production of goods formerly imported.
Income elasticity of demand	A proportionate change in demand brought about by a proportionate change in income.
Indifference curve	A graphical representation of sets of different combinations of commodities which yield to the consumer the same level of satisfaction.
Indirect investment	Made up of equity investment, private debt investment and intergovernmental transfers, e.g. economic aid.
Indivisible/lumpy cost	A production cost which is not divisible into smaller units.
Infant industry argument	An argument in support of protection. Tariffs should be imposed to protect an industry which is trying to get started. The presumption is that once the 'infant industry' is established and technologically efficient, then the tariff barrier can be removed.
Intellectual property	Ideas which have commercial value. These ideas may be expressed in designs, computer programmes, textbooks, etc.
International Monetary Fund (IMF)	An inter-governmental body that oversees the operation of the international monetary system. Acts as a creditor to countries that find themselves in balance of payments difficulties.
Irrevocable credits	Letters of credit which cannot be amended during the life of the credit except with the agreement of the beneficiary.
Joint venture	A business formed by two or more companies or institutions to achieve a common goal.
Keynesian	A branch of economics associated with J. M. Keynes. Its main features are that: Aggregate demand plays a decisive role in determining the level of real output. Economics can settle at positions with high unemployment. Governments can influence aggregate demand through fiscal policy to cut unemployment.

Laissez faire	The principle of non-intervention by Government in economic affairs as proposed by classical economists.
Leontief paradox	Wassily Leontief's study of US trade which indicated that the US was exporting labour intensive products. This was a paradox because of the general belief that the US was a capital intensive country which should be exporting capital intensive products.
Limited option	Similar to an option except that currency has to be exchanged within a thirty day period beginning at a specified future date.
Liner trade	A ship or ships which make regular voyages on dates made known in advance between certain ports. The opposite of a tramp freighter that keeps no regular route or timetable.
Log rolling	A means of increasing the political power of disparate groups or individuals through co-operation to achieve mutually beneficial objectives.
Maastricht Treaty	The agreement signed in December 1991 in which European Community Members agreed to a specific timetable and set of necessary conditions to create a single currency.
Macroeconomics	The study of national economies and the determination of national income.
Maquiladoras	Plants that made goods for exports back to the United States.
Marginal product	The output created by the employment of one additional unit of a factor of production.
Marginal rate of substitution	The rate at which a consumer needs to substitute one commodity for another in order to maintain constant total utility from the commodities taken together, i.e. the slope of an indifference curve.
Marine underwriter	A person/firm that accepts marine insurance contracts.

Market segmentation	The act of dividing a market into distinct groups of buyers who may require separate products of marketing mixes.
Marshall plan	Economic help given by the USA mainly to countries in Europe to help re-build their economies after World War II. This three year plan was administered in the USA by the ECA (European Co-operation Administration) and in Europe by the OEEC (Organisation for European Economic Co-operation).
Mercantilism	A policy originating in the 17th and early 18th centuries aimed at increasing a nation's wealth and power by encouraging the export of goods in return for gold.
Monetarist/monetarism	The name applied to a theory of macro-economics which holds that money supply increases are a necessary and sufficient condition for inflation.
Monopoly	A market in which there is only one seller.
Most favoured nation (MFN)	The status granted to a trading partner which entitles it to the same privileges granted to other most favoured nations.
Multilateral agreement	Agreement between a number of different countries.
Multinational company or transnational corporation	A company or enterprise operating in a number of countries and having production or service facilities outside the country of origin.
National treatment	Foreign suppliers and foreign goods to be given equitable treatment with domestic suppliers and goods in Government procurement contracts.
Neoclassical economics	A school of economic thought in the tradition of classical economics characterized by microeconomic systems constructed to explore conditions of static equilibrium.
Niche market	A comparatively small segment of a market in which a company concentrates its efforts.
Open accounts	A sort of trade credit that allows a buyer to purchase goods or services and pay for

them within a specified period of time without the penalty of interest rates being charged.

Open economy — An economic system in which the proportion of exports and imports to GDP is high.

Opportunistic recontracting — *See* Post-contractual opportunistic behaviour.

Opportunity cost — Cost incurred by a firm by not undertaking an alternative strategy.

Option — The right to buy or sell at a specified future date or within a specified period.

Organization of Petroleum Exporting Countries (OPEC) — A cartel formed by the principal oil producing and exporting countries with the purpose of setting output quotas and fixing prices.

Patent — An exclusive right granted by a government to an inventor for a specified period.

Per diem — Per day.

Perfect competition — A market structure in which neither the buyer's nor seller's individual decisions have an effect on the market price and output. Price and output are determined by the market.

Post-contractual-opportunistic behaviour (PCOB) — Purposeful re-negotiation of an agreement for economic gain.

Predatory pricing — Setting prices at very low levels with the aim of weakening or eliminating competitors or to keep out new entrants to a market.

Price discrimination — The selling of the same good or service to different buyers at different prices.

Primary products — The output of the agriculture, forestry, fishing and extractive industries.

Principal-Agent relationship — In essence, a principal employs an agent to work on the principal's behalf. This involves delegation of some decision making authority to the agent which he may exploit to his advantage.

Producers surplus	The difference between the price a producer receives for a good or service and what he would be willing to accept.
Product differentiation	A way of distinguishing essentially the same products from one another by real or illusory means.
Product life cycle	A theory which suggests that products pass through four stages: introduction, growth, maturity and decline.
Production possibility frontier	A curve showing the various alternative combinations of two goods that a nation or community can produce by fully utilizing all of its resources.
Profit	The residual return to the entrepreneur.
Protectionism	The name applied to the imposition of tariffs or quotas to restrict the flow of imports.
Real income	Money income adjusted for changes in prices.
Recession	A term given to a sharp slow down in the rate of economic growth.
Regional trade association	A number of countries which come together to form an association in which mutual concessions on trade are agreed.
Resource mobility	The relative ease/difficulty with which resources can be allocated/transferred from industry to industry or area to area.
Returns to scale	The proportionate increase in output resulting from proportionate increases in all inputs.
Revocable credits	Letters of credit which may be amended at the option of the applicant.
Ricardian goods	Goods which require heavy natural resource, are climatic influenced or need unsophisticated labour inputs. Goods from extractive industries (coal, petroleum, minerals) or food, e.g. wheat and corn.
Rules of origin requirements	Regulations which specify that a proportion of the value of the good sold in a country must have been added in that country.

Second best	The best solution when the first is not available or unattainable.
Senile industry	A once thriving industry which has lost its comparative advantage and is suffering decline.
Serious prejudice	A concept introduced to prevent suits over minor trade distortions caused by the introduction of a subsidy.
Shipbroker	A broker who acts as agent for ship owners and shipping companies arranging bill of lading contracts, charter parties and insurance, finding cargoes and in some cases passengers. The shipbroker receives a commission as a percentage of business he gets for his principals.
Single voyage charter	A contract between the shipowner and charterer covering one trip only.
Sogoshosha	A large Japanese trading company.
Spot rates	Contracts that provide for two parties to exchange currencies with delivery in two business days.
State trading agencies	Organizations specifically authorized to make purchases and sales internationally by the Government.
Subsidiaries	Companies legally controlled by other companies.
Subsidies	Payments by Government to a firm or an industry in order to prevent its decline or in order to avoid an increase in the prices of its products or to enable its exports to compete more effectively on the international markets.
Sunk costs	Cost incurred in acquiring specific assets which have no or limited alternative use.
Switching costs	The cost which will be incurred by a firm in changing production from one set of goods/services to another set of goods or services.
Tariffication	The process by which quantitative restrictions such as quotas are converted to tariff duties having equivalent effect.

Tariffs	Taxes on imported goods and services levied by Governments as a means of raising revenue and barriers to trade.
Terms of trade	The ratio of the indexes of export prices and import prices.
Time charter	One by which the ship/aircraft is hired for an agreed period of time during which the charterer may use the ship as he wishes paying a monthly rate of hire based on the deadweight tonnage of the ship. The ship is operated by the owners but the charterer pays the cost of fuel and stores consumed during the period of the charter.
Trade creation	The benefit accruing to a country when a group of countries trade freely amongst themselves but maintain barriers to trade with non-members.
Trade diversion	The cost to a country when a group of countries freely trade a product amongst themselves, but maintain barriers against lower cost non-members.
Trade liberalization	A policy aimed at the removal of tariffs or quotas to encourage trade in goods and services.
Trade related investment measures (TRIMS)	Economic policies that restrict foreign companies in their operations, i.e. restriction on ownership, repatriation of profits, etc.
Trading bloc	Established by agreement among countries to further links through trade in goods and services and the movement of capital across borders.
Trading house	Companies that specialize in arranging international transactions, e.g. Hutchinson Whampoa.
Tramp freighter	A ship travelling an irregular route scheduled only by demand conditions.
Transfer pricing	Internal (as opposed to market) prices used in large organizations for transactions between semi-autonomous divisions.
Unconfirmed credit	A letter of credit which relies solely upon the good name of the issuing bank.

United Nations Conference on Trade and Development (UNCTAD)	A UN conference established to actively develop trade relations between developed and developing countries.
Utility	The satisfaction derived by an individual from consuming goods or services.
Variable levies	A tax on goods not set at a fixed level but which vary according to world prices to keep the domestic price stable.
Vertical integration	The extent to which successive stages of production and distribution are placed under the control of a sole enterprise. Firms can integrate forward towards retailing or backwards towards the source of raw materials.
Voyage charter	One by which the ship/aircraft is hired for a single voyage between agreed ports to carry stated cargo at a fixed rate of freight. The owner bears responsibility for operating the ship and all expenses.
Winner's curse	A situation where the highest bidder of a good or contract pays more than it is actually worth.
Working capital	This includes work in progress and components.
World Trade Organization (WTO)	The new organization set to replace GATT with the purpose of promoting and policing trade between countries.
X-inefficiency	Originated by H. Liebenstein to explain the discrepancy between the efficiency of firms as implied by economic theory and practice.

Index

Page numbers appearing in **bold** refer to figures and page numbers appearing in *italic* refer to tables.

Absolute advantage *20*, 20–21
  see also Comparative advantage
Accepted retaliation 98
Acquisitions 145–6
Adjudication procedures 98, 123–5
  see also Arbitration services
Ad valorem tariffs 107, *108*
Agreement on Government Procurement 246–7
Agreement on Trade-Related Aspects of Intellectual Property Rights 244–5
Agreement on Trade Related Investment Measures (TRIMS) 146
Air transport 198
  growth of 198–9
  supply of 199
Animal welfare issues 250
APEC 90
Arbitration services
  enforcement of awards 217–19
  formalization of 210–11
  growth of 210, *211*
  information available on 212
  institutions 211–12
    International Chamber of Commerce (ICC) 212–17
  and national legal systems 201–9
  see also Adjudication procedures
Asia-Pacific Economies Co-operation forum (APEC) 90
Asset specificity 141, *142*

Banks
  documentary collection services 174–5
  documentary letters of credit 175–8
  exchange rate management 190, 191
  sources of information 165
Bareboat charters 196, 197
Barriers, *see* Restrictions on trade
Barter agreements 153–4
Bilateral agreements 71, 72, 73, 74, 91
Black market operations 187–8
Borrowing foreign currency 191
Bulk cargoes 193, 194
Businesses, input to trade issues 36, 248–50
Buy-back agreements 154–5

Canada-US Trade Agreement (CUSTA) 88, 124
Carrier of origin requirements 115, 119–20
Cartels 142–3
Chartering
  aircraft 199
  ships 196, 197
c.i.f. 197
Classical trade theory 20–23
Classification 28, 29, *29*
CMEA 87–8
Command economies, *see* Former command economies
Commodity agreements 100–2
Common markets 76
Community indifference curves 40, 41, **41**, 42, **42**, 43
Comparative advantage *21*, 21–3
Competitive advantage 19, 33–5, **34**
  see also Trade theories

Components, international sourcing of 232
Conciliation 206, 207–8
Consumer protection legislation 113–14
Consumers surplus 79
Containerized carriage 196
Contingent protection 126
  see also Countervail; Dumping
Contracts 200
Contracts of affreightment 196–7
Control of trade restrictions 117–25
Convention on the Recognition and Enforcement of Foreign Arbitral Awards 218
Convertible currencies 185–6
Cost, insurance and freight (c.i.f.) 197
Cost of search 164–5
Council for Mutual Economic Assistance (CMEA) 87–8
Counterfeiting 140, 245
  see also Intellectual property
Counter-purchase agreements 155
Countertrade 104–6, 152–5
Countervail 128–9
Cultural differences 162–4
Currency accounts 190
Currency devaluations 51, 52, 189
CUSTA 88, 124
Customs unions 76

Debt collection 184
  see also Discounting; Factoring; Forfaiting; Payment methods
Decoupled subsidies 128

Devaluation, currency 51, 52, 189
Developing countries
  growth of trade 10–11
  protection measures 55–6
  role in international trade 233–4
Development, see Research and development
Differentiated goods, intra-industry trade 30
Discounting 178
Disequilibrium and change 229
Disputes
  causes 200
  settlement 200–1
    see also Adjudication procedures; Arbitration services
Diversifying 231–2
Documentary collection services 174–5
Documentary letters of credit 175–8
Dumping 53–4, 126–7

Economic blocs 75, 77, 89–91, 237
  common markets 76
  customs unions 76
  dynamic factors 81
  economic union 76, 77
  effect on foreign direct investment 13
  enhancement of power 81–2
  Europe 82–8
  free trade areas 75–6
  future issues 247–8
  governments' interests 91
  North America 88–9
  static factors 77, 77–81
Economic sovereignty 65–6
Economic union 76, 77
Economies of scale 25–6
EEA 86–7
EFTA 86, 87
Enforcement costs 136, 137
Enforcement of arbitration awards 217–19
Entrepôt trade 29
Environmental issues 249, 250
Equity joint ventures 144, 145
Equivalence 120–21
  see also Harmonization
Espionage, industrial 139–40
EU, see European Union
European Economic Area (EEA) 86–7

European Free Trade Area (EFTA) 86, 87
European Union (EU) 83–6, 87
  dispute settlement procedures 85–6, 123–4
Exchange rate management 190–92
Expertise 206
Exporting rights 103, 104
Export restrictions 111
Externalities 46–7

Factoring 178–9
Factor proportion theory 23–5
'Fair' trade
  contingent protection 126
  countervail 128–9
  dumping 53–4, 126–7
f.a.s. 197
FDI, see Foreign direct investment
Financing 184
  see also Discounting; Factoring; Forfaiting
Fixed exchange rates 188–9
Flat rate tariffs 107, 108
Flexible exchange rates 188, 189–90
f.o.b. 175, 197
Foreign direct investment (FDI)
  growth of 12–13
  restrictions 146
  see also Transnational firms
Foreign exchange
  acquisition of foreign currencies 184–5
  black market operations 187–8
  controlled access 186, 187, 188
  convertible currencies 185–6
  fixed exchange rates 188–9
  flexible exchange rates 188, 189–90
  internationally accepted currency 185
  spot rates 190
  see also Exchange rate management
Forfaiting 179–82
Former command economies 11–12, 234
  see also Council for Mutual Economic Assistance; State trading agencies
Forward exchange contracts 190
Franchises 140–41
Free along side (f.a.s.) 197
Free on board (f.o.b.) 175, 197

Free trade areas 75–6
Future issues 225–7, 229
  business input to trade issues 36, 248–50
  growth areas 234
Futures market 191–2

GATS 241–2
General Agreement on Tariffs and Trade (GATT) 93, 94, 96–9
  dispute settlement procedures 98, 123
  see also World Trade Organization
General Agreement on Trade in Services (GATS) 241–2
General cargoes 193–4
Gold standard system 185
Goodwill 140–41
Government procurement
  liberalization 245–7
  national treatment 120
  restrictions 115–16
Governments
  cost of search programmes 165
  economic interests 66–7, 91
  economic sovereignty 65–6
  export financing guarantees 184
  influence on international trading system 30, 34–5, 36, 67–9
  procurement contracts, see Government procurement
  see also Political risk; State trading agencies
Greenfield investments 145–6

Harmonization 118–19
  see also Equivalence
Health regulations 111–13, 119
Hedging 191–2
Hegemony 68–9
High quality products 142
Historical development of world trade 6–8, 70–71
Homogeneous goods, intra-industry trade 29–30
Horizontal integration 139
Human skills 25

ICC, arbitration services 212–17
Identifying new markets 164–5
IMF 6, 189
Immigration policies 238, 239

Import/export firms, *see* Trading houses
Import licences 109
Import quotas 108–9
Import substitution 55
Income elasticity of demand 9
Income similarity theory 27
Indifference curves 40, 41, **41**, 42, **42**, 43
Indivisible costs 162
Industrial espionage 139–40
Infant economies, protection measures 55–6
Infant industries, protection measures 54, 55
Information costs 136
Insurance, shipping services 198
Intellectual property 10, *10*
 protection of rights 139, 140, 242–5
International Chamber of Commerce (ICC), arbitration services 212–17
International commodity arrangements 100–2
Internationally accepted currency 185
International Monetary Fund (IMF) 6, 189
International terms of trade line **42**, 42–3
Intra-industry trade 27–8
 aggregation and classification of goods 28–9
 explanations for 29, 30–31
  differentiated goods 30
  homogeneous goods 29–30
 measurement of 28
Irrevocable confirmed credits 177
Irrevocable credits 177

Joint ventures 144–5

Keynesian techniques 7

Lateral integration 139
Letters of credit 175–8
Liberalization
 government procurement 245–7
 growth of 235, 236, 237, 238
 services trade 238–42
Limited option contracts 190
Liner trade 195–6
Log rolling 45

Long-term contracts 143–4
Lumpy costs 162

Managed trade 39
Marginal product 48–9, 50
Mercantilism 39–40
MFN principle 71–2, 97–8
Monetarist policies 7
Most favoured nation (MFN) principle 71–2, 97–8
Multilateral agreements 71–2, 73, 91, 93, 236, 237–8
 see also General Agreement on Tariffs and Trade; United Nations Conference on Trade and Development; World Trade Organization
Multinational firms, *see* Transnational firms

NAFTA 88–9
National character of firms 232
National legal systems and arbitration services 201–9
National security measures 52
National treatment 119–20, 240–41
Nation state, *see* Governments
Negotiation costs 136, 137
Neo-classical trade theory 23–5
Non-discrimination 71–2, 97–8
Non-tariff barriers 110–16
North American Free Trade Agreement (NAFTA) 88–9

OPEC, raising of prices 8
Open account 173–4
Open trading system 40–43
 effect on social stability 66–7
 indicators of 69–70
 see also Liberalization
Opportunistic recontracting 141–2
Opportunity cost 40
Optimum tariffs 52–3
Option contracts 190
Orderly markets, need for 100
 see also Countertrade; International commodity arrangements; Voluntary export restraints
Organization of Petroleum Exporting Countries (OPEC), raising of prices 8

Patents 10, *10*, 139, 140, 243, 244
Patterns of world trade, *see* Trade patterns
Payment in kind 104–6, 152–5
Payment methods 173, 174–8
 opportunistic behaviour 173
 see also Forfaiting; Payment in kind
PCOB 141–2
Phytosanitary regulations 111–13, 119
Political risk 182–4
Porter's diamond 33–5, **34**
Post-contractural-opportunistic-behaviour (PCOB) 141–2
Predatory pricing 53–4, 126–7
Price line **42**, 42–3
Principal-agent problems 156
Procurement contracts, *see* Government procurement
Producers surplus 79
Production possibility frontier 40, 41, **41**, 42, **42**, 43
Product life cycle theory 26–7
Professional services 239–41
Protectionism 56–7
 countering strategic behaviour 53–4
 decline of 235, 236, 249
 distortions in commodity and factor markets 46–50
 environmental issues 249, 250
 full employment and the balance of payments 50–52
 infant economies 55–6
 infant industries 54, 55
 national security 52
 optimum tariffs 52–3
 political forces 43–6
 revenue requirements 53
 senile industries 55
 trade sanctions 250
 see also Restrictions on trade

Quotas, import 108–9

Recontracting, opportunistic 141–2
Re-export trade 29
Regional trade associations, *see* Economic blocs
Research and development
 returns on investment 138–40, 243

Research and development (cont.)
  see also Intellectual property
Resource mobility 229–31
Restrictions on trade 107
  control of 117–25
  export restrictions 111
  import quotas 108–9
  non-tariff barriers 110–16
  tariffs 107–8
  unilateral action 107
  see also Protectionism
Retraining of workers 51
Revenue raising tariffs 53
Revocable credits 177
Rules of origin requirements 114, 119
Rules of trade, effectiveness of 130

Safeguard procedures 121–3
Sanctions 250
Sanitary regulations 111–13, 119
Senile industries, protection measures 55
Serious prejudice 129
Services trade 9–10, *10*
  future developments 232
  GATS 241–2
  liberalization 238–41
Shipping services 10, *10*
  brokers 194–5
  bulk cargoes 193, 194
  chartering 196, 197
  conditions of carriage and service 197–8
  containerized carriage 196
  contracts of affreightment 196–7
  general cargoes 193–4
  insurance 198
  liner trade 195–6
Single voyage charters 196, 197
Social stability, effect of open trade 66–7
Sourcing of components, international 232
Spot rates 190

Standard International Trade Classification 29, *29*
State trading agencies 148, 156
  command economies 148–51
  countertrade arrangements 152–5
  mixed economies 151–2
  opportunistic behaviour 155–6
Stockpiling, essential goods 52
Subsidiaries, setting up 145–6
Subsidies
  benefits of 47, 48, 50
  decoupled 128
  important business sectors 52
  infant industries 54
  see also Countervail
Substitution, import 55

Tariffication 117–18
Tariffs 50, 52–3, 107–8
  see also General Agreement on Tariffs and Trade; Tariffication
Taxes, benefits of 47, 48, 50
Technical joint ventures 144, 145
Technological theories 26
Time charters 196, 197
Trade blocs, see Economic blocs
Trade creation and diversion 77–81
Trade dependency, determinants of 33
Trademarks 10, 140, 245
Trade patterns 31–2
  see also Trade theories
Trade related investment measures (TRIMS) 146
Trade shows 164–5
Trade theories 19, 35–6
  classical 20–23
  determinants of dependency and competitiveness 33–5
  economies of scale 25–6
  human skills 25
  income similarity 27
  intra-industry trade 27–31

neo-classical 23–5
product life cycle 26–7
technological 26
trade patterns 31–2
Trading houses 157–8, 165
  cost of search 164–5
  cultural differences 162–4
  indivisible costs 162
  market characteristics 159–61
  market importance 162
  product characteristics 158–9, 161
Transaction costs 135–8
  see also Transnational firms
Transfer prices, strategic use of 143
Transnational firms 135–47
  see also Foreign direct investment
Transportation 10, *10*, 193
  see also Air transport; Shipping services
TRIMS 146
Trip charters 196, 197

United Nations Conference on Trade and Development (UNCTAD) 95–6

Variable levies 110
VERs 102–4
Vertical integration 136, 137
  see also Transnational firms
Voluntary export restraints (VERS) 102–4
Vulnerable assets 141, 142

World trade
  distribution and concentration of 10–12
  historical development of 6–8, 70–71
  structure of *9*, 9–10, *10*
World Trade Organization (WTO) 94–5, 98
  adjudication procedures 95, 124–5
  see also General Agreement on Tariffs and Trade